# FREE VIDEO  FREE  FREE VIDEO

## *Essential Test Tips* Video from Trivium Test Prep

Dear Customer,

Thank you for purchasing from Trivium Test Prep! We're honored to help you prepare for your PECT PAPA exam.

To show our appreciation, we're offering a **FREE *PECT PAPA Essential Test Tips* Video by Trivium Test Prep**.* Our video includes 35 test preparation strategies that will make you successful on the PECT PAPA. All we ask is that you email us your feedback and describe your experience with our product. Amazing, awful, or just so-so: we want to hear what you have to say!

To receive your **FREE *PECT PAPA Essential Test Tips* Video**, please email us at 5star@ triviumtestprep.com. Include "Free 5 Star" in the subject line and the following information in your email:

1. The title of the product you purchased.
2. Your rating from 1 – 5 (with 5 being the best).
3. Your feedback about the product, including how our materials helped you meet your goals and ways in which we can improve our products.
4. Your full name and shipping address so we can send your **FREE *PECT PAPA Essential Test Tips* Video**.

If you have any questions or concerns please feel free to contact us directly at 5star@triviumtestprep.com.

Thank you!

- Trivium Test Prep Team

*To get access to the free video please email us at 5star@triviumtestprep.com, and please follow the instructions above.

# PECT PAPA Study Guide 2019–2020

EXAM PREP AND PRACTICE TEST QUESTIONS FOR THE PENNSYLVANIA EDUCATOR CERTIFICATION TESTS PRE-SERVICE ACADEMIC PERFORMANCE ASSESSMENT

# Table of Contents

# Online Resources

To help you fully prepare for your PECT PAPA exam, Cirrus includes online resources with the purchase of this study guide.

## Practice Test

In addition to the practice test included in this book, we also offer an online exam. Since many exams today are computer based, getting to practice your test-taking skills on the computer is a great way to prepare.

## Flash Cards

A convenient supplement to this study guide, Cirrus's flash cards enable you to review important terms easily on your computer or smartphone.

## Cheat Sheets

Review the core skills you need to master the exam with easy-to-read Cheat Sheets.

## From Stress to Success

Watch From Stress to Success, a brief but insightful YouTube video that offers the tips, tricks, and secrets experts use to score higher on the exam.

## Reviews

Leave a review, send us helpful feedback, or sign up for Cirrus promotions—including free books!

Access these resources at:

**www.cirrustestprep.com/pect-papa-online-resources**

# Introduction

Congratulations on choosing to take the Pre-service Academic Performance Assessment! By purchasing this book, you've taken the first step toward becoming a teacher, an enriching and satisfying career.

This guide will provide you with a detailed overview of the Pre-service Academic Performance Assessment (PAPA) so you know exactly what to expect on test day. It will prepare you for all three of the PAPA modules: Mathematics, Reading, and Writing. We'll take you through all the concepts covered on these tests and give you the opportunity to test your knowledge with practice questions. Even if it's been a while since you last took a major test, don't worry; we'll make sure you're more than ready!

## What is the PAPA?

The PAPA is used by teacher preparation programs in Pennsylvania to measure applicants' aptitude in mathematics, reading, and writing. You may take the modules individually on separate dates, or you may take them all on the same date. While you may also be required to take other Pennsylvania Education Certification Tests for specific academic subjects, these core subjects are essential for anyone entering the teaching profession.

## What's on the PAPA?

The PAPA gauges college-level skills in mathematics, reading and, writing in accordance with the Common Core State Standards. Each module—Mathematics, Reading, and Writing—is broken down into different categories based on the skills needed to succeed in a teacher preparation program.

On the Reading test, you will read and answer questions about fiction and nonfiction passages of varying length. Some will be paired. They may be taken from any reading material an educated adult is likely to encounter, including novels, newspapers, magazines, articles on current events, and visual representations.

The Mathematics test focuses on numbers, algebra and functions, geometry, problem solving and mathematical communication, and statistics and probability.

The Writing test tests your ability to analyze purpose, production and types of text, and your language and research skills. You will complete two sentence correction assignments, write one essay, and answer multiple-choice questions.

### What's on the PAPA?

| Section | Concepts | Number of Questions | Time |
|---|---|---|---|
| Mathematics | Numbers; algebraic expressions, equations, linear and nonlinear functions; measurement and geometry; data, probability, and statistics | 36 selected-response questions | 75 minutes |
| Reading | Words and phrases; main idea; organization, analysis, and evaluation of ideas; inferences | 36 selected-response questions following paired, long and short passages, and brief statements | 45 minutes |
| Writing | Effectiveness, clarity, conciseness, and coherence of writing; conventions of American English; ability to develop well-organized writing | 36 selected-response questions, 2 sentence correction assignments, and 1 constructed response (essay) | 75 minutes |
| **Total** | | **108 (and 2 sentence correction assignments, 1 essay)** | **3 hours, 15 minutes** |

# How is the PAPA Scored?

Your scores for the Mathematics and Reading modules are provided immediately after you complete the test. Your official score report for these modules will be available within 10 days after the exam. Your score on the Writing module will be available within 20 days after the exam. You can elect to have your scores emailed to you, or you can download them from your account, where they will remain for 2 years after being posted. Your PAPA scores will automatically be sent to the

Pennsylvania Department of Education; however to have them sent to a college or university, you must make a request when you register for the exam.

Each selected-response (or multiple-choice) question is worth one raw point. The total number of questions you answer correctly is added up to obtain your raw score.

Essay responses are scored holistically by two separate graders who are unaware of each other's evaluations of your work. If they differ substantially, to ensure fairness a third scorer determines your final essay score. This number is added to your raw score, which is then converted to a scale of 100 – 300. In order to pass the PAPA, you must receive at least a score of 220 on Reading, 193 on Mathematics, and 220 on Writing. Alternatively, you can opt for composite scoring. In this case, you would need to receive a total of 657, including at least one minimum qualifying score.

Keep in mind that a small number of selected-response questions are experimental and will not count toward your overall score. PECT uses these to test out new questions for future exams. However, as those questions are not indicated on the test, you must respond to every question.

There is no penalty for guessing on the test, so be sure to eliminate answer choices and answer every question. If you still do not know the answer, guess; you may get it right!

# How is the PAPA Administered?

The PAPA is a computer-based test offered continuously at a range of universities and testing centers. It may be taken in its individual parts or all at once. Check https://home.pearsonvue.com/ for more information. You will need to print your registration ticket from your online account and bring it, along with your identification, to the testing site on test day. No pens, pencils, erasers, or calculators are allowed; on the Mathematics portion of the exam, a calculator will automatically appear on the computer screen for certain questions. You may take the test once every 21 days.

# About Cirrus Test Prep

Cirrus Test Prep study guides are designed by current and former educators and are tailored to meet your needs as an incoming educator. Our guides offer all of the resources necessary to help you pass teacher certification tests across the nation.

Cirrus clouds are graceful, wispy clouds characterized by their high altitude. Just like cirrus clouds, Cirrus Test Prep's goal is to help educators "aim high" when it comes to obtaining their teacher certification and entering the classroom.

# About This Guide

This guide will help you master the most important test topics and also develop critical test-taking skills. We have built features into our books to prepare you for your tests and increase your score. Along with a detailed summary of the test's format, content, and scoring, we offer an in-depth overview of the content knowledge required to pass the test. Our sidebars provide interesting information, highlight key concepts, and review content so that you can solidify your understanding of the exam's concepts. Test your knowledge with sample questions and detailed answer explanations in the text that help you think through the problems on the exam, and with two full-length practice tests that reflect the content and format of the PAPA. We're pleased you've chosen Cirrus to be a part of your professional journey!

I

# Part I: Reading

# Reading Skills

## Introduction

The Reading test assesses overall proficiency in several key reading skills, including building inferences, understanding themes, and describing the organization and craft of writing.

The Reading test contains fifty-six multiple-choice questions, presented following brief passages of text or other types of media, such as graphs. The number of questions following each passage depends on the length of the passage: four to seven questions follow a 200-word passage or a pair of passages may be followed by four to seven questions; three questions follow a 100-word passage; and single questions follow statements and briefer passages. Question stems may be presented as fill-in-the-blank sentences, straightforward questions, or *LEAST/NEVER/EXCEPT* questions, which ask the test taker to choose the answer that does not fit.

The PECT PAPA Reading test consists of three main question categories based on the Common Core State Standards. In the sections that follow, several strategies and terms will be briefly discussed, and they will be fully addressed throughout this book.

### KEY IDEAS AND DETAILS

Questions in this category focus on the text as a whole; they ask for explanations of the main ideas and how those ideas lead to specific inferences and conclusions. Answers should reflect connections between various sections of the text, discuss the consistency and overall meaning of the author's argument, and identify the piece's theme, summarizing it accurately. To accomplish this, the test taker should incorporate details that support the author's argument and are considered the most important.

Strategies for approaching this type of question include previewing the questions and outlining. Reading through the questions before reading the passage is a way to find a focus. The questions describe what to look for, and wrong answer choices can be eliminated quickly by identifying the main ideas and supporting details. Building an outline of the text assists in accurately identifying these things: jotting down words or phrases that describe the main idea of each paragraph and underlining important details that uphold that idea.

## Craft, Structure, and Language Skills

This category tests understanding of the craft of writing, including the use of language, point of view, and organization. Questions may require relating the details of a passage to the overall organization and meaning of that passage. Such questions ask for evaluations of specific areas of the text as they relate to the author's purpose and argument, and descriptions of how the author uses specific words, figurative language, or transitions.

For these craft-related questions, the best strategy entails returning to the passage after reading each question and looking for the specific context and location of each question in order to be as accurate as possible. Marking out incorrect answers plus circling the important aspects of the question stem and answer are also helpful strategies.

## Integrating Knowledge and Skills

This final category blends the strategies used with the other two categories. The synthesis of skills employed with previous questions extends in these questions into evaluation and judgment.

Questions may require an assessment of a text, a comparison of multiple texts, or an examination of other kinds of texts, such as visual media. In order to compare two texts, for example, the test taker must understand the purpose and main idea of each text as well as specific details. Determining what to pay attention to is accomplished by reviewing each question before reading its relative passage and returning to the passage as needed. A passage that employs diverse media, such as visuals, requires the same skills used while reading text. Carefully considering each question resolves which skills and knowledge should be integrated to answer it, and deconstructing the question stem best determines what sort of question it is.

The rest of this book will focus on describing in detail the skills, terms, and general content familiarity needed to approach the PECT PAPA Reading test. Each section contains examples of the sorts of questions the test may ask about each of these topics. These examples are meant to exercise the skills needed for each type of question.

# The Main Idea

The **main idea** of a text describes the author's main topic and general concept; it also generalizes the author's point of view about a subject. It is contained within and throughout the text. The reader can easily find the main idea by considering how the main topic is addressed throughout a passage. In the reading test, the expectation is not only to identify the main idea but also to differentiate it from a text's theme and to summarize the main idea clearly and concisely.

The main idea is closely connected to topic sentences and how they are supported in a text. Questions may deal with finding topic sentences, summarizing a text's ideas, or locating supporting details. The sections and practice examples that follow detail the distinctions between these aspects of text.

## IDENTIFYING THE MAIN IDEA

To identify the main idea, first identify the **topic**. The difference between these two things is simple: the **topic** is the overall subject matter of a passage; the **main idea** is what the author wants to say about that topic. The main idea covers the author's direct perspective about a topic, as distinct from the **theme**, which is a generally true idea that the reader might derive from a text. Most of the time, fiction has a theme, whereas nonfiction has a main idea. This is the case because in a nonfiction text, the author speaks more directly to the audience about a topic—his or her perspective is more visible. For example, the following passage conveys the topic as well as what the author wants to communicate about that topic.

> **HELPFUL HINT**
>
> The author's perspective on the subject of the text and how he or she has framed the argument or story hints at the main idea. For example, if the author framed the story with a description, image, or short anecdote, this suggests a particular idea or point of view.

The "shark mania" of recent years can be largely pinned on the sensationalistic media surrounding the animals: from the release of *Jaws* in 1975 to the week of ultra-hyped shark feeding frenzies and "worst shark attacks" countdowns known as Shark Week, popular culture both demonizes and fetishizes sharks until the public cannot get enough. Swimmers and beachgoers may look nervously for the telltale fin skimming the surface, but the reality is that shark bites are extremely rare and they are almost never unprovoked. Sharks attack people at very predictable times and for very predictable reasons. Rough surf, poor visibility, or a swimmer sending visual and physical signals that mimic a shark's normal prey are just a few examples.

Of course, some places are just more dangerous to swim. Shark attack "hot spots," such as the coasts of Florida, South Africa, and New Zealand try a variety of solutions to protect tourists and surfers. Some beaches employ "shark nets," meant to keep sharks away from the beach, though these are controversial because they frequently trap other forms of marine life as well. Other beaches use spotters in helicopters and boats to alert beach officials when there are sharks in the area. In addition, there is an array of products that claim to offer personal protection from sharks, ranging from wetsuits in different colors to devices that broadcast electrical signals in an attempt to confuse the sharks' sensory organs. At the end of the day, though, beaches like these remain dangerous, and swimmers must assume the risk every time they paddle out from shore.

The author of this passage has a clear topic: sharks and the relationship between humans and sharks. In order to identify the main idea of the passage, the reader must ask what the author wants to say about this topic, what the reader is meant to think or understand. The author makes sure to provide information about several different aspects of the relationship between sharks and humans, and points out that humans must respect sharks as dangerous marine animals, without sensationalizing the risk of attack. This conclusion results from looking at the various pieces of information the author includes as well as the similarities between them. The passage describes sensationalistic media, then talks about how officials and governments try to protect beaches, and ends with the observation that people must take personal responsibility. These details clarify what the author's main idea is. Summarizing that main idea by focusing on the connection between the different details helps the reader draw a conclusion.

## HELPFUL HINT

Readers should identify the topic of a text and pay attention to how the details about it relate to one another. A passage may discuss, for example, topic similarities, characteristics, causes, and/or effects.

## SAMPLE QUESTIONS

The art of the twentieth and twenty-first centuries demonstrates several aspects of modern societal advancement. A primary example is the advent and ascendancy of technology: New technologies have developed new avenues for art making, and the globalization brought about by the Internet has both diversified the art world and brought it together simultaneously. Even as artists are able to engage in a global conversation about the categories and characteristics of art, creating a more uniform understanding, they can now express themselves in a diversity of ways for a diversity of audiences. The result has been a rapid change in how art is made and consumed.

1) **This passage is primarily concerned with**

    A.    the importance of art in the twenty-first century.

    B.    the use of art to communicate overarching ideals to diverse communities.

    C.    the importance of technology to art criticism.

    D.    the change in understanding and creation of art in the modern period.

**Answers:**

    A.    Incorrect. The focus of the passage is what the art of the twentieth and twenty-first centuries demonstrates.

    B.    Incorrect. Although the passage mentions a diversity of audiences, it discusses the artists expressing themselves, not attempting to communicate overarching ideals.

    C.    Incorrect. The passage discusses how new technologies have "developed new avenues for art making," but nothing about criticism.

    **D.**    **Correct.** The art of the modern period reflects the new technologies and globalization possible through the Internet.

2) **Which of the following best describes the main idea of the passage?**

    A.    Modern advances in technology have diversified art making and connected artists to distant places and ideas.

    B.    Diversity in modern art is making it harder for art viewers to understand and talk about that art.

    C.    The use of technology to discuss art allows us to create standards for what art should be.

    D.    Art making before the invention of technology such as the Internet was disorganized and poorly understood.

**Answers:**

    **A.**    **Correct.** According to the text, technology and the Internet have "diversified the art world and brought it together simultaneously."

    B.    Incorrect. The passage explains that the global conversation about art has created a more uniform understanding.

    C.    Incorrect. The passage indicates that artists now engage in a global conversation about art, but this is one detail in the passage. The main idea of the passage concerns the advances in art in the twentieth and twenty-first centuries.

    D.    Incorrect. The invention of technology and the Internet have diversified art; however, that does not mean it was disorganized previously.

## TOPIC AND SUMMARY SENTENCES

Identifying the main idea requires understanding the structure of a piece of writing. In a short passage of one or two paragraphs, the topic and summary sentences quickly relate what the paragraphs are about and what conclusions the author wants the reader to draw. These sentences function as bookends to a paragraph or passage, telling readers what to think and keeping the passage tied tightly together.

Generally, the **topic sentence** is the first, or very near the first, sentence in a paragraph. It is a general statement that introduces the topic, clearly and specifically directing the reader to access any previous experience with that topic.

### QUICK REVIEW

A **summary** is a very brief restatement of the most important parts of an argument or text. Building a summary begins with the most important idea in a text. A longer summary also includes supporting details. The text of a summary should be much shorter than the original.

The **summary sentence**, on the other hand, frequently—but not always!—comes at the end of a paragraph or passage, because it wraps up all the ideas presented. This sentence provides an understanding of what the author wants to say about the topic and what conclusions to draw about it. While a topic sentence acts as an introduction to a topic, allowing the reader to activate his or her own ideas and experiences, the summary statement asks the reader to accept the author's ideas about that topic. Because of this, a summary sentence helps the reader quickly identify a piece's main idea.

### SAMPLE QUESTIONS

Altogether, Egypt is a land of tranquil monotony. The eye commonly travels either over a waste of waters, or over a green plain unbroken by elevations. The hills which inclose (*sic*) the Nile valley have level tops, and sides that are bare of trees, or shrubs, or flowers, or even mosses. The sky is generally cloudless. No fog or mist enwraps the distance in mystery; no rainstorm sweeps across the scene; no rainbow spans the empyrean; no shadows chase each other over the landscape. There is an entire absence of picturesque scenery. A single broad river, unbroken within the limits of Egypt even by a rapid, two flat strips of green plain at its side, two low lines of straight-topped hills beyond them, and a boundless open space where the river divides itself into half a dozen sluggish branches before reaching the sea, constitute Egypt, which is by nature a southern Holland—"weary, stale, flat and unprofitable."

—from *Ancient Egypt* by George Rawlinson

3)    **Which of the following best explains the general idea and focus indicated by the topic sentence?**

   A.    Egypt is a boring place without much to do.

   B.    The land of Egypt is undisturbed; the reader will read on to find out what makes it so dull.

   C.    Egypt is a peaceful place; its people live with a sense of predictability.

   D.    The land of Egypt is quiet; the reader wants to know what is missing.

**Answers:**

   A.    Incorrect. The word *monotony* does suggest the idea of being bored; however, the focus is the land of Egypt, not what people have to do. In addition, tranquility is part of the general idea.

   **B.    Correct.** This option indicates both the main idea and what the reader will focus on while reading.

   C.    Incorrect. This option leaves out what the focus will be.

   D.    Incorrect. This option leaves out the general idea of monotony.

4)    **Which of the following best states what the author wants the reader to understand after reading the summary sentence?**

   A.    There is not much to get excited about while visiting Egypt.

   B.    Egypt is a poverty-stricken wasteland.

   C.    The land of Egypt is worn out from overuse.

   D.    The land of Egypt lacks anything fresh or inspiring.

**Answers:**

   A.    Incorrect. The summary describes the place, not a visit to the place.

   B.    Incorrect. The word *unprofitable* suggests that the land of Egypt is unrewarding, not poverty stricken.

   C.    Incorrect. The reason the land is stale and weary may not be due to overuse. This summary describes; it does not explain the reasons the land is worn.

   **D.    Correct.** The words *weary*, *stale*, and *unprofitable* suggest a lack of freshness or anything that stimulates enthusiasm.

# Supporting Details

Between a topic sentence and a summary sentence, the rest of a paragraph is built with **supporting details**. Supporting details come in many forms; the purpose of the passage dictates the type of details that will support the main idea. A persuasive passage may use facts and data or detail specific reasons for the author's opinion. An informative passage will primarily use facts about the topic to support the main idea. Even a narrative passage will have supporting details—specific things the author says to develop the story and characters.

The most important aspect of supporting details is exactly what the term states: They support the main idea. Examining the various supporting details and how they work with one another will solidify how the author views a topic and what the main idea of the passage is. Supporting details are key to understanding a passage.

## IDENTIFYING SUPPORTING DETAILS

How can the reader identify the most important pieces of information in a passage? Supporting details build an argument and contain the concepts upon which the main idea rests. While supporting details will help the reader determine the main idea, it is actually easier to find the most important supporting details by first understanding the main idea; the pieces that make up the main argument then become clear.

**Signal words**—transitions and conjunctions—explain to the reader how one sentence or idea is connected to another. These words and phrases can be anywhere in a sentence, and it is important to understand what each signal word means. Signal words can add information, provide counterarguments, create organization in a passage, or draw conclusions. Some common signal words include *in particular, in addition, besides, contrastingly, therefore,* and *because*.

### SAMPLE QUESTIONS

The war is inevitable—and let it come! I repeat it, sir, let it come! It is in vain, sir, to extenuate the matter. Gentlemen may cry, "Peace! Peace!"—but there is no peace. The war is actually begun! The next gale that sweeps from the north will bring to our ears the clash of resounding arms! Our brethren are already in the field! Why stand we here idle? What is it that gentlemen wish? What would they have? Is life so dear, or peace so sweet, as to be purchased at the price of chains and slavery? Forbid it, Almighty God! I know not what course others may take; but as for me, give me liberty or give me death!

—from "Give Me Liberty or Give Me Death" speech
by Patrick Henry

5)   **In the fourth sentence of the text, the word *but* signals**

   A.   an example.

   B.   a consequence.

   C.   an exception.

   D.   a counterargument.

**Answers:**

A.      Incorrect. The author includes an example that the war has begun when he says "Our brethren are already in the field!" The word *but* does not signal this example.

B.      Incorrect. The phrase "but there is no peace" is a fact, not a consequence.

C.      Incorrect. In order to be an exception, the word *but* would have to be preceded by a general point or observation. In this case, *but* is preceded by a demand for peace.

**D.      Correct.** The argument or claim that the country should be at peace precedes the word *but*. *But* counters the demand for peace with the argument that there is no peace; the war has begun.

6)      **What argument does the author use to support his main point?**

A.      Life in slavery is not the goal of the country.

B.      To die bravely is worthwhile.

C.      Life without freedom is intolerable.

D.      The cost of going to war is too great.

**Answers:**

A.      Incorrect. The main point is that the country has to go to war with England to be free. The author does not support his point with a discussion of the goals of the country.

B.      Incorrect. This does not relate to the main point of going to war.

**C.      Correct.** The author indicates that life is not so dear, or peace so sweet, "as to be purchased at the price of chains and slavery."

D.      Incorrect. This is inaccurate. The author insists that the cost of not fighting for freedom is too great.

## EVALUATING SUPPORTING DETAILS

Besides using supporting details to help understand a main idea, the reader must evaluate them for relevance and inconsistency. An author selects details to help organize a passage and support its main idea. Sometimes, the author's bias results in details left out that don't directly support the main idea or that support an opposite idea. The reader has to be able to notice not only what the author says but also what the author leaves out.

To understand how a supporting detail relates to the main idea, the purpose of the passage should be discerned: what the author is trying to communicate and what the author wants from the reader. Every passage has a specific goal, and each paragraph in a passage is meant to support that goal. For each supporting detail, the position in the text, the signal words, and the specific content work together to alert the reader to the relationship between the supporting ideas and the main idea.

Close reading involves noticing the striking features of a text. For example, does a point made in the text appeal to the reader's sense of justice? Does a description seem rather exaggerated or overstated? Do certain words—such as *agonizing*—seem emotive? Are rhetorical questions being used to lead the reader to a certain conclusion?

Though the author generally includes details that support the text's main idea, the reader must decide how those details relate to one another as well as find any gaps in the support of the author's argument. This is particularly important in a persuasive piece of writing, when an author may allow bias to show through. Discovering the author's bias and how the supporting details reveal that bias is also key to understanding a text.

## SAMPLE QUESTIONS

In England in the 'fifties came the Crimean War, with the deep stirring of national feeling which accompanied it, and the passion of gratitude and admiration which was poured forth on Miss Florence Nightingale for her work on behalf of our wounded soldiers. It was universally felt that there was work for women, even in war—the work of cleansing, setting in order, breaking down red tape, and soothing the vast sum of human suffering which every war is bound to cause. Miss Nightingale's work in war was work that never had been done until women came forward to do it, and her message to her countrywomen was educate yourselves, prepare, make ready; never imagine that your task can be done by instinct, without training and preparation. Painstaking study, she insisted, was just as necessary as a preparation for women's work as for men's work; and she bestowed the whole of the monetary gift offered her by the gratitude of the nation to form training-schools for nurses at St. Thomas's and King's College Hospitals.

—from *Women's Suffrage: A Short History of a Great Movement*
by Millicent Garrett Fawcett

7) **Which of the following best states the bias of the passage?**

    A.    Society underestimates the capacity of women.

    B.    Generally, women are not prepared to make substantial contributions to society.

    C.    If women want power, they need to prove themselves.

    D.    One strong woman cannot represent all women.

**Answers:**

    **A.**    **Correct.** The author is suggesting that the work Florence Nightingale did had not been done before women came forward. Up till that point, what a woman could do had not been recognized.

    B.    Incorrect. This fact may have been true at the time this text was written, but only because educational opportunities were not available to women, and women were not encouraged to develop their abilities.

Including this fact reveals the bias that women should be granted opportunities to train and to contribute.

C.   Incorrect. This option does not apply; Florence Nightingale did more than prove herself.

D.   Incorrect. The fact that Florence Nightingale donated the money awarded her to the training of women indicates that other women were preparing themselves to contribute.

8)   **Which of the following best summarizes what the author left out of the passage?**

A.   Women can fight in wars.

B.   Other women should be recognized.

C.   Women need to stop wasting time giving speeches at conventions and start proving themselves.

D.   Without the contributions of women, society suffers.

**Answers:**

A.   Incorrect. "It was universally felt that there was work for women, even in war" suggests that women had much to offer and didn't need to be sheltered; however, "there was work" does not mean the author thought women should engage in combat.

B.   Incorrect. Since the passage is specifically about Florence Nightingale, nothing in it suggests the author included information about what other women did.

C.   Incorrect. Information about women's suffrage conventions is unrelated to the topic of the paragraph.

D.   **Correct.** The author emphasizes that "Miss Nightingale's work in war was work that never had been done until women came forward to do it."

## FACTS AND OPINIONS

Authors use both facts and opinions as supporting details. While it is usually a simple task to identify the two, authors may mix facts with opinions or state an opinion as if it were a fact. The difference between the two is simple: A **fact** is a piece of information that can be verified as true or false, and it retains the quality of truthfulness or falsity no matter who verifies it. An **opinion** reflects a belief held by the author and may or may not be something each reader agrees with.

---

**HELPFUL HINT**

To distinguish between fact and opinion, the reader should rely on what can be proven. Subjectivity is determined by asking if an observation varies according to the situation or the person observing.

## SAMPLE QUESTIONS

I remember thinking how comfortable it was, this division of labor which made it unnecessary for me to study fogs, winds, tides, and navigation, in order to visit my friend who lived across an arm of the sea. It was good that men should be specialists, I mused. The peculiar knowledge of the pilot and captain sufficed for many thousands of people who knew no more of the sea and navigation than I knew. On the other hand, instead of having to devote my energy to the learning of a multitude of things, I concentrated it upon a few particular things, such as, for instance, the analysis of Poe's place in American literature—an essay of mine, by the way, in the current *Atlantic*. Coming aboard, as I passed through the cabin, I had noticed with greedy eyes a stout gentleman reading the *Atlantic*, which was open at my very essay. And there it was again, the division of labor, the special knowledge of the pilot and captain which permitted the stout gentleman to read my special knowledge on Poe while they carried him safely from Sausalito to San Francisco.

—from *The Sea-Wolf* by Jack London

9) **Which of the following best summarizes an opinion stated by the narrator?**

   A.    Poe has a place in American literature.

   B.    People have the time to read magazines like the *Atlantic* because there are other people to take care of other tasks.

   C.    The narrator has no knowledge of the sea and navigation.

   D.    Division of labor is a beneficial practice.

   **Answers:**

   A.    Incorrect. This is a fact. The *significance* of Poe's place in American literature is an opinion.

   B.    Incorrect. This is a fact. The reader is expected to agree with the point that if someone else had not been managing the boat, the people who wanted to get across the water would have had to do the work of getting themselves across.

   C.    Incorrect. This is a fact. The narrator admits to "this division of labor which made it unnecessary for me to study fogs, winds, tides, and navigation."

   **D.**    **Correct.** The narrator provides several facts proving that he and the other passengers benefit from the specialized knowledge and labor of others.

10) **Which of the following is an opinion expressed by the narrator that is not supported by facts within the passage?**

   A.    People should live life focusing on and learning about only a few things.

   B.    Having general knowledge is good.

   C.    He has time to focus on writing about literature.

   D.    People depend on other people.

**Answers:**

A.   **Correct.** When the narrator says "instead of having to devote my energy to the learning of a multitude of things, I concentrated it upon a few particular things," he conveys his view that he does not have to learn much. There are no facts to support the view that he has to learn only a few particular things in life.

B.   Incorrect. The narrator does not express this opinion. He is speaking about specialized knowledge.

C.   Incorrect. This is a fact that the narrator shares about his life.

D.   Incorrect. The passage does offer facts to support this; both the narrator and the passenger reading depend on the pilot to navigate the boat safely.

# Text Structure

The structure of a text determines how the reader understands the argument and how the various details interact to form the argument. There are many ways to arrange text, and various types of arrangements have distinct characteristics.

The organizing structure of a passage is defined by the order in which the author presents information and the transitions used to connect those pieces. Problem-and-solution and cause-and-effect structures use transitions that show causal relationships: *because, as a result, consequently, therefore*. These two types of structures may also use transitions that show contradiction. A problem-and-solution structure may provide alternative solutions; a cause-and-effect structure may explain alternative causes: *however, alternatively, although*.

> **HELPFUL HINT**
>
> Authors often use repetition to reinforce an idea, including repeated words, phrases, or images.

Specific text structures include not only problem and solution and cause and effect but also compare and contrast, descriptive, order of importance, and chronological. When analyzing a text, the reader should consider how text structure influences the author's meaning. Most important, the reader needs to be aware of how an author emphasizes an idea by the way he or she presents information. For instance, including a contrasting idea makes a central idea stand out, and including a series of concrete examples creates a force of facts to support an argument.

## SAMPLE QUESTIONS

It was the green heart of the canyon, where the walls swerved back from the rigid plan and relieved their harshness of line by making a little sheltered nook and filling it to the brim with sweetness and roundness and softness. Here all things rested. Even the narrow stream ceased its turbulent down-rush long enough to form a quiet pool….On one side, beginning at the very lip of the pool, was a tiny meadow, a cool, resilient surface of green that extended to the base of the frowning wall. Beyond the pool a gentle slope of earth ran up and up to meet the opposing wall. Fine grass covered the slope—grass that was spangled with flowers, with here and there patches of color, orange and purple and golden. Below, the canyon was shut in. There was no view. The walls leaned together abruptly and the canyon ended in a chaos of rocks, moss-covered and hidden by a green screen of vines and creepers and boughs of trees. Up the canyon rose far hills and peaks, the big foothills, pine-covered and remote. And far beyond, like clouds upon the border of the slay, towered minarets of white, where the Sierra's eternal snows flashed austerely the blazes of the sun.

—from "All Gold Canyon" by Jack London

11) **The organizational structure of the passage is**

  A.  order of importance.
  B.  cause and effect.
  C.  problem and solution.
  D.  descriptive.

**Answers:**

  A.  Incorrect. A series of reasons is not presented from most to least or least to most important. The passage describes a restful nook in the canyon.
  B.  Incorrect. The passage does not explain the origin of this nook or its effect on anything, although the reader understands from the details what makes the nook so restful.
  C.  Incorrect. The description of the nook presents no problem, although time in the nook could be seen as a solution for many problems.
  **D.  Correct.** The description of the nook begins with a general impression, moves from one side, to the area beyond the pool, to below the heart of the canyon, and finally to what is above the canyon.

12) **How does the text structure emphasize the central idea of the passage?**

  A.  The logical reasons for needing to rest while hiking make the author's argument compelling.
  B.  By explaining the activities within the canyon, the author convinces the reader that the canyon is safe.
  C.  By describing the areas to the side, below, and above the canyon, the author is able to emphasize the softness at the heart of the canyon.
  D.  The concrete examples included in the passage demonstrate the author's view that beauty is found in nature.

**Answers:**

A.    Incorrect. The passage does not indicate anything about a hike, although the valley is described as a restful place.

B.    Incorrect. The heart of the canyon is still, without activity; even the water stops rushing and forms a pool.

C.    **Correct.** The little restful nook is surrounded by the wall of the mountain, a "chaos of rocks," "boughs of trees," "far hills and peaks."

D.    Incorrect. The central idea of the passage is not finding beauty in nature but simply the restfulness of this nook.

# Drawing Conclusions

Reading text begins with making sense of the explicit meanings of information or a narrative. Understanding occurs as the reader draws conclusions and makes logical inferences. To draw a conclusion, the reader considers the details or facts. He or she then comes to a conclusion—the next logical point in the thought sequence. For example, in a Hemingway story, an old man sits alone in a café. A young waiter says that the café is closing, but the old man continues to drink. The waiter starts closing up, and the old man signals for a refill. Based on these details, the reader might conclude that the old man has not understood the young waiter's desire for him to leave.

An inference is distinguished from a conclusion drawn. An **inference** is an assumption the reader makes based on details in the text as well as his or her own knowledge. It is more of an educated guess that extends the literal meaning. Inferences begin with the given details; however, the reader uses the facts to determine additional facts. What the reader already knows informs what is being suggested by the details of decisions or situations in the text. Returning to the example of the Hemingway story, the reader might infer that the old man is lonely, enjoys being in the café, and is reluctant to leave.

> **DID YOU KNOW?**
>
> When considering a character's motivations, the reader should ask what the character wants to achieve, what the character will get by accomplishing this, and what the character seems to value the most.

When reading fictional text, inferring character motivations is essential. The actions of the characters move the plot forward; a series of events is understood by making sense of why the characters did what they did. Hemingway includes contrasting details as the young waiter and an older waiter discuss the old man. The older waiter sympathizes with the old man; both men have no one at home and experience a sense of emptiness in life, which motivates them to seek the café.

Another aspect of understanding text is connecting it to other texts. Readers may connect the Hemingway story about the old man in the café to other Hemingway stories about individuals struggling to deal with loss and loneliness in a dignified way. They can extend their initial connections to people they know or their personal experiences. When readers read a persuasive text, they often connect the arguments made to counterarguments and opposing evidence of which they are aware. They use these connections to infer meaning.

> **HELPFUL HINT**
>
> Conclusions are drawn by thinking about how the author wants the reader to feel. A group of carefully selected facts can cause the reader to feel a certain way.

## SAMPLE QUESTIONS

I believe it is difficult for those who publish their own memoirs to escape the imputation of vanity; nor is this the only disadvantage under which they labor: it is also their misfortune, that what is uncommon is rarely, if ever, believed, and what is obvious we are apt to turn from with disgust, and to charge the writer with impertinence. People generally think those memoirs only worthy to be read or remembered which abound in great or striking events, those, in short, which in a high degree excite either admiration or pity: all others they consign to contempt and oblivion. It is therefore, I confess, not a little hazardous in a private and obscure individual, and a stranger too, thus to solicit the indulgent attention of the public; especially when I own I offer here the history of neither a saint, a hero, nor a tyrant. I believe there are few events in my life, which have not happened to many: it is true the incidents of it are numerous; and, did I consider myself an European, I might say my sufferings were great: but when I compare my lot with that of most of my countrymen, I regard myself as a *particular favorite of Heaven*, and acknowledge the mercies of Providence in every occurrence of my life. If then the following narrative does not appear sufficiently interesting to engage general attention, let my motive be some excuse for its publication. I am not so foolishly vain as to expect from it either immortality or literary reputation. If it affords any satisfaction to my numerous friends, at whose request it has been written, or in the smallest degree promotes the interests of humanity, the ends for which it was undertaken will be fully attained, and every wish of my heart gratified. Let it therefore be remembered, that, in wishing to avoid censure, I do not aspire to praise.

—from *The Interesting Narrative of the Life of Olaudah Equiano, or Gustavus Vassa, The African* by Olaudah Equiano

13) **Which of the following best explains the primary motivation of the narrator?**

   A. He wants his audience to know that he is not telling his story out of vanity.

   B. He is hoping people will praise his courage.

   C. He wants to give credit to God for protecting him.

   D. He is not seeking personal notoriety; he is hoping people will be influenced by his story and the human condition will improve.

**Answers:**

A. Incorrect. That motive is how the passage begins, but it is not his primary motive.

B. Incorrect. He says he does not aspire to praise, and he does not suggest that he was courageous.

C. Incorrect. He does state that the "mercies of Providence" were always with him; however, that acknowledgement is not his primary motive.

**D. Correct.** In the passage "If it…in the smallest degree promotes the interests of humanity, the ends for which it was undertaken will be fully attained, and every wish of my heart gratified," the narrator's use of the word *humanity* could mean he wants to improve the human condition or he wants to increase human benevolence, or brotherly love.

14) **Given the details of what the narrator says he is *not*, as well as what he claims his story is *not*, it can be inferred that his experience was**

A. a story that could lead to his success.

B. an amazing story of survival and struggle that will be unfamiliar to many readers.

C. an adventure that will thrill the audience.

D. a narrow escape from suffering.

**Answers:**

A. Incorrect. The narrator says that what is obvious in his story is what people "are apt to turn from with disgust, and to charge the writer with impertinence." The narrator is telling a story that his audience couldn't disagree with and might consider rude.

**B. Correct.** By saying "what is uncommon is rarely, if ever, believed, and what is obvious we are apt to turn from with disgust," the narrator suggests that his experience wasn't common or ordinary and could cause disgust.

C. Incorrect. The reader can infer that the experience was horrific; it will inspire disgust, not excitement.

D. Incorrect. The narrator admits he suffered; he indicates that he narrowly escaped death. This is not an inference.

# Understanding the Author

Many questions on the PECT PAPA Reading test will ask for an interpretation of an author's intentions and ideas. This requires an examination of the author's perspective and purpose as well as the way the author uses language to communicate these things.

In every passage, an author chooses words, structures, and content with specific purpose and intent. With this in mind, the reader can begin to comprehend why an author opts for particular words and structures and how these ultimately relate to the content.

## THE AUTHOR'S PURPOSE

The author of a passage sets out with a specific goal in mind: to communicate a particular idea to an audience. The **author's purpose** is determined by asking why the author wants the reader to understand the passage's main idea. There are four basic purposes to which an author can write: narrative, expository, technical, and persuasive. Within each of these general purposes, the author may direct the audience to take a clear action or respond in a certain way.

The purpose for which an author writes a passage is also connected to the structure of that text. In a **narrative**, the author seeks to tell a story, often to illustrate a theme or idea the reader needs to consider. In a narrative, the author uses characteristics of storytelling, such as chronological order, characters, and a defined setting, and these characteristics communicate the author's theme or main idea.

In an **expository** passage, on the other hand, the author simply seeks to explain an idea or topic to the reader. The main idea will probably be a factual statement or a direct assertion of a broadly held opinion. Expository writing can come in many forms, but one essential feature is a fair and balanced representation of a topic. The author may explore one detailed aspect or a broad range of characteristics, but he or she mainly seeks to prompt a decision from the reader.

Similarly, in **technical** writing, the author's purpose is to explain specific processes, techniques, or equipment in order for the reader to use that process or equipment to obtain a desired result. Writing like this employs chronological or spatial structures, specialized vocabulary, and imperative or directive language.

> **HELPFUL HINT**
>
> Reading persuasive text requires an awareness of what the author believes about the topic.

In **persuasive** writing, though the reader is free to make decisions about the message and content, the author actively seeks to convince him or her to accept an opinion or belief. Much like expository writing, persuasive writing is presented in many organizational forms, but the author will use specific techniques, or **rhetorical strategies**, to build an argument. Readers can identify these strategies in order to clearly understand what an author wants them to believe, how the author's perspective and purpose may lead to bias, and whether the passage includes any logical fallacies.

Common rhetorical strategies include the appeals to ethos, logos, and pathos. An author uses these to build trust with the reader, explain the logical points of his or her argument, and convince the reader that his or her opinion is the best option.

An **ethos—ethical—appeal** uses balanced, fair language and seeks to build a trusting relationship between the author and the reader. An author might explain his or her credentials, include the reader in an argument, or offer concessions to an opposing argument.

A **logos—logical—appeal** builds on that trust by providing facts and support for the author's opinion, explaining the argument with clear connections and reasoning. At this point, the reader should beware of logical fallacies that connect unconnected ideas and build arguments on incorrect premises. With a logical appeal, an author strives to convince the reader to accept an opinion or belief by demonstrating that not only is it the most logical option but it also satisfies his or her emotional reaction to a topic.

> **TEACHING TIP**
>
> Readers should consider how different audiences will react to a text. For example, how a slave owner's reactions to the narrative of Olaudah Equiano (on page 19) will differ from a slave trader's.

A **pathos—emotional—appeal** does not depend on reasonable connections between ideas; rather, it seeks to remind the reader, through imagery, strong language, and personal connections, that the author's argument aligns with his or her best interests.

Many persuasive passages seek to use all three rhetorical strategies to best appeal to the reader.

Clues will help the reader determine many things about a passage, from the author's purpose to the passage's main idea, but understanding an author's purpose is essential to fully understanding the text.

## SAMPLE QUESTIONS

Evident truth. Made so plain by our good Father in Heaven, that all *feel* and *understand* it, even down to brutes and creeping insects. The ant, who has toiled and dragged a crumb to his nest, will furiously defend the fruit of his labor, against whatever robber assails him. So plain, that the most dumb and stupid slave that ever toiled for a master, does constantly *know* that he is wronged. So plain that no one, high or low, ever does mistake it, except in a plainly *selfish* way; for although volume upon volume is written to prove slavery a very good thing, we never hear of the man who wishes to take the good of it, *by being a slave himself.*

*Most governments* have been based, practically, on the denial of the equal rights of men, as I have, in part, stated them; *ours* began, by *affirming* those rights. *They* said, some men are too *ignorant*, and *vicious*, to share in government. Possibly so, said we; and, by your system, you would always keep them ignorant and vicious. We proposed to give *all* a chance; and we expected the weak to grow stronger, the ignorant, wiser; and all better, and happier together.

We made the experiment; and the fruit is before us. Look at it. Think of it. Look at it, in its aggregate grandeur, of extent of country, and numbers of population, of ship, and steamboat.

—from Abraham Lincoln's speech fragment on slavery

**15)  The author's purpose is to**

A.    explain ideas.

B.    narrate a story.

C.    describe a situation.

D.    persuade to accept an idea.

**Answers:**

A.    Incorrect. The injustice of slavery in America is made clear, but only to convince the audience that slavery cannot exist in America.

B.    Incorrect. The author briefly mentions the narrative of America in terms of affirming the equal rights of all people, but he does not tell a story or relate the events that led to slavery.

C.    Incorrect. The author does not describe the conditions of slaves or the many ways their human rights are denied.

**D.    Correct.** The author provides logical reasons and evidence that slavery is wrong, that it violates the American belief in equal rights.

**16)  To achieve his purpose, the author primarily uses**

A.    concrete analogies.

B.    logical reasoning.

C.    emotional appeals.

D.    images.

**Answers:**

A.    Incorrect. The author mentions the ant's willingness to defend what is his but does not make an explicit and corresponding conclusion about the slave; instead, he says, "So plain, that the most dumb and stupid slave that ever toiled for a master, does constantly *know* that he is wronged." The implied parallel is between the ant's conviction about being wronged and the slave knowing he is wronged.

**B.    Correct.** The author uses logic when he points out that people who claim slavery is good never wish "to take the good of it, *by being a slave.*" The author also points out that the principle of our country is to give everyone, including the "ignorant," opportunity; then he challenges his listeners to look at the fruit of this principle, saying, "Look at it, in its aggregate grandeur, of extent of country, and numbers of population, of ship, and steamboat."

C.    Incorrect. The author relies on logic and evidence, and makes no emotional appeals about the suffering of slaves.

D.    Incorrect. The author does offer evidence of his point with an image of the grandeur of America, but his primary appeal is logic.

## THE AUDIENCE

The structure, purpose, main idea, and language of a text all converge on one target: the intended audience. An author makes decisions about every aspect of a piece of writing based on that audience, and readers can evaluate the writing through the lens of that audience. By considering the probable reactions of an intended audience, readers can determine many things: whether or not they are part of that intended audience; the author's purpose for using specific techniques or devices; the biases of the author and how they appear in the writing; and how the author uses rhetorical strategies. While readers evaluate each of these things separately, identifying and considering the intended audience adds depth to the understanding of a text and helps highlight details with more clarity.

> **TEACHING TIP**
>
> When reading a persuasive text, students should maintain awareness of what the author believes about the topic.

Several aspects identify the text's intended audience. First, when the main idea of the passage is known, the reader considers who most likely cares about that idea, benefits from it, or needs to know about it. Many authors begin with the main idea and then determine the audience in part based on these concerns.

Then the reader considers language. The author tailors language to appeal to the intended audience, so the reader can narrow down a broad understanding of that audience. The figurative language John Steinbeck uses in his novel *The Grapes of Wrath* reveals the suffering of the migrant Americans who traveled to California to find work during the Great Depression of the 1930s. Steinbeck spoke concretely to the Americans who were discriminating against the migrants.

> **QUICK REVIEW**
>
> A logical argument includes a claim, a reason that supports the claim, and an assumption that the reader makes based on accepted beliefs. All parts of the argument need to make sense to the reader, so authors often consider the beliefs of their audience as they construct their arguments.

Instead of finding work in the "land of milk and honey," migrants faced unbearable poverty and injustice. The metaphor that gives the novel its title is "and in the eyes of the people there is the failure; and in the eyes of the hungry there is a growing wrath. In the souls of the people the grapes of wrath are filling and growing heavy, growing heavy for the vintage." Steinbeck, used the image of ripening grapes, familiar to those surrounded by vineyards, to condemn this harsh treatment, provide an education of the human heart, and inspire compassion in his audience. Readers who weren't directly involved in the exodus of people from Oklahoma to the West, could have little difficulty grasping the meaning of Steinbeck's language in the description: "66 is the path of a people in flight, refugees from dust and shrinking land, from the thunder of tractors and invasion, from the twisting winds that howl up out of Texas, from floods that bring no richness to the land and steal what little richness is there."

## SAMPLE QUESTIONS

*In the following text, consideration should be made for how an English political leader of 1729 might have reacted.*

It is a melancholy object to those, who walk through this great town, or travel in the country, when they see the streets, the roads and cabin-doors crowded with beggars of the female sex, followed by three, four, or six children, all in rags, and importuning every passenger for an alms. These mothers instead of being able to work for their honest livelihood, are forced to employ all their time in strolling to beg sustenance for their helpless infants who, as they grow up, either turn thieves for want of work, or leave their dear native country, to fight for the Pretender in Spain, or sell themselves to the Barbados.

I shall now therefore humbly propose my own thoughts, which I hope will not be liable to the least objection.

I have been assured by a very knowing American of my acquaintance in London, that a young healthy child well nursed, is, at a year old, a most delicious nourishing and wholesome food, whether stewed, roasted, baked, or boiled; and I make no doubt that it will equally serve in a fricassee.

I do therefore humbly offer it to public consideration, that of the hundred and twenty thousand children, already computed, twenty thousand may be reserved for breed, whereof only one fourth part to be males; which is more than we allow to sheep, black cattle, or swine, and my reason is, that these children are seldom the fruits of marriage, a circumstance not much regarded by our savages, therefore, one male will be sufficient to serve four females. That the remaining hundred thousand may, at a year old, be offered in sale to the persons of quality and fortune, through the kingdom, always advising the mother to let them suck plentifully in the last month, so as to render them plump, and fat for a good table. A child will make two dishes at an entertainment for friends, and when the family dines alone, the fore or hind quarter will make a reasonable dish, and seasoned with a little pepper or salt, will be very good boiled on the fourth day, especially in winter.

—from *A Modest Proposal for Preventing the Children of Poor People in Ireland From Being a Burden on Their Parents or Country, and for Making Them Beneficial to the Public* by Jonathan Swift

**17)   Which of the following best states the central idea of the passage?**

A.   Irish mothers are not able to support their children.

B.   The Irish people lived like savages.

C.   The people of England are quality people of fortune.

D.   The kingdom of England has exploited the weaker country of Ireland to the point that the Irish people cannot support their families.

**Answers:**

A.    Incorrect. This is a fact alluded to in the passage, not a central idea.

B.    Incorrect. Although the author does refer to the Irish as savages, the reader recognizes that the author is being outrageously satirical.

C.    Incorrect. The author does say "That the remaining hundred thousand may, at a year old, be offered in sale to the persons of quality and fortune, through the kingdom," referring to the English. However, this is not the central idea; the opposite is, given that this is satire.

**D.    Correct.** The author is hoping to use satire to shame England.

18)  **The author's use of phrases like "humbly propose," "liable to the least objection," "wholesome food" suggests which of the following purposes?**

A.    to inform people about the attitudes of the English

B.    to use satire to reveal the inhumane treatment of the Irish by the English

C.    to persuade people to survive by any means

D.    to express his admiration of the Irish people

**Answers:**

A.    Incorrect. The author's subject is the poverty of the Irish, and his audience is the English who are responsible for the suffering of the Irish.

**B.    Correct.** The intended meaning of a satire sharply contradicts the literal meaning. Swift's proposal is not humble; it is meant to humble the arrogant. He expects the audience to be horrified. The children would make the worst imaginable food.

C.    Incorrect. The author is not serious. His intent is to shock his English audience.

D.    Incorrect. The author is expressing sympathy for the Irish.

## TONE AND MOOD

Two important aspects of the communication between author and audience occur subtly. The **tone** of a passage describes the author's attitude toward the topic, distinct from the **mood**, which is the pervasive feeling or atmosphere in a passage that provokes specific emotions in the reader. The distinction between these two aspects lies once again in the audience: the mood influences the reader's emotional state in response to the piece, while the tone establishes a relationship between the audience and the author. Does the author intend to instruct the audience? Is the author more experienced than the audience, or does he or she wish to convey a

**TEACHING TIP**

To determine the author's tone, students should examine what overall feeling they are experiencing.

friendly or equal relationship? In each of these cases, the author uses a different tone to reflect the desired level of communication.

Primarily **diction**, or word choice, determines mood and tone in a passage. Many readers make the mistake of thinking about the ideas an author puts forth and using those alone to determine particularly tone; a much better practice is to separate specific words from the text and look for patterns in connotation and emotion. By considering categories of words used by the author, the reader can discover both the overall emotional atmosphere of a text and the attitude of the author toward the subject.

### HELPFUL HINT

To decide the connotation of a word, the reader examines whether the word conveys a positive or negative association in the mind. Adjectives are often used to influence the feelings of the reader, such as in the phrase "an ambitious attempt to achieve."

Every word has not only a literal meaning but also a **connotative meaning**, relying on the common emotions, associations, and experiences an audience might associate with that word. The following words are all synonyms: *dog, puppy, cur, mutt, canine, pet.* Two of these words—*dog* and *canine*—are neutral words, without strong associations or emotions. Two others—*pet* and *puppy*—have positive associations. The last two—*cur* and *mutt*—have negative associations. A passage that uses one pair of these words versus another pair activates the positive or negative reactions of the audience.

### SAMPLE QUESTIONS

Day had broken cold and grey, exceedingly cold and grey, when the man turned aside from the main Yukon trail and climbed the high earth-bank, where a dim and little-travelled trail led eastward through the fat spruce timberland. It was a steep bank, and he paused for breath at the top, excusing the act to himself by looking at his watch. It was nine o'clock. There was no sun nor hint of sun, though there was not a cloud in the sky. It was a clear day, and yet there seemed an intangible *pall* over the face of things, a subtle gloom that made the day dark, and that was due to the absence of sun. This fact did not worry the man. He was used to the lack of sun. It had been days since he had seen the sun, and he knew that a few more days must pass before that cheerful orb, due south, would just peep above the sky-line and dip immediately from view.

—from "To Build a Fire" by Jack London

19)    **Which of the following best describes the mood of the passage?**

A.    exciting and adventurous

B.    fierce and determined

C.    bleak and forbidding

D.    grim yet hopeful

**Answers:**

A.    Incorrect. The man is on some adventure as he turns off the main trail, but the context is one of gloom and darkness, not excitement.

B.    Incorrect. The cold, dark day is fierce, and the man may be determined; however, the overall mood of the entire passage is one of grim danger.

**C.    Correct.** The man is oblivious to the gloom and darkness of the day, which was "exceedingly cold and grey."

D.    Incorrect. The atmosphere is grim, and there is no indication the man is hopeful about anything. He is aware only of his breath and steps forward.

20)  **The connotation of the words intangible *pall* is**

A.    a death-like covering.

B.    a vague sense of familiarity.

C.    an intimation of communal strength.

D.    an understanding of the struggle ahead.

**Answers:**

**A.    Correct.** Within the context of the sentence "It was a clear day, and yet there seemed an intangible *pall* over the face of things, a subtle gloom that made the day dark," the words *gloom* and *dark* are suggestive of death; the words *over the face* suggest a covering.

B.    Incorrect. The word *intangible* can mean a vague sense, but there is nothing especially familiar about a clear day that is dark, with no sunlight.

C.    Incorrect. The word *intangible* suggests intimation; however, from the beginning, the author shows the man alone, and reports, "the man turned aside from the main Yukon trail."

D.    Incorrect. A struggle may be indicated by the darkness and gloom, but the man has no understanding of this possibility. The text refers to the darkness, saying, "This fact did not worry the man. He was used to the lack of sun."

# Meaning of Words and Phrases

## CONTEXT CLUES

Vocabulary in context questions ask about the meaning of specific words in the passage. The questions will ask which answer choice is most similar in meaning to the specified word, or which answer choice could be substituted for that word in the passage.

When confronted with unfamiliar words, the passage itself can help clarify their meaning. Often, identifying the tone or main idea of the passage can help eliminate answer choices. For example, if the tone of the passage is generally positive, try eliminating the answer choices with a negative connotation. Or, if the passage is about a particular occupation, rule out words unrelated to that topic.

Passages may also provide specific **context clues** that can help determine the meaning of a word.

One type of context clue is a **definition**, or **description**, **clue**. Sometimes, authors use a difficult word, then include *that is* or *which is* to signal that they are providing a definition. An author also may provide a synonym or restate the idea in more familiar words:

> *Teachers often prefer teaching students with intrinsic motivation; these students have an internal desire to learn.*

The meaning of *intrinsic* is restated as an *internal desire*.

Similarly, authors may include an **example clue**, providing an example phrase that clarifies the meaning of the word:

> *Teachers may view extrinsic rewards as efficacious; however, an individual student may not be interested in what the teacher offers. For example, a student who is diabetic may not feel any incentive to work when offered a sweet treat.*

*Efficacious* is explained with an example that demonstrates how an extrinsic reward may not be effective.

Another commonly used context clue is the **contrast**, or **antonym**, **clue**. In this case, authors indicate that the unfamiliar word is the opposite of a familiar word:

> *In contrast to intrinsic motivation, extrinsic motivation is contingent on teachers offering rewards that are appealing.*

The phrase "in contrast" tells the reader that *extrinsic* is the opposite of *intrinsic*.

## SAMPLE QUESTIONS

21) **One challenge of teaching is finding ways to incentivize, or to motivate, learning.**

**Which of the following is the meaning of *incentivize* as used in the sentence?**

   A.  encourage

   B.  determine

   C.  challenge

   D.  improve

**Answers:**

A. **Correct.** The word *incentivize* is defined immediately with the synonym *motivate*, or *encourage*.

B. Incorrect. *Determine* is not a synonym for *motivate*. In addition, the phrase "to determine learning" does not make sense in the sentence.

C. Incorrect. *Challenge* is not a synonym for motivate.

D. Incorrect. *Improve* is closely related to motivation, but it is not the best synonym provided.

22) **If an extrinsic reward is extremely desirable, a student may become so apprehensive he or she cannot focus. The student may experience such intense pressure to perform that the reward undermines its intent.**

**Which of the following is the meaning of *apprehensive* as used in the sentence?**

A. uncertain

B. distracted

C. anxious

D. forgetful

**Answers:**

A. Incorrect. Nothing in the sentence suggests the student is uncertain.

B. Incorrect. *Distracted* is related to the clue "focus" but does not address the clue "pressure to perform."

C. **Correct.** The reader can infer that the pressure to perform is making the student anxious.

D. Incorrect. Nothing in the sentence suggests the student is forgetful.

# WORD STRUCTURE

In addition to the context of a sentence or passage, an unfamiliar word itself can give the reader clues about its meaning. Each word consists of discrete pieces that determine meaning; the most familiar of these pieces are word roots, prefixes, and suffixes.

**Word roots** are the bases from which many words take their form and meaning. The most common word roots are Greek and Latin, and a broad knowledge of these roots can greatly improve a reader's ability to determine the meaning of words in context. The root of a word does not always point to the word's exact meaning, but combined with an understanding of the word's place in a sentence and the context of a passage, it will often be enough to answer a question about meaning or relationships.

## Table 1.1. Common Word Roots

| Root | Meaning | Examples |
| --- | --- | --- |
| alter | other | alternate, alter ego |
| ambi | both | ambidextrous |
| ami, amic | love | amiable |
| amphi | both ends, all sides | amphibian |
| anthrop | man, human, humanity | misanthrope, anthropologist |
| apert | open | aperture |
| aqua | water | aqueduct, aquarium |
| aud | to hear | audience |
| auto | self | autobiography |
| bell | war | belligerent, bellicose |
| bene | good | benevolent |
| bio | life | biology |
| ced | yield, go | secede, intercede |
| cent | one hundred | century |
| chron | time | chronological |
| circum | around | circumference |
| contra, counter | against | contradict |
| crac, crat | rule, ruler | autocrat, bureaucrat |
| crypt | hidden | cryptogram, cryptic |
| curr, curs, cours | to run | precursory |
| dict | to say | dictator, dictation |
| dyna | power | dynamic |
| dys | bad, hard, unlucky | dysfunctional |
| equ | equal, even | equanimity |
| fac | to make, to do | factory |
| form | shape | reform, conform |
| fort | strength | fortitude |
| fract | to break | fracture |
| grad, gress | step | progression |
| gram | thing written | epigram |
| graph | writing | graphic |
| hetero | different | heterogeneous |
| homo | same | homogenous |
| hypo | below, beneath | hypothermia |
| iso | identical | isolate |
| ject | throw | projection |
| logy | study of | biology |
| luc | light | elucidate |

| Root | Meaning | Examples |
| --- | --- | --- |
| mal | bad | malevolent |
| meta, met | behind, between | metacognition (behind the thinking) |
| meter, metr | measure | thermometer |
| micro | small | microbe |
| mis, miso | hate | misanthrope |
| mit | to send | transmit |
| mono | one | monologue |
| morph | form, shape | morphology |
| mort | death | mortal |
| multi | many | multiple |
| phil | love | philanthropist |
| port | carry | transportation |
| pseudo | false | pseudonym |
| psycho | soul, spirit | psychic |
| rupt | to break | disruption |
| scope | viewing instrument | microscope |
| scrib, scribe | to write | inscription |
| sect, sec | to cut | section |
| sequ, secu | follow | consecutive |
| soph | wisdom, knowledge | philosophy |
| spect | to look | spectator |
| struct | to build | restructure |
| tele | far off | telephone |
| terr | earth | terrestrial |
| therm | heat | thermal |
| vent, vene | to come | convene |
| vert | turn | vertigo |
| voc | voice, call | vocalize, evocative |

In addition to understanding the base of a word, it is vital to recognize common affixes that change the meaning of words and demonstrate their relationships to other words. **Prefixes** are added to the beginning of words and frequently change their meaning, sometimes to an opposite meaning.

Go on

**Table 1.2. Common Prefixes**

| Prefix | Meaning | Examples |
| --- | --- | --- |
| a, an | without, not | anachronism, anhydrous |
| ab, abs, a | apart, away from | abscission, abnormal |
| ad | toward | adhere |
| agere | act | agent |
| amphi, ambi | round, both sides | ambivalent |
| ante | before | antedate, anterior |
| anti | against | antipathy |
| archos | leader, first, chief | oligarchy |
| bene | well, favorable | benevolent, beneficent |
| bi | two | binary, bivalve |
| caco | bad | cacophony |
| circum | around | circumnavigate |
| corpus | body | corporeal |
| credo | belief | credible |
| demos | people | demographic |
| di | two, double | dimorphism, diatomic |
| dia | across, through | dialectic |
| dis | not, apart | disenfranchise |
| dynasthai | be able | dynamo, dynasty |
| ego | I, self | egomaniac, egocentric |
| epi | upon, over | epigram, epiphyte |
| ex | out | extraneous, extemporaneous |
| geo | earth | geocentric, geomancy |
| ideo | idea | ideology, ideation |
| in | in | induction, indigenous |
| in, im | not | ignoble, immoral |
| inter | between | interstellar |
| lexis | word | lexicography |
| liber | free, book | liberal |
| locus | place | locality |
| macro | large | macrophage |
| micro | small | micron |
| mono | one, single | monocle, monovalent |
| mortis | death | moribund |
| olig | few | oligarchy |
| peri | around | peripatetic, perineum |
| poly | many | polygamy |
| pre | before | prescient |

| Prefix | Meaning | Examples |
|--------|---------|----------|
| solus | alone | solitary |
| subter | under, secret | subterfuge |
| un | not | unsafe |
| utilis | useful | utilitarian |

**Suffixes**, on the other hand, are added to the end of words, and they generally point out a word's relationship to other words in a sentence. Suffixes might change a part of speech or indicate if a word is plural or related to a plural.

### Table 1.3. Common Suffixes

| Suffix | Meaning | Examples |
|--------|---------|----------|
| able, ible | able, capable | visible |
| age | act of, state of, result of | wreckage |
| al | relating to | gradual |
| algia | pain | myalgia |
| an, ian | native of, relating to | riparian |
| ance, ancy | action, process, state | defiance |
| ary, ery, ory | relating to, quality, place | aviary |
| cian | processing a specific skill or art | physician |
| cule, ling | very small | sapling, animalcule |
| cy | action, function | normalcy |
| dom | quality, realm | wisdom |
| ee | one who receives the action | nominee |
| en | made of, to make | silken |
| ence, ency | action, state of, quality | urgency |
| er, or | one who, that which | professor |
| escent | in the process of | adolescent, senescence |
| esis, osis | action, process, condition | genesis, neurosis |
| et, ette | small one, group | baronet, lorgnette |
| fic | making, causing | specific |
| ful | full of | frightful |
| hood | order, condition, quality | adulthood |
| ice | condition, state, quality | malice |
| id, ide | connected with, belonging to | bromide |
| ile | relating to, suited for, capable of | puerile, juvenile |
| ine | nature of | feminine |
| ion, sion, tion | act, result, state of | contagion |
| ish | origin, nature, resembling | impish |
| ism | system, manner, condition, characteristic | capitalism |

**Table 1.3. Common Suffixes (continued)**

| Suffix | Meaning | Examples |
|---|---|---|
| ist | one who, that which | artist, flautist |
| ite | nature of, quality of, mineral product | graphite |
| ity, ty | state of, quality | captivity |
| ive | causing, making | exhaustive |
| ize, ise | make | idolize, bowdlerize |
| ment | act of, state or, result | containment |
| nomy | law | autonomy, taxonomy |
| oid | resembling | asteroid, anthropoid |
| some | like, apt, tending to | gruesome |
| strat | cover | strata |
| tude | state of, condition of | aptitude |
| um | forms single nouns | spectrum |
| ure | state of, act, process, rank | rupture, rapture |
| ward | in the direction of | backward |
| y | inclined to, tend to | faulty |

## SAMPLE QUESTIONS

Width and intensity are leading characteristics of his writings—width both of subject-matter and of comprehension, intensity of self-absorption into what the poet contemplates and expresses. He scans and presents an enormous panorama, unrolled before him as from a mountain-top; and yet, whatever most large or most minute or casual thing his eye glances upon, that he enters into with a depth of affection which identifies him with it for a time, be the object what it may. There is a singular interchange also of actuality and of ideal substratum and suggestion. While he sees men, with even abnormal exactness and sympathy, as men, he sees them also "as trees walking," and admits us to perceive that the whole show is in a measure spectral and unsubstantial, and the mask of a larger and profounder reality beneath it, of which it is giving perpetual intimations and auguries.

—from "Prefatory Notice," in the first edition of Walt Whitman's *Leaves of Grass,* by W. M. Rossetti

23) **Which of the following is the best definition of the word** *substratum*?

    A.    meaningful crest

    B.    distracting idea

    C.    reduction

    D.    underlying foundation

**Answers:**

    A.    Incorrect. Within the context of the sentence "There is a singular interchange also of actuality and of ideal substratum and suggestion," to say an "ideal meaningful crest" would be inaccurate because the *sub* prefix suggests *under*, a foundation.

    B.    Incorrect. Within the context, an "ideal distracting idea" sounds contradictory.

    C.    Incorrect. The word *reduction* suggests less than, not under.

    **D.**    **Correct.** Combining the prefix *sub* (*under*) and the root *strata* (*cover*) with the singular suffix *um*, the word *substratum* means underlying layer or substance. An "ideal underlying foundation" makes sense.

24) **The prefix *un* in a word like *unsubstantial* indicates the meaning of the word is**

    A.    not whatever the root word is.

    B.    suggestive of an undercurrent of whatever the root word is.

    C.    a lower value of the root word.

    D.    in opposition to whatever the root word is.

**Answers:**

    **A.**    **Correct.** The prefix *un* means not, and the root word *substantial* means real. *Unsubstantial* means not of physical reality.

    B.    Incorrect. The prefix *un* does not suggest under.

    C.    Incorrect. The prefix *un* does not suggest less than; it is the opposite of the root word.

    D.    Incorrect. "In opposition to" suggests working against something, not being the opposite of.

## FIGURATIVE LANGUAGE

A figure of speech is an expression that is understood to have a nonliteral meaning. Instead of meaning what is actually said, figurative language suggests meaning by pointing to something else. When Shakespeare says "All the world's a stage, / And all men and women merely players," he is speaking of the world as if it were a stage. Since the world is not literally a stage, the reader has to ask how the world is a stage and what Shakespeare is implying about the world.

Figurative language extends the meaning of words by giving readers a new way to view a subject. Thinking of the world as a stage on which people are performing is a new way of thinking about life. After reading Shakespeare's metaphor, people may reflect on how often they play a role, act a part. Their minds may go in many directions; they may wonder when their behavior is genuine, whether they're too worried about others evaluating their performance, and so on. Figurative language—such as metaphors and similes—generates thought after thought; with just a few words, it engages the reader's imagination and adds emphasis to different aspects of the text's subject.

A **metaphor** describes a *topic* that may be unfamiliar to the reader as though it were something else—a *vehicle*—that is probably familiar to the reader. The familiar vehicle is used to help the reader understand a new or unfamiliar topic. As the reader reflects on the similarities between the topic and the vehicle, he or she forms a new idea about the topic. For example, if a person refers to an issue as "the elephant in the room," the topic is the issue, and "the elephant in the room" is a vehicle communicating how overwhelming the issue is or that the issue is undeniable.

> **HELPFUL HINT**
>
> Aristotle claimed that "the greatest thing by far is to have a command of metaphor. This alone cannot be imparted by another; it is the mark of genius, for to make good metaphors implies an eye for resemblances." The resemblance between two unlike things enables understanding of the ideas suggested by metaphoric language.

Similarly, in **personification** an object is anthropomorphized in some way or receives a human attribute. In the sentence "The earth swallowed him whole," *earth* is personified because it is described as carrying out a human action. Personification may also represent an abstract quality. For instance, a timid individual may be the "personification of cowardice."

A **simile** directly points to similarities between two things. The author uses a familiar vehicle to express an idea about the topic. For example, in his poem "The Rime of the Ancient Mariner," Samuel Taylor Coleridge describes his ship as "Idle as a painted ship upon a painted ocean." Readers have most likely seen a painting of a ship; Coleridge has used this knowledge to convey that the ship was completely motionless. Like a simile, an **analogy** is a correspondence between two things; it shows a partial similarity.

**SAMPLE QUESTIONS**

In shape Egypt is like a lily with a crooked stem. A broad blossom terminates it at its upper end; a button of a bud projects from the stalk a little below the blossom, on the left-hand side. The broad blossom is the Delta, extending from Aboosir to Tineh, a direct distance of a hundred and eighty miles, which the projection of the coast—the graceful swell of the petals—enlarges to two hundred and thirty. The bud is the Fayoum, a natural depression in the hills that shut in the Nile valley on the west, which has been rendered cultivable for many thousands of years.... The long stalk of the lily is the Nile valley itself, which is a ravine scooped in the rocky soil for seven hundred miles from the First Cataract to the apex of the Delta, sometimes not more than a mile broad, never more than eight or ten miles. No other country in the world is so strangely shaped, so long compared to its width, so straggling, so hard to govern from a single center.

—from *Ancient Egypt* by George Rawlinson

25) **What kind of figurative language does the author of *Ancient Egypt* use?**

    A.    a metaphor

    B.    a simile

    C.    a comparison

    D.    an analogy

**Answers:**

    A.    Incorrect. A metaphor involves speaking of one thing as if it is something else, not just like something else.

    **B.**    **Correct.** To describe Egypt, the author uses a simile. "Egypt is like a lily with a crooked stem." The blossom is the Delta region of Egypt, the bud is the hills on the west, and the long stalk is the Nile valley.

    C.    Incorrect. Similes show only how one thing is similar to another. A comparison usually shows both similarities and differences.

    D.    Incorrect. An analogy is a correspondence between two things; it shows a partial similarity.

26) **What does the figurative language used in *Ancient Egypt* help the reader understand?**

    A.    how outsiders perceive Egypt

    B.    the dominance of the Nile River

    C.    how difficult it is to live in Egypt

    D.    how strange the shape of the country is

**Answers:**

    A.    Incorrect. The problem with this option is the word *outsiders*. Anyone looking at a map can see the similarity between the shape of Egypt and a lily.

    B.    Incorrect. The Nile River does run through Egypt, but this does not account for the hills or Delta region.

    C.    Incorrect. Egypt being shaped like a lily does not suggest difficulty in living there. Something like a lack of rainfall could create difficulty.

    **D.**    **Correct.** By showing the similarities between a lily and the shape of the country, the author puts a memorable image in the mind of the reader and provides a clear understanding of his point: that there is no center from which to govern the country.

# Comparing Passages

Some of the questions in the PECT PAPA Reading exam require test takers to compare texts that have similar themes or topics. Questions involve identifying the similarities and differences in main ideas, styles, supporting details, and text structures. Test takers will find it helpful to preview the questions and to note pertinent similarities and differences in texts while reading.

The following example passages discuss Walt Whitman's text *Leaves of Grass*. The first is from the preface of *Leaves of Grass* and is written by Whitman himself. The second is from a critical essay by Ed Folsom and Kenneth M. Price about *Leaves of Grass*.

Readers should keep in mind the following questions:

▶   What central idea about Whitman's response to slavery is being expressed in the passages?

▶   How does Folsom and Price's explanation of Whitman's response to the issue of slavery in America differ from Whitman's own statement of his intention?

## SAMPLE QUESTIONS

### One

No great literature, nor any like style of behavior or oratory or social intercourse or household arrangements or public institutions, can long elude the jealous and passionate instinct of American standards. Whether or not the sign appears from the mouths of the people, it throbs a live interrogation in every freeman's and freewoman's heart after that which passes by.

Are its disposals without ignominious distinctions? Is it for the ever-growing communes of brothers and lovers, large, well united, proud beyond the old models, generous beyond all models?

I know that what answers for me, an American, must answer for any individual or nation that serves for a part of my materials. Does this answer? Or is it without reference to universal needs?

Does this acknowledge liberty with audible and absolute acknowledgment, and set slavery at naught, for life and death? Will it help breed one good-shaped man, and a woman to be his perfect and independent mate?

—from preface to *Leaves of Grass* by Walt Whitman

### Two

A pivotal and empowering change came over Whitman at this time of poetic transformation. His politics—and especially his racial attitudes—underwent a profound alteration. As we have noted, Whitman the journalist spoke to the interests of the day and from a particular class perspective when he advanced the interests of white workingmen while seeming, at times, unconcerned about the plight of blacks. Perhaps the New Orleans experience had prompted a change in attitude, a change that was intensified by an increasing number of friendships with radical thinkers and writers who led Whitman to rethink his attitudes toward the issue of race. Whatever the cause, in Whitman's future-oriented poetry blacks become central to his new literary project and central to his understanding of democracy.…His first notebook lines in the manner of *Leaves of Grass* focus directly on the fundamental issue dividing the United States. His notebook breaks into free verse for the first time in lines that seek to bind opposed categories, to link black and white, to join master and slave:

> *I am the poet of the body*
> *And I am the poet of the soul*
> *I go with the slaves of the earth equally with the masters*
> *And I will stand between the masters and the slaves,*
> *Entering into both so that both shall understand me alike.*

The audacity of that final line remains striking. While most people were lining up on one side or another, Whitman placed himself in that space—…*between* master and slave. His extreme political despair led him to replace what he now named the "scum" of corrupt American politics in the 1850s with his own persona—a shaman, a culture-healer, an all-encompassing "I."

—from "Walt Whitman: Racial Politics and the Origins of *Leaves of Grass*" by Ed Folsom and Kenneth M. Price, http://www.whitmanarchive.org/biography/walt_whitman/index.html#racial

**27)  What main idea do both sources make about Walt Whitman's perspective?**

    A.    Slavery is anti-American.

    B.    Democracy is a force of brotherhood.

    C.    Walt Whitman is the voice of American individuality.

    D.    American politics is corrupt.

**Answers:**

    **A.**    **Correct.** The main idea of both passages reveals that Whitman's perspective about the issue of slavery is that slavery is anti-American because it is undemocratic. Whitman saw the liberty of America as a unifying force, a force of brotherhood that could not permit slavery to continue.

    B.    Incorrect. Whitman does view democracy this way; however, he is speaking specifically about slavery being undemocratic.

    C.    Incorrect. This option is true but far too broad an interpretation of the passages. A main idea is more specific statement.

    D.    Incorrect. This option is mentioned in only one passage.

**28)  What is the main difference between the passages?**

    A.    In the first passage, the writer is concerned about slavery, but in the second passage the writers reveal the American confusion about slavery.

    B.    The first passage is a biography of Whitman; the second passage discusses Whitman's poetry.

    C.    The second passage reveals Whitman's consistent opposition to slavery; the first passage details Whitman's pain in relation to slavery.

    D.    In the first passage, Whitman states his perspective on slavery, but the second passage is about Whitman's change of perspective on slavery.

**Answers:**

A.    Incorrect. In the first passage, Whitman explains his viewpoint. In the second passage, the authors critique Whitman's changing views on slavery. Initially, as a journalist, Whitman was sympathetic to the white working class, not the blacks. The authors go on to explain that, in time, Whitman's poetic response to the issue of slavery in America displayed his sympathy for the slave that originated in his soul and his ability to form a union with what he observed. He could see the spiritual significance of different aspects of life and nature, including slavery.

B.    Incorrect. The first passage is written by Whitman; he is expressing his own perspective.

C.    Incorrect. The second passage clearly states that Whitman's view of slavery changed. The first passage is not about pain.

D.    **Correct.** Whitman's perspective is abstract. The second passage helps to make Whitman's thinking clear.

# Part II: Writing

# Language and Research Skills

## Parts of Speech

The **parts of speech** are the building blocks of sentences, paragraphs, and entire texts. Grammarians have typically defined eight parts of speech—nouns, pronouns, verbs, adverbs, adjectives, conjunctions, prepositions, and interjections—all of which play unique roles in the context of a sentence. Thus, a fundamental understanding of the parts of speech is necessary in order to form an understanding of basic sentence construction.

> **DID YOU KNOW?**
>
> Although some words fall easily into one category or another, many words can function as different parts of speech based on their usage within a sentence.

### NOUNS AND PRONOUNS

**Nouns** are the words used to give names to people, places, things, and ideas. Most often, nouns fill the position of subject or object within a sentence. The category of nouns has several subcategories: common nouns (*chair, car, house*), proper nouns (*Julie, David*), abstract nouns (*love, intelligence, sadness*), concrete nouns (*window, bread, person*), compound nouns (*brother-in-law, rollercoaster*), non-countable nouns (*money, water*), countable nouns (*dollars, cubes*), and verbal nouns (*writing, diving*). There is much crossover between these subcategories (for example, *chair* is common, concrete, and countable).

Sometimes, a word that is typically used as a noun will be used to modify another noun. The word then would be labeled as an adjective because of its usage within the sentence. In the following example, *cabin* is a noun in the first sentence and an adjective in the second:

The family visited the <u>cabin</u> by the lake.

> Our <u>cabin</u> stove overheated during vacation.

**Pronouns** replace nouns in a sentence or paragraph, allowing a writer to achieve a smooth flow throughout a text by avoiding unnecessary repetition. The unique aspect of the pronoun as a part of speech is that the list of pronouns is finite: while there are innumerable nouns in the English language, the list of pronouns is rather limited in contrast. The noun that a pronoun replaces is called its **antecedent**.

Pronouns fall into several distinct categories. **Personal pronouns** act as subjects or objects in a sentence:

> <u>She</u> received a letter; I gave the letter to <u>her</u>.

**Possessive pronouns** indicate possession:

> <u>My</u> coat is red; <u>our</u> car is blue.

**Reflexive** (intensive) **pronouns** intensify a noun or reflect back upon a noun:

> I <u>myself</u> made the dessert. I made the dessert <u>myself</u>.

**HELPFUL HINT**

The subject performs the action of a sentence, while the object has the action performed on it.

Personal, possessive, and reflexive pronouns must all agree with the noun that they replace both in gender (male, female, or neutral), number (singular or plural), and person. **Person** refers to the point of view of the sentence. First person is the point of view of the speaker (I, me), second person is the person being addressed (you), and third person refers to a person outside the sentence (he, she, they).

### Table 2.1. Personal, Possessive, and Reflexive Pronouns

| Case | First Person | | Second Person | | Third Person | |
|------|-------------|--------|---------------|---------|-------------------------|------------------|
| Subject | singular | plural | singular | plural | singular | plural |
| | I | we | you | you (all) | he, she, it, | they |
| Object | me | us | you | you (all) | him, her, it | them |
| Possessive | my | our | your | your | his, her, its | their |
| Reflexive | myself | ourselves | yourself | yourselves | himself, herself, itself | themselves |

**Relative pronouns** begin dependent clauses. Like other pronouns, they may appear in subject or object case, depending on the clause. Take, for example, the sentence below:

> Charlie, <u>who</u> made the clocks, works in the basement.

Here, the relative pronoun *who* is substituting for Charlie; that word indicates that Charlie makes the clocks, and so *who* is in the subject case because it is performing the action (*makes the clocks*).

In cases where a person is the object of a relative clause, the writer would use the relative pronoun *whom*. For example, read the sentence below:

My father, <u>whom</u> I care for, is sick.

Even though *my father* is the subject of the sentence, in the relative clause the relative pronoun *whom* is the object of the preposition *for*. Therefore that pronoun appears in the object case.

When a relative clause refers to a non-human, *that* or *which* is used. (*I live in Texas, which is a large state.*) The relative pronoun *whose* indicates possession. (*I don't know whose car that is.*)

### Table 2.2. Relative Pronouns

| Pronoun Type | Subject | Object |
|---|---|---|
| Person | who | whom |
| Thing | which, that | |
| Possessive | whose | |

**Interrogative pronouns** begin questions (*Who worked last evening?*). They request information about people, places, things, ideas, location, time, means, and purposes.

### Table 2.3. Interrogative Pronouns

| Interrogative Pronoun | Asks About | Example |
|---|---|---|
| who | person | <u>Who</u> lives there? |
| whom | person | To <u>whom</u> shall I send the letter? |
| what | thing | <u>What</u> is your favorite color? |
| where | place | <u>Where</u> do you go to school? |
| when | time | <u>When</u> will we meet for dinner? |
| which | selection | <u>Which</u> movie would you like to see? |
| why | reason | <u>Why</u> are you going to be late? |
| how | manner | <u>How</u> did the ancient Egyptians build the pyramids? |

**Demonstrative pronouns** point out or draw attention to something or someone. They can also indicate proximity or distance.

→
Go on

## Table 2.4. Demonstrative Pronouns

| Number | Subject/ Proximity | Example | Object/ Distance | Example |
|---|---|---|---|---|
| Singular | this (subject) | This is my apartment—please come in! | that (object) | I gave that to him yesterday. |
| | this (proximity) | This is the computer you will use right here, not the one in the other office. | that (distance) | That is the Statue of Liberty across the harbor. |
| Plural | these (subject) | These are flawless diamonds. | those (object) | Give those to me later. |
| | these (proximity) | These right here are the books we want, not the ones over there. | those (distance) | Those mountains across the plains are called the Rockies. |

Indefinite pronouns simply replace nouns to avoid unnecessary repetition:

Several came to the party to see both.

Indefinite pronouns can be either singular or plural (and some can act as both depending on the context). If the indefinite pronoun is the subject of the sentence, it is important to know whether that pronoun is singular or plural so that the verb can agree with the pronoun in number.

## Table 2.5. Common Indefinite Pronons

| Sigular | | Plural | Singular or Plural |
|---|---|---|---|
| each | everybody | both | some |
| either | nobody | few | any |
| neither | somebody | several | none |
| one | anybody | many | all |
| everyone | everything | | most |
| no one | nothing | | more |
| someone | something | | *These pronouns take their singularity or plurality from the object of the prepositions that follow: Some of the pies were eaten.* |
| anyone | anything | | |
| | another | | *Some of the pie was eaten.* |

# VERBS

**Verbs** express action (*run, jump, play*) or state of being (*is, seems*). The former are called action verbs, and the latter are linking verbs. Linking verbs join the subject of the sentence to the subject complement, which follows the verb and provides more information about the subject. See the sentence below:

> The dog is cute.

*The dog* is the subject, *is* is the linking verb, and *cute* is the subject complement.

Verbs can stand alone or they can be accompanied by **helping verbs**, which are used to indicate tense. Verb tense indicates the time of the action. The action may have occurred in the past, present, or future. The action may also have been simple (occurring once) or continuous (ongoing). The perfect and perfect continuous tenses describe when actions occur in relation to other actions.

**Table 2.6. Verb Tenses**

| Tense | Past | Present | Future |
|---|---|---|---|
| Simple | I <u>answered</u> the question. | I <u>answer</u> your questions in class. | I <u>will answer</u> your question. |
| Continuous | I <u>was answering</u> your question when you interrupted me. | I <u>am answering</u> your question; please listen. | I <u>will be answering</u> your question after the lecture. |
| Perfect | I <u>had answered</u> all questions before class ended. | I <u>have answered</u> the questions already. | I <u>will have answered</u> every question before the class is over. |
| Perfect Continuous | I <u>had been answering</u> questions when the students started leaving. | I <u>have been answering</u> questions for 30 minutes and am getting tired. | I <u>will have been answering</u> students' questions for 20 years by the time I retire. |

Helping Verbs: is/am/are/was/were, be/being/been, has/had/have, do/does/did, should, would, could, will

Changing the spelling of the verb and/or adding helping verbs is known as **conjugation**. In addition to being conjugated for tense, verbs are conjugated to indicate *person* (first, second, and third person) and *number* (whether they are singular or plural). The conjugation of the verb must agree with the subject of the sentence. A verb that has not be conjugated is called an infinitive and begins with *to* (*to swim, to be*).

> **HELPFUL HINT**
>
> A noun that receives the direct object is the indirect object.
> The pitcher will throw <u>Antoine</u> the ball.

$\longrightarrow$
## Go on

### Table 2.7. Verb Conjugation (Present Tense)

| Person | Singular | Plural |
|---|---|---|
| First Person | I answer | we answer |
| Second Person | you answer | you (all) answer |
| Third Person | he/she/it answers | they answer |

Verbs may be regular, meaning they follow normal conjugation patterns, or irregular, meaning they do not follow a regular pattern.

### Table 2.8. Regular and Irregular Verbs

| | Simple Present | Present Participle | Simple Past | Past Participle |
|---|---|---|---|---|
| Regular | help | helping | helped | (have) helped |
| | jump | jumping | jumped | (have) jumped |
| Irregular | am | been | was | (have) been |
| | swim | swimming | swam | (have) swum |
| | sit | sitting | sat | (have) sat |
| | set | setting | set | (have) set |
| | lie | lying | lay | (have) lain |
| | lay | laying | laid | (have) laid |
| | rise | rising | rose | (have) risen |
| | raise | raising | raised | (have) raised |

Verbs can be written in the active or passive voice. In the **active voice**, the subject of the sentence performs the main action of the sentence. In the sentence below, Alexis is performing the action:

Alexis played tennis.

In the passive voice, the subject of the sentence is receiving the action of the main verb. In the sentence below, the subject is *tennis*, which receives the action *played*:

Tennis was played.

Note that, in the passive voice, there is no indication of who performed the action. For this reason, passive voice is used when the subject is unknown or unimportant. For example, in science, it is common to use the passive voice:

The experiment was performed three times.

At most other times, it is considered more appropriate to use the active voice because it is more dynamic and gives more information.

Finally, verbs can be classified by whether they take a **direct object**, which is a noun that receives the action of the verb. Transitive verbs require a direct object. In the sentence below, the transitive verb *throw* has a direct object (ball):

The pitcher will throw <u>the ball</u>.

Intransitive verbs do not require a direct object. Verbs like *run*, *jump*, and *go* make sense without any object:

He will run.

She jumped.

Many sets of similar verbs include one transitive and one intransitive verb, which can cause confusion. These troublesome verbs include combinations such as *lie* or *lay*, *rise* or *raise*, and *sit* or *set*.

**Table 2.9. Intransitive and Transitive Verbs**

| Intransitive Verbs | Transitive Verbs | |
| --- | --- | --- |
| lie – to recline | lay – to put | lay <u>something</u> |
| rise – to go or get up | raise – to lift | raise <u>something</u> |
| sit – to be seated | set – to put | set <u>something</u> |
| Hint: These intransitive verbs have *i* as the second letter. *Intransitive* begins with *i*. | Hint: The word *transitive* begins with a *t*, and it *TAKES* an object. | |

## ADJECTIVES AND ADVERBS

**Adjectives** modify or describe nouns and pronouns. In English, adjectives are usually placed before the word being modified, although they can also appear after a linking verb such as is or smells.

<u>The</u> <u>beautiful</u> <u>blue</u> <u>jade</u> necklace will go perfectly with my dress.

I think that lasagna smells <u>delicious</u>.

When multiple adjectives are used, they should be listed in the following order:

1. Determiners: articles (*a*, *an*, and *the*), possessive adjectives (e.g., *my*, *her*), and descriptors of quantity (e.g., *three*, *several*)

2. Opinions: modifiers that imply a value (e.g., *beautiful*, *perfect*, *ugly*)

3. Size: descriptions of size (e.g., *small*, *massive*)

4. Age: descriptions of age (e.g., *young*, *five-year-old*)

5. Shape: descriptions of appearance or character (e.g., *smooth*, *loud*)

**HELPFUL HINT**

Adverbs typically answer the questions Where? When? Why? How? How often? To what extent? Under what conditions?

6.   Color: descriptions of color (e.g., *blue, dark*)

7.   Origin: modifiers that describe where something came from (e.g., *American, homemade*)

8.   Material: modifiers that describe what something is made from (e.g., *cotton, metallic*)

9.   Purpose: adjectives that function as part of the noun to describe its purpose (e.g., *sewing machine, rocking chair*)

**Adverbs**, which are often formed by adding the suffix *–ly*, modify any word or set of words that isn't a noun or pronoun. They can modify verbs, adjectives, other adverbs, phrases, or clauses.

> He <u>quickly</u> ran to the house next door. (*Quickly* modifies the verb *ran*.)
>
> Her <u>very</u> effective speech earned her a promotion. (*Very* modifies the adjective *effective*.)
>
> <u>Finally</u>, the table was set and dinner was ready. (*Finally* modifies the clause *the table was set and dinner was ready*.)

## CONJUNCTIONS

**Conjunctions** join words into phrases, clauses, and sentences by use of three mechanisms. There are three main types of conjunctions. **Coordinating conjunctions** join together two independent clauses (i.e., two complete thoughts). These include *and, but, or, for, nor, yet, so* (FANBOYS). Note that some of these can also be used to join items in a series.

> I'll order lunch, <u>but</u> you need to go pick it up.
>
> Make sure to get sandwiches, chips, <u>and</u> sodas.

**Correlative conjunctions** (whether/or, either/or, neither/nor, both/and, not only/but also) work together to join items:

> <u>Both</u> the teacher <u>and</u> the students needed a break after the lecture.

**Subordinating conjunctions** join dependent clauses (thoughts that cannot stand alone as sentences) to the related independent clause. They usually describe some sort of relationship between the two parts of the sentence, such as cause/ effect or order. They can appear at the beginning or in the middle of a sentence:

> We treat ourselves during football season to several orders <u>because</u> we love pizza.
>
> <u>Because</u> we love pizza, we treat ourselves during football season to several orders.

### Table 2.10 Subordinating Conjunctions

| Subordinating Conjunctions | |
|---|---|
| Time | after, as, as long as, as soon as, before, since, until, when, whenever, while |
| Manner | as, as if, as though |
| Cause | because |
| Condition | although, as long as, even if, even though, if, provided that, though, unless, while |
| Purpose | in order that, so that, that |
| Comparison | as, than |

When using correlative conjunctions, be sure that the structure of the word, phrase, or clause that follows the first part of the conjunction mirrors the structure of the word, phrase, or clause that follows the second part.

> I will neither mow the grass nor pull the weeds today. (correct)
>
> I will neither mow the grass nor undertake the pulling of the weeds today. (incorrect)

## PREPOSITIONS

**Prepositions** set up relationships in time (*after the party*) or space (*under the cushions*) within a sentence. A preposition will always function as part of a prepositional phrase, which includes the preposition along with the object of the preposition. If a word that usually acts as a preposition is standing alone in a sentence, the word is likely functioning as an adverb:

> She hid <u>underneath</u>.

### Table 2.11 Common Prepositions

| Prepositions | Compound Prepositions |
|---|---|
| along, among, around, at, before, behind, below, beneath, beside, besides, between, beyond, by, despite, down, during, except, for, from, in, into, near, of, off, on, onto, out, outside, over, past, since, through, till, to, toward, under, underneath, until, up, upon, with, within, without | according to, as of, as well as, aside from, because of, by means of, in addition to, in front of, in place of, in respect to, in spite of, instead of, on account of, out of, prior to, with regard to |

## INTERJECTIONS

**Interjections** have no grammatical attachment to the sentence itself other than to add expressions of emotion. These parts of speech may be punctuated with commas or exclamation points and may fall anywhere within the sentence itself:

> <u>Ouch</u>! He stepped on my toe.
>
> She shopped at the stores after Christmas and, <u>hooray</u>, found many items on sale.
>
> I have seen his love for his father in many expressions of concern—<u>Wow</u>!

### SAMPLE QUESTIONS

1) **List all of the adjectives used in the following sentence:**

   **Her camera fell into the turbulent water, so her frantic friend quickly grabbed the damp item.**

   A.    turbulent, frantic, damp

   B.    turbulent, frantic, quickly, damp

   C.    her, turbulent, frantic, damp

   D.    her, the, turbulent, frantic, damp

   **Answers:**

   A.    Incorrect. This list is incomplete ; it does not include the articles or possessive adjectives.

   B.    Incorrect. This list is incomplete and inaccurate; *quickly* is an adverb.

   C.    Incorrect. This list is incomplete ; it does not include the articles.

   **D.    Correct.** *Turbulent, frantic,* and *damp* are adjectives; *her* is modifying first *camera* and then *friend*; and *the* is always a limiting adjective—the definite article.

2) **List all of the pronouns used in the following sentence:**

   **Several of the administrators who had spoken clearly on the budget increase gave both of the opposing committee members a list of their ideas.**

   A.    several, of, their

   B.    several, who, both

   C.    several, who, both, their

   D.    several, both

   **Answers:**

   A.    Incorrect. The word *of* is a preposition; the word *their* is being used as a possessive adjective.

B.    **Correct.** *Several* is an indefinite plural pronoun; *who* is a relative pronoun introducing the adjectival clause *who had spoken clearly on the budget increase*; *both* is an indefinite plural pronoun.

C.    Incorrect. The word *their* is being used as a possessive adjective.

D.    Incorrect. The list is missing the word *who* which is a relative pronoun introducing the adjectival clause *who had spoken clearly on the budget increase*.

3)    **Which of the following words is functioning as a coordinating conjunction in the sentence below?**

**The political parties do not know if the most popular candidates will survive until the election, but neither the voters nor the candidates will give up their push for popularity.**

A.    if

B.    until

C    but

D.    neither

**Answers:**

A.    Incorrect. *If* is a subordinating conjunction.

B.    Incorrect. *Until* is a preposition.

C.    **Correct.** *But* is a coordinating conjunction joining two clauses.

D.    Incorrect. *Neither* is half of the correlative conjunction pair neither/nor.

# Constructing Sentences

**Syntax** is the study of how words are combined to create sentences. In English, words are used to build phrases and clauses, which, in turn, are combined to create sentences. By varying the order and length of phrases and clauses, writers can create sentences that are diverse and interesting.

Phrases and clauses are made up of either a subject, a predicate, or both. The **subject** is what the sentence is about. It will be a noun that is usually performing the main action of the sentence, and it may be accompanied by modifiers. The **predicate** describes what the subject is doing or being. It contains the verb(s) and any modifiers or objects that accompany it.

## PHRASES

A **phrase** is a group of words that communicates a partial idea and lacks either a subject or a predicate. Several phrases may be strung together, one after another, to add detail and interest to a sentence.

> The animals crossed <u>the large bridge to eat the fish on the wharf</u>.

Phrases are categorized based on the main word in the phrase. A **prepositional phrase** begins with a preposition and ends with an object of the preposition; a **verb phrase** is composed of the main verb along with its helping verbs; and a **noun phrase** consists of a noun and its modifiers.

> prepositional phrase: The dog is hiding <u>under the porch</u>.
>
> verb phrase: The chef <u>would have created</u> another soufflé, but the staff protested.
>
> noun phrase: *The big, red barn* rests beside <u>the vacant chicken house</u>.

An **appositive phrase** is a particular type of noun phrase that renames the word or group of words that precedes it. Appositive phrases usually follow the noun they describe and are set apart by commas.

> My dad, <u>a clock maker</u>, loved antiques.

**Verbal phrases** begin with a word that would normally act as a verb but is instead filling another role within the sentence. These phrases can act as nouns, adjectives, or adverbs. **Gerund phrases** begin with gerunds, which are verbs that end in *–ing* and act as nouns. The word *gerund* has an *n* in it, a helpful reminder that the gerund acts as a noun. Therefore, the gerund phrase might act as the subject, the direct object, or the object of the preposition just as another noun would.

> gerund phrase: <u>Writing numerous Christmas cards</u> occupies her aunt's time each year.

A **participial phrase** is a verbal phrase that acts as an adjective. These phrases start with either present participles (which end in *–ing*) or past participles (which usually end in *–ed*). Participial phrases can be extracted from the sentence, and the sentence will still make sense because the participial phrase is playing only a modifying role:

> <u>Enjoying the stars that filled the sky</u>, Dave lingered outside for quite a while.

Finally, an **infinitive phrase** is a verbal phrase that may act as a noun, an adjective, or an adverb. Infinitive phrases begin with the word *to*, followed by a simple form of a verb (to eat, to jump, to skip, to laugh, to sing).

> <u>To visit Europe</u> had always been her dream.

## Clauses

**Clauses** contain both a subject and a predicate. They can be either independent or dependent. An **independent** (or main) **clause** can stand alone as its own sentence:

The dog ate her homework.

Dependent (or subordinate) clauses cannot stand alone as their own sentences. They start with a subordinating conjunction, relative pronoun, or relative adjective, which will make them sound incomplete:

Because the dog ate her homework

### Table 2.12. Words That Begin Dependent Clauses

| Subordinating Conjunctions | Relative Pronouns and Adjectives |
| --- | --- |
| after, before, once, since, until, when, whenever, while, as, because, in order that, so, so that, that, if, even if, provided that, unless, although, even though, though, whereas, where, wherever, than, whether | who, whoever, whom, whomever, whose, which, that, when, where, why, how |

## TYPES OF SENTENCES

Sentences can be classified based on the number and type of clauses they contain. A **simple sentence** will have only one independent clause and no dependent clauses. The sentence may contain phrases, complements, and modifiers, but it will comprise only one independent clause, one complete idea.

The cat under the back porch jumped against the glass yesterday.

A **compound sentence** has two or more independent clauses and no dependent clauses:

The cat under the back porch jumped against the glass yesterday, and he scared my grandma.

A **complex sentence** has only one independent clause and one or more dependent clauses:

The cat under the back porch, who loves tuna, jumped against the glass yesterday.

A **compound-complex sentence** has two or more independent clauses and one or more dependent clause:

The cat under the back porch, who loves tuna, jumped against the glass yesterday; he left a mark on the window.

→

Go on

Table 2.13. Sentence Structure and Clauses

| Sentence Structure | Independent Clauses | Dependent Clauses |
|---|---|---|
| Simple | 1 | 0 |
| Compound | 2 + | 0 |
| Complex | 1 | 1 + |
| Compound-complex | 2 + | 1 + |

Writers can diversify their use of phrases and clauses in order to introduce variety into their writing. Variety in **sentence structure** not only makes writing more interesting but also allows writers to emphasize that which deserves emphasis. In a paragraph of complex sentences, a short, simple sentence can be a powerful way to draw attention to a major point.

### SAMPLE QUESTIONS

4) Identify the prepositional phrase in the following sentence:

Wrapping packages for the soldiers, the kind woman tightly rolled the t-shirts to see how much space remained for the homemade cookies.

A. Wrapping packages for the soldiers

B. the kind woman

C. rolled the t-shirts

D. for the homemade cookies

**Answers:**

A. Incorrect. This is a participial phrase that begins with the participle *wrapping*.

B. Incorrect. This is a noun phrase that contains the noun *woman* and modifiers.

C. Incorrect. This is a verb phrase that contains the verb and its object.

**D. Correct.** This phrase begins with the preposition *for*.

5) Which of the following sentences is complex?

A. The grandchildren and their cousins enjoyed their day at the beach.

B. Most of the grass has lost its deep color despite the fall lasting into December.

C. The committee members cheered when the amendment passed.

D. The recipes calls for many ingredients that are hard to find or too expensive.

**Answers:**

A.   Incorrect. This sentence is simple with only one independent clause.

B.   Incorrect. This sentence is simple with one independent clause but several phrases.

**C.   Correct.** This sentence is complex. It has an indpendent clause (The committee members cheered) and a dependent clause (when the amendment passed).

D.   Incorrect. This sentence is simple with only one independent clause.

# Punctuation

Many of the choices writers must make relate to **punctuation**. While creative writers have the liberty to play with punctuation to achieve their desired ends, academic and technical writers must adhere to stricter conventions. The main punctuation marks are periods, question marks, exclamation marks, colons, semicolons, commas, quotation marks, and apostrophes.

> **DID YOU KNOW?**
>
> Many people are taught that a comma represents a pause for breath. While this trick is useful for helping young readers, it is not a helpful guide for comma usage when writing.

There are three terminal punctuation marks that can be used to end sentences. The **period** is the most common and is used to end declarative (statement) and imperative (command) sentences. The **question mark** is used to end interrogative sentences, and exclamation marks are used to indicate that the writer or speaker is exhibiting intense emotion or energy.

> Sarah and I are attending a concert.
>
> How many people are attending the concert?
>
> What a great show that was!

The **colon** and the **semicolon**, though often confused, have a unique set of rules surrounding their respective uses. While both punctuation marks are used to join clauses, the construction of the clauses and the relationship between them varies.

The **semicolon** is used to show a general relationship between two independent clauses (IC; IC):

> The disgruntled customer tapped angrily on the counter; she had to wait nearly ten minutes to speak to the manager.

Coordinating conjunctions (FANBOYS) cannot be used with semi-colons. However, conjunctive adverbs can be used following a semi-colon:

> She may not have to take the course this year; however, she will eventually have to sign up for that specific course.

The **colon**, somewhat less limited than the semicolon in its usage, is used to introduce a list, definition, or clarification. While the clause preceding the colon must be an independent clause, the clause that follows does not have to be one:

> The buffet offers three choices that include: ham, turkey, or roast. (incorrect)
>
> The buffet offers three choices: ham, turkey, or roast. (correct)
>
> The buffet offers three choices that include the following: ham, turkey, or roast. (correct)

Note that neither the semicolon nor the colon should be used to set off an introductory phrase from the rest of the sentence.

> After the trip to the raceway; we realized that we should have brought ear plugs. (incorrect)
>
> After the trip to the raceway: we realized that we should have brought ear plugs. (incorrect)
>
> After the trip to the raceway, we realized that we should have brought ear plugs. (correct)

**DID YOU KNOW?**

Exclamation points should be used sparingly or not at all in formal writing.

The **comma** is a complicated piece of punctuation that can serve many different purposes within a sentence. Many times comma placement is an issue of style, not mechanics, meaning there is not necessarily one correct way to write the sentence. There are, however, a few important hard-and-fast comma rules to be followed.

1. Commas should be used to separate two independent clauses along with a coordinating conjunction.

   > George ordered the steak, but Bruce preferred the ham.

2. Commas should be used to separate coordinate adjectives (two different adjectives that describe the same noun).

   > The shiny, regal horse ran majestically through the wide, open field.

3. Commas should be used to separate items in a series. The comma before the conjunction is called the Oxford or serial comma, and is optional.

   > The list of groceries included cream, coffee, donuts, and tea.

4. Commas should be used to separate introductory words, phrases, and clauses from the rest of the sentence.

   > Slowly, Nathan became aware of his surroundings after the concussion.

> Within an hour, the authorities will descend on the home.
>
> After Alice swam the channel, nothing intimidated her.

5. Commas should be used to set off non-essential information and appositives.

> Estelle, our newly elected chairperson, will be in attendance.
>
> Ida, my neighbor, watched the children for me last week.

6. Commas should be used to set off titles of famous individuals.

> Charles, Prince of Wales, visited Canada several times in the last ten years.

7. Commas should be used to set off the day and month of a date within a text.

> My birthday makes me feel quite old because I was born on February 16, 1958, in Minnesota.

8. Commas should be used to set up numbers in a text of more than four digits.

> We expect 25,000 visitors to the new museum.

**Quotation marks** are used for many purposes. First, quotation marks are used to enclose direct quotations within a sentence. Terminal punctuation that is part of the quotation should go inside the marks, and terminal punctuation that is part of the larger sentence goes outside:

> She asked him menacingly, "Where is my peanut butter?"
>
> What is the original meaning of the phrase "king of the hill"?

In American English, commas are used to set quotations apart from the following text and are placed inside the marks:

> "Although I find him tolerable," Arianna wrote, "I would never want him as a roommate."

Additionally, quotation marks enclose titles of short, or relatively short, literary works such as short stories, chapters, and poems. (The titles of longer works, like novels and anthologies, are italicized.) Writers also use quotation marks to set off words used in special sense or for a non-literary purpose:

> The shady dealings of his Ponzi scheme earned him the ironic name "Honest Abe."

**Apostrophes**, sometimes referred to as single quotation marks, show possession; replace missing letters, numerals, and signs; and form plurals of letters, numerals, and signs in certain instances.

1. To signify possession by a singular noun not ending in *s*, add *'s*.
   
   *boy* → *boy's*

2. To signify possession by a singular noun ending in *s*, add *'s*.
   *class → class's*

3. To signify possession by an indefinite pronoun not ending in *s*, add *'s*.
   *someone → someone's*

4. To signify possession by a plural noun not ending in *s*, add *'s*.
   *children → children's*

5. To signify possession by a plural noun ending in *s*, add only the apostrophe.
   *boys → boys'*

6. To signify possession by singular, compound words and phrases, add *'s* to the last word in the phrase.
   *everybody else → everybody else's*

7. To signify joint possession, add *'s* only to the last noun.
   *John and Mary's house*

8. To signify individual possession, add *'s* to each noun.
   *John's and Mary's houses*

9. To signify missing letters in a contraction, place the apostrophe where the letters are missing.
   *do not → don't*

10. To signify missing numerals, place the apostrophe where the numerals are missing.
    *1989 → '89*

11. There are differing schools of thought regarding the pluralization of numerals and dates, but be consistent within the document with whichever method you choose.
    *1990's/1990s; A's/As*

Other marks of punctuation include:

> ▸ **en dash** (–) to indicate a range of dates
>
> ▸ **em dash** (—) to indicate an abrupt break in a sentence and emphasize the words within the em dashes
>
> ▸ **parentheses** ( ) to enclose insignificant information
>
> ▸ **brackets** [ ] to enclose added words to a quotation and to add insignificant information within parentheses

▸ **slash** (/) to separate lines of poetry within a text or to indicate interchangeable terminology

▸ **ellipses** (…) to indicate information removed from a quotation, to indicate a missing line of poetry, or to create a reflective pause

**DID YOU KNOW?**

If a quotation is within another quotation, then the inner quotation uses single quotation marks.

## SAMPLE QUESTIONS

6)    Which of the following is the correct version of the underlined portion of the sentence below?

Freds brother wanted the following items for <u>Christmas a</u> red car a condo and a puppy.

A.    Christmas a

B.    Christmas, a

C.    Christmas. A

D.    Christmas: a

**Answers:**

A,    Incorrect. The sentence needs punctuation to introduce the list.

B.    Incorrect. A comma should not be used to introduce a list.

C.    Incorrect. Adding a period creates a sentence fragment (A red car, a condo, and a puppy).

**D.    Correct.** A colon can be used to introduce a list.

7)    **Which of the following sentences contains a comma usage error?**

A)    On her way home she stopped to pick up groceries, pay her electric bill, and buy some flowers.

B.    I used to drink coffee every morning but my office took away the coffee machine.

C.    Elizabeth will order the cake for the party after she orders the hats.

D.    My cousin, who lives in Indiana, is coming to visit this weekend.

**Answers:**

A.    Incorrect. The commas are used correctly in this series.

**B.    Correct.** This compound sentence requires a comma before the conjunction *but*.

C.    Incorrect. This complex sentence does not require a comma.

D.    Incorrect. The appositive phrase *who lives in Indiana* is appropriately set apart by commas.

# Avoiding Common Usage Errors

## ERRORS IN AGREEMENT

Some of the most common grammatical errors are those involving agreement between subjects and verbs, and between nouns and pronouns. While it is impossible to cover all possible errors, the lists below include the most common agreement rules to look for on the test.

### SUBJECT/VERB AGREEMENT

1. Single subjects agree with single verbs; plural subjects agree with plural verbs.

   The girl walks her dog.

   The girls walk their dogs.

2. Compound subjects joined by *and* typically take a plural verb unless considered one item.

   Correctness and precision are required for all good writing.

   Macaroni and cheese makes a great snack for children.

3. Compound subjects joined by *or* or *nor* agree with the nearer or nearest subject.

   Neither I nor my friends are looking forward to our final exams.

   Neither my friends nor I am looking forward to our final exams.

4. For sentences with inverted word order, the verb will agree with the subject that follows it.

   Where are Bob and his friends going? Where is Bob going?

5. All single, indefinite pronouns agree with single verbs.

   Neither of the students is happy about the play.

   Each of the many cars is on the grass.

   Every one of the administrators speaks highly of Trevor.

6. All plural, indefinite pronouns agree with plural verbs.

   Several of the students are happy about the play.

   Both of the cars are on the grass.

   Many of the administrators speak highly of Trevor.

7. Collective nouns agree with singular verbs when the collective acts as one unit. Collective nouns agree with plural verbs when the collective acts as individuals within the group.

   The band plans a party after the final football game.

   The band play their instruments even if it rains.

   The jury announces its decision after sequestration.

   The jury make phone calls during their break time.

8. The linking verbs agree with the subject and the predicate.

   My favorite is strawberries and apples.

   My favorites are strawberries and apples.

9. Nouns that are plural in form but singular in meaning will agree with singular verbs.

<u>Measles is</u> a painful disease.

<u>Sixty dollars is</u> too much to pay for that book.

10. Singular verbs come after titles, business corporations, and words used as terms.

<u>"Three Little Kittens" is</u> a favorite nursery rhyme for many children.

<u>General Motors is</u> a major employer for the city.

### PRONOUN/ANTECEDENT AGREEMENT

1. Antecedents joined by *and* typically require a plural pronoun.

   The <u>children and their dogs</u> enjoyed <u>their</u> day at the beach.

2. For compound antecedents joined by *or*, the pronoun agrees with the nearer or nearest antecedent.

   Either the resident mice <u>or the manager's cat</u> gets <u>itself</u> a meal of good leftovers.

3. When indefinite pronouns function in a sentence, the pronoun must agree with the number of the pronoun.

   <u>Neither</u> student finished <u>his or her</u> assignment.

   <u>Both</u> of the students finished <u>their</u> assignments.

4. When collective nouns function as antecedents, the pronoun choice will be singular or plural depending on the function of the collective.

   The <u>audience</u> was cheering as <u>it</u> rose to <u>its</u> feet in unison.

   Our <u>family</u> are spending <u>their</u> vacations in Maine, Hawaii, and Rome.

5. When *each* and *every* precede the antecedent, the pronoun agreement will be singular.

   <u>Each and every man, woman, and child</u> brings unique qualities to <u>his or her</u> family.

   <u>Every creative writer, technical writer, and research writer</u> is attending <u>his or her</u> assigned lecture.

## ERRORS IN SENTENCE CONSTRUCTION

**Errors in parallelism** occur when items in a series are not put in the same form. For example, if a list contains two nouns and a verb, the sentence should be rewritten so that all three items are the same part of speech. Parallelism should be maintained in words, phrases, and clauses:

> The walls were painted <u>green</u> and <u>gold</u>.
>
> Her home is <u>up the hill</u> and <u>beyond the trees</u>.

> If we shop on Friday and if we have enough time, we will then visit the aquarium.

**Sentence errors** fall into three categories: fragments, comma splices (comma fault), and fused sentences (run-on). A **fragment** occurs when a group of words does not have both a subject and verb as needed to construct a complete sentence or thought. Many times a writer will mirror conversation and write down only a dependent clause, for example, which will have a subject and verb but will not have a complete thought grammatically.

> Why are you not going to the mall? Because I do not like shopping. (incorrect)
>
> Because I do not like shopping, I will not plan to go to the mall. (correct)

A **comma splice** (comma fault) occurs when two independent clauses are joined together with only a comma to "splice" them together. To fix a comma splice, a coordinating conjunction should be added, or the comma can be replaced by a semicolon:

> My family eats turkey at Thanksgiving, we eat ham at Christmas. (incorrect)
>
> My family eats turkey at Thanksgiving, and we eat ham at Christmas. (correct)
>
> My family eats turkey at Thanksgiving; we eat ham at Christmas. (correct)

**Fused** (run-on) sentences occur when two independent clauses are joined with no punctuation whatsoever. Like comma splices, they can be fixed with a comma and conjunction or with a semicolon:

> My sister lives nearby she never comes to visit. (incorrect)
>
> My sister lives nearby, but she never comes to visit. (correct)
>
> My sister lives nearby; she never comes to visit. (correct)

## COMMONLY CONFUSED WORDS

**a, an**: *a* is used before words beginning with consonants or consonant sounds; *an* is used before words beginning with vowels or vowel sounds.

**affect, effect**: *affect* is most often a verb; *effect* is usually a noun (*The experience affected me significantly* OR *The experience had a significant effect on me.*)

**among, amongst, between**: *among* is used for a group of more than two people; *amongst* is archaic and not commonly used in modern writing; *between* is reserved to distinguish two people, places, things, or groups.

**amount, number**: *amount* is used for non-countable sums; *number* is used with countable nouns (*She had a large amount of money in her purse, nearly fifty dollars.*)

**cite, site**: *cite* is a verb used in documentation to credit an author of a quotation, paraphrase, or summary; *site* is a location.

**elicit, illicit**: *elicit* means to draw out a response from an audience or a listener; *illicit* refers to illegal activity.

**every day, everyday**: *every day* is an indefinite adjective modifying a noun—*each day* could be used interchangeably with *every day*; *everyday* is a one-word adjective to imply frequent occurrence (*Our visit to the Minnesota State Fair is an everyday activity during August.*)

**fewer, less**: *fewer* is used with a countable noun; *less* is used with a non-countable noun (*Fewer parents are experiencing stress since the new teacher was hired; parents are experiencing less stress since the new teacher was hired.*)

**firstly, secondly**: These words are archaic; today, *first* and *second* are more commonly used.

**good, well**: *good* is always the adjective; *well* is always the adverb except in cases of health (*She felt well after the surgery.*)

**implied, inferred**: *implied* is something a speaker does; *inferred* is something the listener does after assessing the speaker's message (*The speaker implied something mysterious, but I inferred the wrong thing.*)

**irregardless, regardless**: *irregardless* is non-standard usage and should be avoided; *regardless* is the proper usage of the transitional statement.

**its, it's**: *its* is a possessive case pronoun; *it's* is a contraction for *it is*.

**moral, morale**: *moral* is a summative lesson from a story or life event; *morale* is the emotional attitude of a person or group of people.

**principal, principle**: *principal* is the leader of a school in the noun usage; *principal* means *main* in the adjectival usage; *principle* is a noun meaning *idea* or *tenet* (*The principal of the school spoke on the principal meaning of the main principles of the school.*)

**quote, quotation**: *quote* is a verb and should be used as a verb; *quotation* is the noun and should be used as a noun.

**reason why**: *reason why* is a redundant expression—use one or the other (*The reason we left is a secret. Why we left is a secret.*)

**should of, should have**: *should of* is improper usage, likely resulting from misunderstood speech—*of* is not a helping verb and can therefore cannot complete the verb phrase; *should have* is the proper usage. (*He should have driven.*)

**than, then**: *than* sets up a comparison of some kind; *then* indicates a reference to a point in time (*When I said that I liked the hat better than the gloves, my sister laughed; then she bought both for me.*)

**their, there, they're**: *their is* the possessive case of the pronoun *they. There* is the demonstrative pronoun indicating location, or place. *They're* is a contraction of the words *they are*, the third-person plural subject pronoun and third-person plural, present-tense conjugation of the verb *to be*. These words are very commonly confused in written English.

**to lie (to recline), to lay (to place)**: *to lie* is the intransitive verb meaning *to recline*, so the verb does not take an object; *to lay* is the transitive verb meaning *to place something*. (*I lie out in the sun; I lay my towel on the beach.*)

**to try and**: *to try and* is sometimes used erroneously in place of *to try to*. (*She should try to succeed daily.*)

**unique**: *unique* is an ultimate superlative. The word *unique* should not be modified technically. (*The experience was ~~very~~ unique.*)

**who, whom**: *who* is the subject relative pronoun. (*My son, who is a good student, studies hard.*) Here, the son is carrying out the action of studying, so the pronoun is a subject pronoun (*who*). *Whom* is the object relative pronoun. (*My son, whom the other students admire, studies hard.*) Here, *son* is the object of the other students' admiration, so the pronoun standing in for him, *whom*, is an object pronoun.

**your, you're**: *your* is the possessive case of the pronoun *you. You're* is a contraction of the words *you are*, the second-person subject pronoun and the second-person singular, present-tense conjugation of the verb *to be*. These words are commonly confused in written English.

## SAMPLE QUESTIONS

8) **Which sentence does NOT contain an error?**

    A.    My sister and my best friend lives in Chicago.

    B.    My parents or my brother is going to pick me up from the airport.

    C.    Neither of the students refuse to take the exam.

    D.    The team were playing a great game until the rain started.

**Answers:**

    A.    Incorrect. Because the sentence reads <u>My sister and my</u> best friend, the subject is plural and needs a plural verb (*live*).

    **B.**    **Correct.** The verb agrees with the closest subject—in this case, the singular *brother*.

    C.    Incorrect. *Neither* is a singular, indefinite pronoun, so the agreement is singular. *Neither refuses*

    D.    Incorrect. In the context of a game, the *team* is functioning as a singular, so it should take a singular verb. *The team was*

9)    **Which sentence does NOT contain an error?**

    A.    The grandchildren and their cousins enjoyed their day at the beach.

    B.    Most of the grass has lost their deep color.

    C.    The jury was cheering as their commitment came to a close.

    D.    Every boy and girl must learn to behave themselves in school.

**Answers:**

    **A.**    **Correct.** *Grandchildren and cousins/their*

    B.    Incorrect. *Most of the grass has lost its deep color.*

    C.    Incorrect. *The jury was cheering as its commitment came to a close.*

    D.    Incorrect. *Every boy and girl must learn to behave himself or herself in school.*

10)    **Which of the following sentences contains a comma splice?**

    A.    Since she went to the store.

    B.    The football game ended in a tie, the underdog caught up in the fourth quarter.

    C.    If we get rid of the bookcase, we'll have enough room for a couch.

    D.    When the players dropped their gloves, a fight broke out on the ice hockey rink floor.

**Answers:**

    A.    Incorrect. The group of words in A is not a complete thought and would be classified as a fragment.

    **B.**    **Correct.** The sentence in B joins two complete thoughts with only a comma and would therefore be classified as a comma splice.

    C.    Incorrect. This sentence correctly joins a dependent and independent clause using a comma.

    D.    Incorrect. The sentence in D is punctuated properly and constructed correctly.

# Evaluating Sources

**Research** is a process of gathering sources containing documented facts that answer specific questions and provide information about an issue. In the twenty-first century, locating sources is easy; however, finding and determining quality sources involves careful evaluation.

It is best to begin by evaluating the credibility of a source's author. Consideration should be given to the author's motivation—the purpose or reason he or she had for writing the text. Next, research involves identifying the author's background and expertise. Although educational credentials are significant, firsthand experience offers equally reliable information.

Questions a researcher should be able to answer about a source include:

▶ Is it current or written fairly recently?

▶ If it is secondary, is it based on both primary as well as other secondary sources?

▶ Is the author an expert in the area of study? Does he or she include or cite relevant information from other authorities on the topic? Are the conclusions based on scientific evidence? How well does the scientifically gathered evidence explain the topic?

▶ Is the purpose of the source clear? Is there any bias?

▶ What does the author assume is true?

▶ Does the author present several viewpoints on issues?

▶ Does the content agree with what other reliable sources on the topic indicate?

Evaluating a website entails determining who the site's intended audience is and if the site has an agenda, such as selling something or promoting a belief system. If the site is educational, researchers should verify whether it was created by authoritative authors and authors that have identified themselves. Grammatically correct content on the site is a helpful indicator. Plus, the site's address should work and be relatively current. (Typing "javascript:alert(document.lastModified)" in the address bar provides a site's most recent modification date.)

## SAMPLE QUESTIONS

11) **What legitimizes the claims made in a source?**

A. Similar information and conclusions are apparent in other sources.

B. The background of the writer is clear.

C. The publisher of the source is a respected organization.

D. A journalist or an admired writer has written the source.

**Answers:**

A. **Correct.** The content is in agreement with what other reliable sources on the topic indicate.

B. Incorrect. The writer's background may be clear, but that background is not the subject of the source.

C.    Incorrect. A respected organization is unrelated to scholarly research, an author's qualifications, or the use of verifiable data.

D.    Incorrect. The writer may be a journalist or admired, but that does not mean the writer is knowledgeable about the subject of the text or has collected data that supports the ideas of the source.

12) **A quality source**

A.    is free of the clutter of citations, quotations, footnotes, and a works-cited page.

B.    is peer-reviewed by scholars who have credentials in a wide variety of areas, not just the subject of the source article.

C.    has remained in publication for decades.

D.    includes accurate, well-documented information.

**Answers:**

A.    Incorrect. A quality source has citations, quotations, footnotes, and a works-cited page.

B.    Incorrect. A peer-reviewed source has been assessed by scholars who have credentials in the same area as the author of the source.

C.    Incorrect. A quality source may be a recent publication.

**D.    Correct.** The author of a quality source is an expert in the source's area of study and will have included or cited relevant information from other authorities on the topic.

## TYPES OF SOURCES

Which sources a researcher uses depends on his or her purpose. If the purpose is to analyze, interpret, or critique an historical event, a creative work, or a natural phenomenon, the researcher will use a **primary**, or **original**, **source**. Examples of primary sources include:

- ▶ letters and e-mails
- ▶ autobiographies, diaries, and memoirs
- ▶ firsthand or eyewitness accounts or descriptions of events
- ▶ interviews, questionnaires, and surveys
- ▶ speeches and lectures
- ▶ photographs, drawings, and paintings
- ▶ news stories written at the time of the event

The written analysis or interpretation of a primary source is considered a **secondary source**. These sources are written by people who do not have firsthand experience of the topic being described. Instead, authors of secondary sources examine primary sources in order to draw conclusions or make generalizations about people, events, and ideas. Examples of secondary sources include:

▶ literary criticism and interpretation essays

▶ biographies

▶ historical criticism

▶ political analyses

▶ essays on ethics and social policies

To research a problem or question that has not been researched before, an analysis of the relevant primary documents is recommended. In addition, researchers can conduct their own observations, interviews, surveys, or experiments.

If the purpose is to report on, explain, or summarize what is known about a topic, the researcher will use texts written by other researchers or secondary sources. Of note, most primary research studies begin with a review of literature, which summarizes what secondary sources are saying about a topic.

Research on topics of interest usually begins with a critical analysis of existing research; researchers draw conclusions from secondary sources that deal with their specific topic. Initially, thought should be given to searching databases. Annotated bibliographies are helpful in locating the most relevant sources for a topic. Web pages created by associations, government agencies, and institutions have a wealth of source material. Although print sources continue to be helpful, most researchers use the Internet to locate digital versions of print sources. Reports by research agencies are often available, particularly in areas concerning the environment. If scholarly sources are required—that is, texts written by those who are highly educated in a particular field—instead of a web search, Google Scholar and databases like JSTOR, EBSCO, and GALE can be more helpful. Public libraries are the best places to avoid the cost of subscription-based databases like JSTOR.

## SAMPLE QUESTIONS

13) **A secondary source**

    A.    summarizes or evaluates an original source or research study.

    B.    is written by a person who conducted an original study or wrote an original text.

    C.    must be peer reviewed.

    D.    is published by the government or a private publisher.

**Answers:**

    **A.**    **Correct.** A secondary source is a written analysis or interpretation of a primary source. Examples include literary and historical criticism.

    B.    Incorrect. This option describes a primary source.

    C.    Incorrect. This is a possibility, but it does not define what a secondary source is.

D.     Incorrect. These are possibilities, but they don't explain what a secondary source is.

**14)  What kind of source is a political speech?**

A.     a secondary source

B.     an authoritative source

C.     a confusing source

D.     a primary source

**Answers:**

A.     Incorrect. A secondary source is a written analysis or interpretation of a primary source. Examples include literary and historical criticism.

B.     Incorrect. The speaker may not be authoritative, or even knowledgeable.

C.     Incorrect. This is possible but hopefully not true.

**D.     Correct.** Primary sources are firsthand accounts of a topic. They are created by authors who have direct experience with the subject and are usually created at the time the authors are involved with the subject. A political speech is written or given by a person who is directly involved with the issues presented in the speech.

## RESEARCH STRATEGIES

Research begins with curiosity about a specific topic, then moves from curiosity to a research question. Doing preliminary reading on the topic refines that question and gains the researcher an overview. A search of *available sources related to the question* is also wise. For example:

- ▶  **Research topic**: Emily Dickinson and feminism
- ▶  **Question**: What feminist ideas did Emily Dickinson express?
- ▶  **Preliminary sources**: Literary criticism on Emily Dickinson, especially feminist interpretations of Dickinson's poetry

Next, the researcher will need to decide which primary sources and critical essays to use. After skim-reading these sources, a preliminary *organizational plan* should be determined. Some considerations include: What basic background information does the reader (also considered the audience) need in order to understand the topic? What is the basis of the ideas to be presented? In other words, what topics need to be explained first so other topics can be understood by the reader? What is the most logical way to present the information that has been located? The reader prefers one topic to lead to the next. Organizational plans detail the characteristics, causes, effects, sequences of events, similarities, and contrasts.

A sample organizational plan for the Emily Dickinson research example could involve presenting in the first section a historical account of the nineteenth-century women's rights movement and a definition of the concept of feminism during Dickinson's life. The next sections could delve into the main feminist ideas Dickinson expressed in her poetry.

Once an organizational plan is outlined, the researcher should start taking *notes* from the sources gathered. Most important, each note must include identifying information about the source, including publication details and page numbers. In addition, the section of the outline that corresponds with the source information noted must be designated above each note. This way, the notes are categorized according to the outline, or organizational plan.

Notes come in four different forms. A **direct quotation** is three or more consecutive words copied precisely from a source. It must be designated by quotation marks or by block indentation if the quotation is longer than four lines of prose or three lines of poetry. A quotation can be a definition or a well-worded or authoritative statement that will amplify a main point. A **paraphrase** is a re-worded version of any sentence in a source. Typically, a sentence with complex or sophisticated wording needs to be paraphrased. The main thoughts are pulled apart and the language is simplified, but the original meaning is retained. A **summary** is a shortened version of a section of a source, containing only the main points or events of the original. Any type of descriptive, detailed, or narrative text, such as news stories, fictional stories, or chronicles of events needs to be summed up. An **idea and list**—the most common form of notes—consists of the key idea of a section of text followed by a bulleted list of related details. Again, all notes should be marked with corresponding outline sections, so it will be easy to put the notes in the order of the outline and use the information to compose the paper.

The following are sample notes for research on feminist ideas expressed by Emily Dickinson:

Cooper, Susan Fenimore. "Female Suffrage: A Letter to the Christian Women of America." *Harper's New Weekly Magazine* XLI (June–November 1870): 594 – 600.

**Outline Section I**

Three Reasons Women Remain in a Subordinate Position:

1. They are physically weaker and depend on men for protection.
2. They are intellectually inferior.
   ▶ This claim is considered debatable.
   ▶ Why women have not educated themselves is of concern.
3. Christianity teaches that men are the head of the household.
   ▶ But protects her more than other systems

**Figure 2.2a. A Primary Source**

Dickinson, Emily. "My Life had stood – a Loaded Gun." Stanzas 1 – 3.

**Outline Section I**

> My Life had stood—a Loaded Gun—
> In Corners—till a Day
> The Owner passed—identified—
> And carried Me away—
>
> And now We roam in Sovereign Woods—
> And now We hunt the Doe—
> And every time I speak for Him—
> The Mountains straight reply—
> And do I smile, such cordial light
> Upon the Valley glow—
> It is as a Vesuvian face
> Had let its pleasure through—

Figure 2.2b. A Primary Source

Rich, Adrienne. "Vesuvius at Home: The Power of Emily Dickinson." Reprinted in *Literary Theories in Praxis*. Edited by Shirley F. Staton. Philadelphia: University of Pennsylvania Press, 1987. pp. 258–59.

**Outline Section I**

Speaking of Emily Dickinson's poem "My Life had stood – a Loaded Gun," Adrienne Rich explains, "But I think that for us, at this time, it is a central poem in understanding Emily Dickinson, and ourselves, and the condition of the woman artist, particularly in the nineteenth century. It seems likely that the nineteenth-century woman poet, especially, felt the medium of poetry as dangerous….Poetry is too much rooted in the unconscious; it presses too close against the barriers of repression; and the nineteenth-century woman had much to repress."

*Paraphrase of the above quotation:*

Nineteenth-century women had to repress many of their thoughts. In other words, they pushed these thoughts into their unconscious minds and weren't aware of them. Since the unconscious mind is the source of poetic expression, writing poetry was dangerous for a nineteenth-century woman; in doing so, she gave expression to these repressed thoughts and feelings.

Figure 2.3. A Secondary Source, Literary Criticism

15) **Which of the following is an example of a secondary source for an article on local highways?**

   A. an online opinion column promoting tax incentives for those who carpool

   B. photographs of traffic accidents

   C. data from the city's transportation department

   D. an autobiography of a city official who led efforts to improve local infrastructure

   **Answers:**

   **A. Correct.** Only this option describes a secondary source, since it offers analysis of a topic, not firsthand experience of it.

   B. Incorrect. Photographs are a primary source.

   C. Incorrect. The analysis or interpretation of data could be considered a secondary source, but the data itself is a primary source.

   D. Incorrect. An autobiography is a primary source.

16) **What is a good reason for a writer of a research paper to include a short section of text copied word for word from a source?**

   A. The text is a secondary source.

   B. The vocabulary is sophisticated.

   C. The text is well worded.

   D. The information relates to several areas of the research.

   **Answers:**

   A. Incorrect. The type of source does not affect whether a direct quote should be included in a research paper.

   B. Incorrect. Sophisticated vocabulary is not a good enough reason to quote text; the text should be still be paraphrased.

   **C. Correct.** Quoting a statement with wording that is emphatic or memorable can be an especially effective way to amplify an argument in a research paper.

   D. Incorrect. Ideally all the information in a research paper is relevant, so this is not a reason to include direct quotations.

# CITATIONS

In general, any ideas or details that are not original to the writer must be documented. Specifically, this includes any information quoted, paraphrased, or summarized from sources.

Information taken from sources is documented with **in-text citations**, **internal documentation**, or **parenthetical references**. These terms are used interchangeably to mean that the source information—usually the author's last name or the first main words of the title plus the page, line, or section number—is put in parentheses right after the paraphrase, quotation, or summary. If the source of the information is introduced in the text with the author's name, the writer puts just the page, line, or section number in the parentheses.

# Writing the Essay

Regardless of the format or topic, a high-scoring essay can be written by following several simple rules. First, identify the type of essay to be written: if the essay doesn't correctly address the prompt, it will always receive a low score. Second, determine what the main point and organizational structure of the essay will be. It is much easier to write using a clear outline than to haphazardly organize along the way. Third, make sure that the essay uses sound evidence while maintaining a style that's appropriate to the test. A good essay doesn't have to be complicated; it just needs to have a clear, well-reasoned position. Finally, all of this must be accomplished within a limited time frame. Fortunately, the essay graders will understand that a first draft written under test conditions does not need to be as polished as a final essay in a classroom assignment.

## Types of Essays

It is important to note that essays do not follow a single format. Rather, the format is determined by the intended purpose of each essay. For example, an essay may attempt to inform or persuade the reader, or perhaps describe or narrate a scene. It is important to use the appropriate type of essay for a given task.

### PERSUASIVE

A **persuasive essay** is meant to convince the reader of the author's point of view on a particular issue. Typically, such an essay will also include a call to action. Thus, a persuasive essay should cause the reader to feel and act in a particular way.

A persuasive essay can be written on any topic on which people can have a difference of opinion. For example, an essay may argue that social media is harmful to teenagers or that a noise ordinance should be adopted in a community. These both seek to sway the reader's opinion to that of the author's. In contrast, essays describing the social media habits of teenagers or telling the story of a neighborhood's attempt to pass local noise ordinances are not persuasive because they do not present a specific opinion.

In writing a persuasive essay, it is vital to take a clear stance on an issue. The reader should be left with no doubt as to which side of an issue the writer supports. In addition, a persuasive essay must include facts and logical reasoning to show that the ideas put forth by the author are superior to other ideas on the topic. This type of essay should be written with a specific audience in mind to tailor the arguments and language to the intended readers.

When writing persuasive essays in an exam setting, keep in mind that the actual stance taken in the essay is not important. The graders don't care about the specific opinion expressed in the essay; they only care that the opinion is well written and supported by logically relevant evidence.

## PERSUASIVE ESSAY EXAMPLE

**PROMPT**: Technology has launched us into a new era and, with it, a new way of living with and relating to one another. It has opened doors and allowed us to accomplish things that would have been impossible in the past: we are able to keep up closely with a large number of people in an easy and comfortable way. As it continues to develop, social media technology will, time and again, offer us new and better ways of staying in touch with one another and, because of it, will make our lives and our relationships fuller and more meaningful.

*Discuss the extent to which you agree or disagree with this opinion. Support your position with specific reasoning and examples from your experience, observations, and reading.*

One would be foolish to argue that technology has not had a real and pervasive impact on our daily lives. Many of us rely daily on cell phones, tablets, and computers that allow us to reach family, friends, and business associates with little to no trouble. However, this ease of access does not necessarily mean our relationships are improving: the impersonal and anonymous nature of social media and other communication technologies make it even more difficult for us to make meaningful, lasting connections with the people around us.

Social media is, by nature, impersonal. Though we are able to build personal profiles that reflect whom we want the world to see, these profiles do little to improve our connection and communication with others. In fact, it is these very tools that are distancing us from our fellow humans. Birthday notifications, for example, remind social media users every day of the "friends" who are celebrating that day. While this tool seems, in theory, to be a great way to keep up with others, it actually desensitizes us. In truth, when I receive birthday notifications via social media, I end up either ignoring them altogether or sending an impersonal "Happy Birthday" just to be able to say I did. In fact, I never send birthday notes via social media to friends and family whose birthdays I actually care about because I do so in a more personal way—via a phone call or in person. Furthermore, I don't need an app to remember those birthdays. Though it may seem more useful or convenient to be able to stay in touch through social media, the relationships that rely on it are, in my experience, rarely very meaningful. By allowing us to stay in touch with larger numbers of people, social media also makes our connections shallower.

In addition to being impersonal, social media and other communication technologies can also be anonymous, creating a world of users that are disconnected from the things they post and read and, ultimately, from each other. Cyber bullying has been a significant concern of the twenty-first century, with numerous incidents leading to depressing outcomes, like teenage suicide. Through the lens of social media, bullies are able to disregard the humanity of the person on the other end and say things that they might never say in real life. A similar effect is clear during important political events: people post, with aggressive fervor, in favor of their own beliefs and respond, with equally aggressive insults, to anyone they disagree with. While this may, on the surface, seem to encourage open dialogue, social media and other communication technologies fail to have any effect on the quality of the conversation itself. Rather than learning to interact with one another respectfully, a tactic that may actually lead to increased understanding and greater acceptance of others, social media users learn that what they say has little to no consequence in real life.

The sense of community created by social media is deceptive. The ease with which people can "connect" often makes those connections meaningless. The friend who "Likes" a photo you post isn't putting any real energy into that friendship—he just clicked once and moved on. Similarly, people can use the anonymity of the internet to just as easily create enemies. One angry comment (that would never be said face-to-face) can launch a hundred nasty replies. These types of relationships don't make our lives fuller or more meaningful. They make our lives empty and shallow.

## EXPOSITORY

An **expository essay** is one in which the author tells the reader something in a straightforward manner. This essay type is meant to explain, inform, or clarify a topic for which the reader may have no prior knowledge. It is also a chance for the writer to display his or her own understanding of a topic. Subjects for an expository essay might include many different sides, but an expository essay doesn't dive into these controversies. Instead, it simply explains a topic with as much neutrality as possible.

To compose a successful expository essay, the author must present facts from verifiable sources and arrange the information in a logical sequence. Language should be clear and precise, and relevant context should be provided since the reader may not be familiar with the topic. It is important that the essay remains objective and does not include the author's opinion.

### DID YOU KNOW?

The word *expository* is related to the word *expose*, which means to show.

## EXPOSITORY ESSAY EXAMPLE

**PROMPT**: Following the Second World War, the United States and the Soviet Union emerged as the dominant world powers, ushering in the Cold War and a "bipolar world." Only a few years before, however, European powers like England and France controlled colonial empires around the world, dominating world affairs; in fact, the Soviet Union itself was only a few decades old.

*Using your knowledge of world history, explain how the two superpowers were able to rapidly dominate world affairs following World War II.*

The United States and the Soviet Union—victorious allies in the Second World War—were not able to maintain a strong relationship for long. Despite losses in the millions, the Soviet Union still had an enormous and powerful military and, in violation of the agreements made at Yalta, Stalin later occupied several Eastern European countries, preventing free elections. The US-led West formed NATO as a result; in response, the USSR organized the Warsaw Pact. This rapid rise in the prominence of the United States and the USSR was a result of both countries' advanced industrial capabilities, large resource reserves, and expanded global military presence.

In the United States, the New Deal and mobilization for the war had strengthened the national economy. At the end of the war, the United States had proven its weapons capacity by using the nuclear bomb: this technology, on the heels of its military domination of Europe and the Pacific, made it an undisputed global superpower.

At the same time, the Soviet Union dominated land throughout Europe, Central, and East Asia. The Soviet Union's Five Year Plans of the 1920s had sped up industrialization, and their wealth included vast mineral, petroleum, timber, and other natural resources. They also developed nuclear weapons and a military with a global reach.

Furthermore, both countries extended their global reach diplomatically and militarily to spread their respective ideologies—communism and democratic capitalism—in order to ensure global security. By promulgating the Marshall Plan and supporting the establishment of the Bretton Woods institutions (the World Bank and the International Monetary Fund), the United States found ways to promote global capitalism. At the same time, the Soviet Union supported Marxist independence movements worldwide in colonies and resistance movements in former colonies; many Cold War battles were fought as proxy wars between the superpowers in Africa, Asia, and Latin America. Each country also had a global presence with bases, officers, diplomats, and military personnel in nearly every country in the world.

Since the European empires had collapsed in the wake of the Second World War, the Soviet Union and the United States dominated the global stage in a way no other country could match. Each used their natural and industrial resources, alongside a growing military and diplomatic presence, to quickly fill the void left by the fall of European powers.

# Writing a Thesis Statement

The thesis, or **thesis statement**, is central to the structure and meaning of an essay: it presents the writer's argument or position on an issue. In other words, it tells readers specifically what the author is going to say in the essay. A strong, direct thesis statement is key to the organization of any essay. It introduces both the central idea of the essay and the main points that will be used to support that idea. Thus, the thesis will mirror the organization of the essay as a whole: each paragraph can elaborate on each supporting point.

In writing a thesis statement, it is important to respond to the prompt provided. The author must identify keywords in the prompt and think about what the prompt is asking. For example, the prompt may be asking for a clear stance to be taken a particular issue, or it may require a detailed explanation of a topic. Once a clear understanding of the task is reached, the author must develop a central idea along with supporting points from relevant sources, including any provided documents and personal knowledge or experience. The central idea and supporting points can then be concisely packaged into a one or two sentence statement. Generally, a thesis statement is no more than two sentences.

> **HELPFUL HINT**
>
> Find an op-ed article in the newspaper. Read it carefully and try to identify the thesis and supporting points.

---

**THESIS STATEMENT EXAMPLES**

**PROMPT**: Many high schools have begun to adopt 1:1 technology programs, meaning that each school provides every student with a computing device, such as a laptop or tablet. Educators who support these initiatives say that the technology allows for more dynamic collaboration and that students need to learn technology skills to compete in the job market. On the other hand, opponents cite increased distraction and the dangers of cyber-bullying or unsupervised internet use as reasons not to provide students with such devices.

*In your essay, take a position on this question. You may write about either one of the two points of view given, or you may present a different point of view on this question. Use specific reasons and examples to support your position.*

**Possible thesis statements:**

1) Providing technology to every student is good for education because it allows students to learn important skills such as typing, web design, and video editing, and it also gives students more opportunities to work cooperatively with their classmates and teachers.

2) I disagree with the idea that schools should provide technology to students because most students will simply be distracted by the free access to games and websites when they should be studying or doing homework.

3) By providing each student with a laptop or tablet, schools can help students apply technology to work more effectively with other students,

communicate with teachers and classmates, and conduct research for class projects.

# Structuring the Essay

There are a lot of different ways to organize an essay. In the limited timeframe of an exam, however, it is best to stick to a basic five-paragraph essay that includes an introduction, body, and conclusion. This structure can be used to discuss nearly any topic and will be easy for graders to follow.

## INTRODUCTIONS

The purpose of an **introduction** is to set the stage for the essay. This is accomplished by capturing the reader's interest, introducing and providing context for the topic, and stating the central idea and main points of the essay. Usually the introductory paragraph ends with a thesis statement, which clearly sets forth the position or point the essay will argue.

### INTRODUCTION EXAMPLE

Technology has changed massively in recent years, but today's generation barely notices—high school students are already experienced with the internet, computers, apps, cameras, cell phones, and more. It's inevitable that these technologies will be begin to make their way into classrooms. Opponents of 1:1 technology programs might argue that students will be distracted or misuse the technology, but that is exactly why schools must teach them to use it. Students need to know how to navigate technology safely and effectively, and schools have a responsibility to ensure they learn these skills. By providing each student with a laptop or tablet, schools can help students learn how to apply technology to work more effectively with other students, communicate with teachers and classmates, and conduct research for class projects.

**Explanation**: This introduction *introduces* the topic in the first sentence. It then provides context by discussing why technology in the classroom is an important—and controversial—topic. The paragraph closes with a thesis statement that takes a firm stance and introduces the supporting ideas that the essay will be organized around.

## THE BODY PARAGRAPHS

The body of the essay should consist of two to four paragraphs, each of which is focused on a single supporting idea. The body of an essay can be organized in a number of ways:

- ▶ Body paragraphs can explain each supporting detail given in the thesis statement.

- ▶ Body paragraphs can describe a problem then discuss the pros and cons of a solution in separate paragraphs.

- ▶ Body paragraphs can tell a story, with the story broken into two to four logical parts.

- ▶ Body paragraphs can compare and contrast the merits of two arguments, possibly drawing a conclusion about which is better at the end.

Each paragraph should be structurally consistent, beginning with a topic sentence to introduce the main idea, followed by supporting ideas and examples. No extra ideas unrelated to the paragraph's focus should appear. Transition words and phrases can be used to connect body paragraphs and to improve the flow and readability of the essay.

**QUICK REVIEW**

Which essay structure would be better suited to a persuasive essay? What about an expository essay?

**BODY PARAGRAPH EXAMPLE**

Technology can be a powerful tool for collaboration. When all of the students in a classroom have access to reliable laptops or tablets, they are able to more effectively share information and work together on projects. Students can communicate quickly via email, share files through a cloud service, and use a shared calendar for scheduling. They also have the opportunity to teach each other new skills since each student may bring to the group unique knowledge about particular apps or programs. When the availability of technology is limited or inconsistent, these opportunities are lost.

**Explanation**: This body paragraph discusses a supporting detail given the thesis (*schools can help students apply technology to work more effectively with other students*). It introduces the topic, then provides concrete examples of how technology makes it easier to work with other students. The final sentence reemphasizes the paragraph's main idea.

## CONCLUSIONS

To end an essay smoothly, the author must compose a conclusion that reminds the reader of the importance of the topic and then restates the essay's thesis and supporting details. The writer should revisit the ideas in the introduction and thesis statement, but these ideas should not be simply repeated word-for-word. Rather, a well-written conclusion will reinforce the argument using wording that differs from the thesis statement but conveys the same idea. The conclusion should leave the reader with a strong impression of the essay's main idea and provide the essay with a sense of closure.

## CONCLUSION EXAMPLE

As technology continues to change and become more incorporated into everyday life, students will need to adapt to it. Schools already teach young people a myriad of academic and life skills, so it makes sense that they would teach students how to use technology appropriately, too. When technology is incorporated into schoolwork, students will learn to collaborate, communicate, and research more effectively. Providing students with their own devices is one part of this important task, and schools that do so should be supported.

> **Explanation:** This conclusion reminds the reader why the topic is important and then restates the thesis and supporting ideas. It ends with a strong, clear statement of the writer's stance on the issue.

# Supporting Evidence

An essay's arguments are made up of claims, which in turn are backed by supporting evidence. This evidence can be drawn from a number of sources. Some essay prompts will include texts from which to draw supporting evidence. Other essays will require the writer to use his or her own background knowledge of the issue. For some essay prompts, it may be appropriate to use personal anecdotes and experiences. Regardless of the source of the evidence, it is important that it be conveyed in a clear, specific, and accurate manner.

## PROVIDING SPECIFIC EXAMPLES

In body paragraphs, general statements should be followed with specific examples that will help to convince the reader that the argument has merit. These specific examples do not bring new ideas to the paragraph; rather, they explain or defend the general ideas that have already been stated. A poorly written essay will be full of general claims supported by little to no evidence or specific examples. Conversely, successful essays will use multiple specific examples to back up general claims.

## EXAMPLES OF GENERAL AND SPECIFIC STATEMENTS

The following are some examples of general statements, followed by examples of specific statements that provide more detailed support of an idea.

> **General:** Students may get distracted online or access harmful websites.
>
> **Specific:** Some students spend too much time using chat features or social media, or they get caught up in online games. Others spend time reading websites that have nothing to do with an assignment.
>
> **Specific:** Teens often think they are hidden behind their computer screens. However, providing personal information online can lead to danger in the real world.
>
> **General:** Schools can teach students how to use technology appropriately and expose them to new tools.

**Specific**: Schools can help students learn how to use technology to work on class projects, communicate with classmates and teachers, and carry out research for classwork.

**Specific**: Providing students with laptops or tablets will allow them to get lots of practice using technology and programs at home, and only school districts can ensure that these tools are distributed widely, especially to students who may not have access to them otherwise.

## INCORPORATING SOURCES

Providing evidence from outside sources is an excellent way to provide support for the claims in an essay. Some essay prompts will include texts that may be cited in the essay, or writers may want to cite sources from memory. In either case, this supporting evidence should be incorporated smoothly into the essay. Context should be provided for the quote, and the quote should always be followed by a discussion of its importance or relevance to the essay.

> **HELPFUL HINT**
>
> In an essay, a quote never speaks for itself; the writer must always explain where it came from and why it is important.

When using outside sources, it is vital to credit the author or source within the text. Usually a full citation isn't needed—it can simply be sufficient to note the author's name in the text. And, as always, the writer must make sure to place direct quotations in quotation marks.

### INCORPORATING SOURCES EXAMPLE

In addition to helping students work better with each other, technology can also help students communicate more effectively with teachers. A recent study from the University of Montana showed that over 75 percent of students have at some point been too intimidated to speak up in class, even if they thought they had something valuable to contribute (Higgins, 2015). But what if technology could provide a way to make speaking up easier? Private online messaging, comment boards for questions, and online tutorials are all made possible by introducing technology to the classroom. A well-trained teacher will be able to use these resources to encourage more effective classroom communication. In my personal experience, I have seen numerous students respond effectively when given the chance to communicate in the privacy of an online interaction.

**Explanation**: This first-person paragraph incorporates two sources: a scientific study and a personal anecdote from the author.

# Writing Well

Although the content of an essay is of primary importance, the writing itself will also factor into the essay's final score. Writing well means that the language and tone are appropriate for the purpose and audience of the essay, the flow of ideas and the relationships among them are logical and clear, and the sentences are varied enough to keep the reader interested.

## Transitions

Transitions are words, phrases, and ideas that help connect ideas throughout a text both between sentences and between paragraphs. Transitions can be used to imply a range of relationships, including cause and effect, sequence, contradictions, and continuance of an idea. Consistent and creative use of transitions will help the essay flow logically from one idea to the next and will make the essay easy for the reader to follow.

Transitions between paragraphs can also be polished by starting paragraphs with references to ideas mentioned in previous paragraphs or by ending them with a transition to the next topic. Such guideposts will guide the reader from one paragraph to the next.

> **HELPFUL HINT**
>
> Common transitions include *then, next, in other words, as well, in addition to, another, because, first, finally, in conclusion, however, in fact, therefore,* and *on the other hand.*

### EXAMPLES OF TRANSITIONS

Teens often think they are hidden behind their computer screens. <u>However,</u> providing personal information online can lead to danger in the real world.

<u>In addition to</u> helping students work better with each other, technology can also help students communicate more effectively with teachers.

They <u>also</u> have the opportunity to teach each other new skills.

## Syntax

A variety of well-written sentences will help maintain the reader's interest in the essay. To create this theme, a writer can use sentences that differ in length and that begin with varying words, rather than repeating the same word at the start of each new sentence. It is also important for the writer to use a mix of different sentence structures, including simple, complex, compound, and compound-complex sentences.

### SYNTAX EXAMPLE

Technology can be a powerful tool for collaboration. When all of the students in a classroom have access to reliable laptops or tablets, they are able to more effectively share information and work together on projects. Students can communicate quickly via email, share files through a cloud service, and use a shared calendar for scheduling. They also have the opportunity to teach each other new skills since each student may bring to the group unique knowledge about particular apps or programs. When the availability of technology is limited or inconsistent, these opportunities are lost.

> **Explanation**: This paragraph starts with a short, simple sentence and follows with a longer, more complex sentence. The next sentence is also long, but it is a simple sentence with a single clause. The second-to-last sentence is complicated with multiple clauses, but it is immediately followed with a short, easy-to-read statement that ends the paragraph.

## WORD CHOICE AND TONE

The words a writer chooses influence the reader's assessment of the essay. When writing essays, it is always necessary to choose words that are appropriate to the task.

For instance, a formal essay on an academic topic may benefit from complex sentences and an expansive vocabulary. However, a first-person essay on a personal topic may use a more causal vocabulary and organization. In general, when writing for exam graders, it is best to use clear, direct vocabulary and avoid using vague, general words such as good, bad, very, or a lot. Showing variety in word choice can also help improve an essay's score. However, it is better to use more familiar vocabulary than to try to impress the exam grader with unfamiliar words or words that do not fit the context of the essay.

### WORD CHOICE EXAMPLES

Technology has changed massively in recent years, but today's generation barely notices—high school students are already experienced with the internet, computers, apps, cameras, cell phones, and more. It is inevitable that these technologies will be begin to make their way into classrooms. Opponents of 1:1 technology programs might argue that students will be distracted or misuse the technology, but that is exactly why schools must teach them to use it. Students need to know how to navigate technology safely and effectively, and schools have a responsibility to ensure they learn these skills. By providing each student with a laptop or tablet, schools can help students apply technology to work more effectively with other students, communicate with teachers and classmates, and conduct research for class projects.

Technology is everywhere in modern life. We've all walked into a coffee shop full of laptops or have seen people walking with their phones in front of their faces. I know I've often looked up from my tablet to realize I've missed a whole conversation. With technology everywhere, it seems obvious that we would start using it in classrooms. Opponents of 1:1 technology programs say that technology will be too distracting or will be abused by students, but it seems like that's an even more important reason for students to learn how to use it. Schools are where students learn all kinds of life skills, and technology is just another skill to learn. By giving students laptops or tablets, schools can help students work better with each other, work better with teachers, and learn to do better research.

**Explanation**: The two paragraphs above discuss the same topic. The first has a word choice and tone for an academic essay; the second is written in a more relaxed, personal style.

## MANAGING TIME

When working on an essay under time constraints, it is important to manage time wisely. Simply launching into the introduction will likely result in a hurried, unorganized essay and a low score. Instead, the writer should take a few minutes to plan.

> **HELPFUL HINT**
>
> Underline key words in the prompt so you can refer to them while writing the essay. This can help keep you and your essay focused.

As a first step, the writer should thoroughly read the prompt and any accompanying texts, and then determine the type of essay that is required. Next, the writer must decide on a thesis and what kind of supporting evidence to use. Once the thesis is clear, it is a good idea for the writer to create a brief outline of the essay. This whole process should only take a few minutes, leaving the bulk of the time for writing. However, it is always a good idea to leave a few minutes at the end to proofread and revise as necessary.

# Example Essays

**PROMPT**: The rise in popularity of e-cigarettes has reduced the overall smoking rate according to the Centers for Disease Control and Prevention. Many hail the new technology for helping smokers quit traditional tobacco cigarettes. However, others raise concerns about the appeal of e-cigarettes to young people and advocate FDA regulation of e-cigarettes to prevent negative side effects of their use on a new generation of smokers.

In your essay, take a position on this question. You may write about either one of the two points of view given, or you may present a different point of view on this question. Use specific reasons and examples to support your position.

### EXAMPLE ESSAY ONE

For decades, youth smoking was a major concern for both parents and public health advocates. With education campaigns informing youth of the dangers of smoking and legal action taken against tobacco producers for their advertising tactics, the number of youth smoking traditional cigarettes has never been lower. But new technology is threatening to overturn that progress as electronic (e-cigarettes) have skyrocketed in popularity among both adults and youth. E-cigarettes should be regulated by the FDA to prevent youth from smoking since the long-term effects of e-cig use are unknown, youth are still becoming addicted to nicotine, and e-cigs could be a gateway to traditional smoking.

Smoking has long been a way for young people to feel cool or sophisticated. Popular culture, including film and television, glamorized smoking and led generations of Americans to pick up the habit. Although traditional smoking is no longer considered cool, the use of e-cigarettes, or vaping, threatens to take the same position in popular culture. Companies which produce traditional cigarettes have long been banned from advertising their products on television, but because e-cigarettes are not regulated by the FDA, there are no restrictions on their advertisement. This allows e-cig companies to reach youth through a wide range of media. Furthermore, the gadget-like design of e-cigs and the variety of candy-like flavors make them especially appealing to youth—a tactic that seems designed to hook a new generation on smoking.

This is particularly concerning as the long-term effects of vaping are not yet known for either adults or youth. The technology is too new to have been studied adequately. The FDA must study a drug for years before it can become available to the general public. Yet a device that delivers a highly-addictive substance remains unregulated. It is true that e-cigarettes are healthier for smokers than traditional cigarettes, but we cannot yet know the impact on youth who would have otherwise not smoked but for the easy access to these drug-delivery devices.

In addition, we do know that nicotine is a highly-addictive drug and that once this habit is established, it is very difficult to quit. If nothing else, this is a wasteful way for young people to spend their money. But even more concerning is the danger that nicotine use could alter the brain chemistry of young people and potentially make them prone to other addictions. Even if vaping does not become a gateway to hard drug use, it does make the leap to traditional smoking much more likely, and we know how harmful cigarettes have been.

The FDA has a responsibility to protect the public's health, and it is clear that regulation is needed to stop the momentum of the e-cigarette industry from getting youth addicted to their products. Although long-term health effects of vaping are unknown at this time, we must be cautious and err on the side of safety. At the very least, youth can be spared from an expensive, addictive habit; at best, an entire generation can live longer, healthier lives.

**Explanation**: This response provides good context for the discussion of the topic and takes a clear stance on the issue raised in the prompt. Strong examples and sound reasoning support the thesis. The essay is cohesive, and strong transitions connect ideas. Vocabulary and tone are appropriate, and the conclusion leaves the reader with a sense of the importance of the issue. Overall, this response would receive a high score.

## EXAMPLE ESSAY TWO

Everyone knows smoking is bad for you. So, it's good that lots of people are quitting, and I think e-cigarettes, or vapes as they are also called, are helping people quit. Even though I don't use them, I know some people who use vapes, and they seem pretty healthy. It may be true that e-cigarettes have harmful side-effects, but it will be too far into the future before we know. The FDA should be studying this so that we do know if vapes are safe to use, especially for kids. No one wants kids to get hooked on drugs or to be unhealthy.

If they do start smoking, it is better for the kids to use e-cigarettes. They are less harmful because they don't use real tobacco or produce the terrible smelling smoke that normal cigarettes do. Some of my friends vape, and I don't even mind being in the same room. They actually smell pretty sweet. I don't think it's good to vape too much, but once in a while is fine, and I hope people make good choices about smoking.

> **Explanation:** This response does not sufficiently address the prompt. The writer seems to disagree with the position of FDA regulation of e-cigarettes but does not develop this into a clear thesis. The writer's position is further confused by stating that the FDA should be studying the matter. The response is short and lacks adequate supporting detail. Although some personal examples are used, they are weak and a divergence from the main point. Although free of most errors, the language is simplistic, personal pronouns are overused, and the tone is not appropriate for academic writing. Overall, this response would receive a low score.

# Part III: Mathematics

# Numbers and Operations

This chapter provides a review of the basic yet critical components of mathematics such as manipulating fractions, comparing numbers, and using units. These concepts will provide the foundation for more complex mathematical operations in later chapters.

## Types of Numbers

Numbers are placed in categories based on their properties.

- A **natural number** is greater than 0 and has no decimal or fraction attached. These are also sometimes called counting numbers {1, 2, 3, 4, ...}.

- **Whole numbers** are natural numbers and the number 0 {0, 1, 2, 3, 4, ...}.

- **Integers** include positive and negative natural numbers and 0 {..., −4, −3, −2, −1, 0, 1, 2, 3, 4, ...}.

- A **rational number** can be represented as a fraction. Any decimal part must terminate or resolve into a repeating pattern. Examples include −12, $-\frac{4}{5}$, 0.36, $7.\overline{7}$, $26\frac{1}{2}$, etc.

- An **irrational number** cannot be represented as a fraction. An irrational decimal number never ends and never resolves into a repeating pattern. Examples include $-\sqrt{7}$, $\pi$, and 0.34567989135...

- A **real number** is a number that can be represented by a point on a number line. Real numbers include all the rational and irrational numbers.

- An **imaginary number** includes the imaginary unit $i$, where $i = \sqrt{-1}$ Because $i^2 = -1$, imaginary numbers produce a negative value when squared. Examples of imaginary numbers include $-4i$, $0.75i$, $i\sqrt{2}$ and $\frac{8}{3}i$.

▶ A **complex number** is in the form $a + bi$, where $a$ and $b$ are real numbers. Examples of complex numbers include $3 + 2i$, $-4 + i$, $\sqrt{3} - i\sqrt[3]{5}$ and $\frac{5}{8} - \frac{7i}{8}$. All imaginary numbers are also complex.

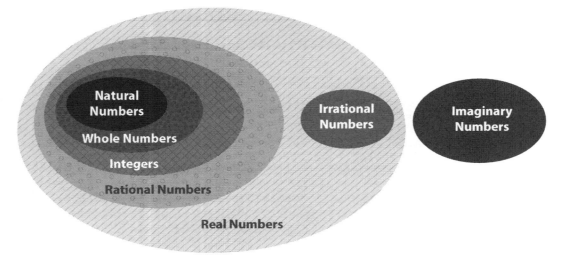

**Figure 4.1. Types of Numbers**

The **factors** of a natural number are all the numbers that can multiply together to make the number. For example, the factors of 24 are 1, 2, 3, 4, 6, 8, 12, and 24. Every natural number is either prime or composite. A **prime number** is a number that is only divisible by itself and 1. (The number 1 is not considered prime.) Examples of prime numbers are 2, 3, 7, and 29. The number 2 is the only even prime number. A **composite number** has more than two factors. For example, 6 is composite because its factors are 1, 6, 2, and 3. Every composite number can be written as a unique product of prime numbers, called the **prime factorization** of the number. For example, the prime factorization of 90 is $90 = 2 \times 3^2 \times 5$. All integers are either even or odd. An even number is divisible by 2; an odd number is not.

HELPFUL HINT

If a real number is a natural number (e.g., 50), then it is also a whole number, an integer, and a rational number.

## PROPERTIES OF NUMBER SYSTEMS

A system is **closed** under an operation if performing that operation on two elements of the system results in another element of that system. For example, the integers are closed under the operations of addition, subtraction, and multiplication but not division. Adding, subtracting, or multiplying two integers results in another integer. However, dividing two integers could result in a rational number that is not an integer $\left(-2 \div 3 = \frac{-2}{3}\right)$.

▶ The rational numbers are closed under all four operations (except for division by 0).

▶ The real numbers are closed under all four operations.

▶ The complex numbers are closed under all four operations.

▶ The irrational numbers are NOT closed under ANY of the four operations.

The **commutative property** holds for an operation if order does not matter when performing the operation. For example, multiplication is commutative for integers: $(-2)(3) = (3)(-2)$.

The **associative property** holds for an operation if elements can be regrouped without changing the result. For example, addition is associative for real numbers: $-3 + (-5 + 4) = (-3 + -5) + 4$

The **distributive property** of multiplication over addition allows a product of sums to be written as a sum of products: $a(b + c) = ab + ac$. The value $a$ is distributed over the sum $(b + c)$. The acronym FOIL (First, Outer, Inner, Last) is a useful way to remember the distributive property.

When an operation is performed with an **identity element** and another element $a$, the result is $a$. The identity element for multiplication on real numbers is $1 (a \times 1 = a)$, and for addition is $0 (a + 0 = a)$.

An operation of a system has an **inverse element** if applying that operation with the inverse element results in the identity element. For example, the inverse element of $a$ for addition is $-a$ because $a + (-a) = 0$. The inverse element of $a$ for multiplication is $\frac{1}{a}$ because $a \times \frac{1}{a} = 1$.

## SAMPLE QUESTIONS

1) Classify the following numbers as natural, whole, integer, rational, or irrational. (The numbers may have more than one classification.)

A.  72

B.  $-\frac{2}{3}$

C.  $\sqrt{5}$

**Answers:**

A.  The number is **natural, whole**, an **integer**, and **rational** (72 can be written as the fraction $\frac{72}{1}$).

B.  The fraction is **rational**.

C.  The number is **irrational**. (It cannot be written as a fraction, and written as a decimal is approximately 2.2360679... Notice this decimal does not terminate nor does it have a repeating pattern.)

2) **Determine the real and imaginary parts of the following complex numbers.**

   A. 20

   B. $10 - i$

   C. $15i$

**Answers:**

A complex number is in the form of $a + bi$, where $a$ is the real part and $b$ is the imaginary part.

   A. $20 = 20 + 0i$
      **The real part is 20, and there is no imaginary part.** (The imaginary part is 0.)

   B. $10 - i = 10 - 1i$
      **The real part is 10, and −1 is the imaginary part.**

   C. $15i = 0 + 15i$
      **The real part is 0, and the imaginary part is 15.**

3) **Answer True or False for each statement:**

   A. The natural numbers are closed under subtraction.

   B. The sum of two irrational numbers is irrational.

   C. The sum of a rational number and an irrational number is irrational.

**Answers:**

   A. **False**. Subtracting the natural number 7 from 2 results in $2 - 7 = -5$, which is an integer, but not a natural number.

   B. **False**. For example, $(5 - 2\sqrt{3}) + (2 + 2\sqrt{3}) = 7$. The sum of two irrational numbers in this example is a whole number, which is not irrational. The sum of a rational number and an irrational number is sometimes rational and sometimes irrational.

   C. **True**. Because irrational numbers have decimal parts that are unending and with no pattern, adding a repeating or terminating decimal will still result in an unending decimal without a pattern.

4) **Answer True or False for each statement:**

   A. The associative property applies for multiplication in the real numbers.

   B. The commutative property applies to all real numbers and all operations.

**Answers:**

   A. **True**. For all real numbers, $a \times (b \times c) = (a \times b) \times c$. Order of multiplication does not change the result.

   B. **False**. The commutative property does not work for subtraction or division on real numbers. For example, $12 - 5 = 7$, but $5 - 12 = -7$ and $10 \div 2 = 5$, but $2 \div 10 = \frac{1}{5}$.

# Scientific Notation

**Scientific notation** is a method of representing very large and small numbers in the form $a \times 10^n$, where $a$ is a value between 1 and 10, and $n$ is a nonzero integer. For example, the number 927,000,000 is written in scientific notation as $9.27 \times 10^8$. Multiplying 9.27 by 10 eight times gives 927,000,000. When performing operations with scientific notation, the final answer should be in the form $a \times 10^n$.

6.5 x $10^7$

.0000987

9.87 x $10^{-5}$

**Figure 4.2. Scientific Notation**

> **HELPFUL HINT**
>
> When multiplying numbers in scientific notation, add the exponents. When dividing, subtract the exponents.

When adding and subtracting numbers in scientific notation, the power of 10 must be the same for all numbers. This results in like terms in which the $a$ terms are added or subtracted and the $10^n$ remains unchanged. When multiplying numbers in scientific notation, multiply the $a$ factors, and then multiply that answer by 10 to the sum of the exponents. For division, divide the $a$ factors and subtract the exponents.

## SAMPLE QUESTIONS

5) Simplify: $(3.8 \times 10^3) + (4.7 \times 10^2)$

**Answer:**

| $(3.8 \times 10^3) + (4.7 \times 10^2)$ | |
|---|---|
| $3.8 \times 10^3 = 3.8 \times 10 \times 10^2 = 38 \times 10^2$ | To add, the exponents of 10 must be the same. Change the first number so the power of 10 is 2. |
| $38 \times 10^2 + 4.7 \times 10^2 = 42.7 \times 10^2$ | Add the $a$ terms together. |
| $= \mathbf{4.27 \times 10^3}$ | Write the number in proper scientific notation. |

6) Simplify: $(8.1 \times 10^{-5})(1.4 \times 10^7)$

**Answer:**

| $(8.1 \times 10^{-5})(1.4 \times 10^7)$ | |
|---|---|
| $= 11.34 \times 10^2$ | Multiply the $a$ factors and add the exponents on the base of 10. |

$$= 1.134 \times 10^3$$

> Write the number in proper scientific notation by placing the decimal so that the first number is between 1 and 10 and adjusting the exponent accordingly.

# Positive and Negative Numbers

**Positive numbers** are greater than 0, and **negative numbers** are less than 0. Both positive and negative numbers can be shown on a **number line**.

**Figure 4.3. Number Line**

The **absolute value** of a number is the distance the number is from 0. Since distance is always positive, the absolute value of a number is always positive. The absolute value of $a$ is denoted $|a|$. For example, $|-2| = 2$ since $-2$ is two units away from 0.

Positive and negative numbers can be added, subtracted, multiplied, and divided. The sign of the resulting number is governed by a specific set of rules shown in the table below.

## Table 4.1. Operations with Positive and Negative Numbers

| Adding Real Numbers | | Subtracting Real Numbers | |
| --- | --- | --- | --- |
| Positive + Positive = Positive | $7 + 8 = 15$ | Negative – Positive = Negative | $-7 - 8 =$ <br> $-7 + (-8) =$ <br> $-15$ |
| Negative + Negative = Negative | $-7 + (-8) =$ <br> $-15$ | Positive – Negative = Positive | $7 - (-8) =$ <br> $7 + 8 = 15$ |
| Negative + Positive OR Positive + Negative = Keep the sign of the number with larger absolute value and subtract the absolute values of the numbers | $-7 + 8 = 1$ <br> $7 + -8 = -1$ | Negative – Negative = Change the subtraction to addition and change the sign of the second number; then use addition rules. | $-7 - (-8) =$ <br> $-7 + 8 = 1$ <br> $-8 - (-7) =$ <br> $-8 + 7 = -1$ |
| Positive × Positive = Positive | $8 \times 4 = 32$ | Positive ÷ Positive = Positive | $8 \div 4 = 2$ |

| Multiplying Real Numbers | | Dividing Real Numbers | |
| --- | --- | --- | --- |
| Negative × Negative = Positive | −8 × (−4) = 32 | Negative ÷ Negative = Positive | −8 ÷ (−4) = 2 |
| Positive × Negative OR Negative × Positive = Negative | 8 × (−4) = −32  −8 × 4 = −32 | Positive ÷ Negative OR Negative ÷ Positive = Negative | 8 ÷ (−4) = −2  −8 ÷ 4 = −2 |

## SAMPLE QUESTIONS

7) **Add or subtract the following real numbers:**

A.    $-18 + 12$

B.    $-3.64 + (-2.18)$

C.    $9.37 - 4.25$

D.    $86 - (-20)$

**Answers:**

A.    Since $|-18| > |12|$, the answer is negative: $|-18| - |12| = 6$. So the answer is **−6**.

B.    Adding two negative numbers results in a negative number. Add the values: **−5.82**.

C.    The first number is larger than the second, so the final answer is positive: **5.12**.

D.    Change the subtraction to addition, change the sign of the second number, and then add: $86 - (-20) = 86 + 20 = $ **106**.

8) **Multiply or divide the following real numbers:**

A.    $\left(\frac{10}{3}\right)\left(-\frac{9}{5}\right)$

B.    $\frac{-64}{-10}$

C.    $(2.2)(3.3)$

D.    $-52 \div 13$

**Answers:**

A.    Multiply the numerators, multiply the denominators, and simplify: $\frac{-90}{15} = $ **−6**.

B.    A negative divided by a negative is a positive number: **6.4**.

C.    The parentheses indicate multiplication: **7.26**.

D.    Dividing a negative by a positive number gives a negative answer: **−4**.

# Order of Operations

The **order of operations** is simply the order in which operations are performed. **PEMDAS** is a common way to remember the order of operations:

- ▶ Parentheses
- ▶ Division
- ▶ Exponents
- ▶ Addition
- ▶ Multiplication
- ▶ Subtraction

Multiplication and division, and addition and subtraction, are performed together from left to right. So, performing multiple operations on a set of numbers is a four-step process:

1. P: Calculate expressions inside parentheses, brackets, braces, etc.
2. E: Calculate exponents and square roots.
3. MD: Calculate any remaining multiplication and division in order from left to right.
4. AS: Calculate any remaining addition and subtraction in order from left to right.

Always work from left to right within each step when simplifying expressions.

## SAMPLE QUESTIONS

9) **Simplify: $2(21 - 14) + 6 \div (-2) \times 3 - 10$**

**Answer:**

| | |
|---|---|
| $2(21 - 14) + 6 \div (-2) \times 3 - 10$ | |
| $= 2(7) + 6 \div (-2) \times 3 - 10$ | Calculate expressions inside parentheses. |
| $14 + 6 \div (-2) \times 3 - 10$ <br> $= 14 + (-3) \times 3 - 10$ <br> $= 14 + (-9) - 10$ | There are no exponents or radicals, so perform multiplication and division from left to right. |
| $5 - 10 = \mathbf{-5}$ | Perform addition and subtraction from left to right. |

10) **Simplify: $-(3)^2 + 4(5) + (5 - 6)^2 - 8$**

**Answer:**

| | |
|---|---|
| $-(3)^2 + 4(5) + (5 - 6)^2 - 8$ | |
| $-(3)^2 + 4(5) + (-1)^2 - 8$ | Calculate expressions inside parentheses. |
| $= -9 + 4(5) + 1 - 8$ | Simplify exponents and radicals. |

| | |
|---|---|
| $= -9 + 20 + 1 - 8$ | Perform multiplication and division from left to right. |
| $= 11 + 1 - 8 = 12 - 8$ <br> $= \mathbf{4}$ | Perform addition and subtraction from left to right. |

**11)** Simplify: $\dfrac{(7-9)^3 + 8(10-12)}{4^2 - 5^2}$

**Answer:**

| | |
|---|---|
| $\dfrac{(7-9)^3 + 8(10-12)}{4^2 - 5^2}$ | |
| $= \dfrac{(-2)^3 + 8(-2)}{4^2 - 5^2}$ | Calculate expressions inside parentheses. |
| $= \dfrac{-8 + (-16)}{16 - 25}$ | Simplify exponents and radicals. |
| $= \dfrac{-24}{-9}$ | Perform addition and subtraction from left to right. |
| $= \dfrac{8}{3}$ | Simplify. |

# Units of Measurement

The standard units for the metric and American systems are shown below, along with the prefixes used to express metric units.

### Table 4.2. Units and conversion factors

| Dimension | American | SI |
|---|---|---|
| length | inch/foot/yard/mile | meter |
| mass | ounce/pound/ton | gram |
| volume | cup/pint/quart/gallon | liter |
| force | pound-force | newton |
| pressure | pound-force per square inch | pascal |
| work and energy | cal/British thermal unit | joule |
| temperature | Fahrenheit | kelvin |
| charge | faraday | coulomb |

**Go on** →

### Table 4.3. Metric Prefixes

| Prefix | Symbol | Multiplication Factor |
|--------|--------|-----------------------|
| tera | T | 1,000,000,000,000 |
| giga | G | 1,000,000,000 |
| mega | M | 1,000,000 |
| kilo | k | 1,000 |
| hecto | h | 100 |
| deca | da | 10 |
| base unit | -- | -- |
| deci | d | 0.1 |
| centi | c | 0.01 |
| milli | m | 0.001 |
| micro | μ | 0.000001 |
| nano | n | 0.000000001 |
| pico | p | 0.000000000001 |

**HELPFUL HINT**

A mnemonic device to help remember the metric system is *King Henry Drinks Under Dark Chocolate Moon* (KHDUDCM).

Units can be converted within a single system or between systems. When converting from one unit to another unit, a conversion factor (a numeric multiplier used to convert a value with a unit to another unit) is used. The process of converting between units using a conversion factor is sometimes known as dimensional analysis.

### Table 4.4. Conversion Factors

| | |
|---|---|
| 1 in. = 2.54 cm | 1 lb. = 0.454 kg |
| 1 yd. = 0.914 m | 1 cal = 4.19 J |
| 1 mi. = 1.61 km | 1 degree F = $\frac{9}{5}$ C + 32 degree C |
| 1 gal. = 3.785 L | 1 cm$^3$ = 1 mL |
| 1 oz. = 28.35 g | 1 hr = 3600 s |

## SAMPLE QUESTIONS

12) **Convert the following measurements in the metric system.**

    A.    4.25 kilometers to meters

    B.    8 m$^2$ to mm$^2$

**Answers:**

A.  $4.25 \text{ km} \left( \frac{1000 \text{ m}}{1 \text{ km}} \right) = \textbf{4250 m}$ (because m is a smaller unit than km, multiply by 1000)

B.  $\frac{8 \text{ m}^2}{} \times \frac{1000 \text{ mm}}{1 \text{ m}} \times \frac{1000 \text{ mm}}{1 \text{ m}} = \textbf{8,000,000 mm}^2$

Since the units are square units (m²), multiply by the conversion factor twice, so that both meters cancel (and mm × mm = mm²).

13) **Convert the following measurements in the American system.**

A.  12 feet to inches

B.  7 yd² to ft²

**Answers:**

A.  $12 \text{ ft} \left( \frac{12 \text{ in}}{1 \text{ ft}} \right) = \textbf{144 in}$ (since inches is a smaller unit, multiply by 12 inches to get feet)

B.  $7 \text{ yd}^2 \left( \frac{9 \text{ ft}^2}{1 \text{ yd}^2} \right) = \textbf{63 ft}^2$

Since the units are square units (ft²), multiply by the conversion factor twice: $\left( \frac{3 \text{ ft}}{1 \text{ yd}} \right) \times \left( \frac{3 \text{ ft}}{1 \text{ yd}} \right) = \left( \frac{9 \text{ ft}^2}{1 \text{ yd}^2} \right)$. Yards squared cancel, leaving square feet.

14) **Convert the following measurements in the metric system to the American system.**

A.  23 meters to feet

B.  10 m² to yd²

**Answers:**

A.  $23 \text{ m}((3.28 \text{ ft})/(1 \text{ m})) = \textbf{75.44 ft}$

B.  $\frac{10 \text{ m}^2}{} \times \frac{1.094 \text{ yd}}{1 \text{ m}} \times \frac{1.094 \text{ yd}}{1 \text{ m}} = \textbf{11.97 yd}^2$

15) **Convert the following measurements in the American system to the metric system.**

A.  8 in³ to milliliters

B.  16 kilograms to pounds

**Answers:**

A.  $8 \text{ in}^3 \left( \frac{16.39 \text{ ml}}{1 \text{ in}^3} \right) = \textbf{131.12 mL}$

Because the conversion factor already has cubic units in it, it only needs to be multiplied once.

B.  $16 \text{ kg} \left( \frac{2.2 \text{ lb}}{1 \text{ kg}} \right) = \textbf{35.2 lb}$

# Decimals and Fractions

## DECIMALS

A **decimal** is a number that contains a decimal point. A decimal number is an alternative way of writing a fraction. The place value for a decimal includes **tenths** (one place after the decimal), **hundredths** (two places after the decimal), **thousandths** (three places after the decimal), etc.

### Table 4.5. Place Values

| | | |
|---|---|---|
| 1,000,000 | $10^6$ | millions |
| 100,000 | $10^5$ | hundred thousands |
| 10,000 | $10^4$ | ten thousands |
| 1,000 | $10^3$ | thousands |
| 100 | $10^2$ | hundreds |
| 10 | $10^1$ | tens |
| 1 | $10^0$ | ones |
| . | | decimal |
| $\frac{1}{10}$ | $10^{-1}$ | tenths |
| $\frac{1}{100}$ | $10^{-2}$ | hundredths |
| 1/1000 | $10^{-3}$ | thousandths |

Decimals can be added, subtracted, multiplied, and divided:

► To add or subtract decimals, line up the decimal point and perform the operation, keeping the decimal point in the same place in the answer.

► To multiply decimals, first multiply the numbers without the decimal points. Then, add the number of decimal places to the right of the decimal point in the original numbers and place the decimal point in the answer so that there are that many places to the right of the decimal.

► When dividing decimals move the decimal point to the right in order to make the divisor a whole number and move the decimal the same number of places in the dividend. Divide the numbers without

$$4.2 \leftarrow \text{quotient}$$
$$2.5\overline{)10.5} \leftarrow \text{dividend}$$
$$\uparrow$$
$$\text{divisor}$$

**Figure 4.4. Division Terms**

regard to the decimal. Then, place the decimal point of the quotient directly above the decimal point of the dividend.

## SAMPLE QUESTIONS

16) Simplify: 24.38 + 16.51 − 29.87

**Answer:**

| 24.38 + 16.51 − 29.87 | |
|---|---|
| 24.38<br>+ 16.51<br>= 40.89 | Align the decimals and apply the order of operations left to right. |
| 40.89<br>− 29.87<br>= **11.02** | |

17) Simplify: (10.4)(18.2)

**Answer:**

| (10.4)(18.2) | |
|---|---|
| $104 \times 182 = 18,928$ | Multiply the numbers ignoring the decimals. |
| 18,928 → 189.28 | The original problem includes two decimal places (one in each number), so move the decimal point in the answer so that there are two places after the decimal point. |

Estimating is a good way to check the answer: $10.4 \approx 10, 18.2 \approx 18$, and $10 \times 18 = 180$.

18) Simplify: 80 ÷ 2.5

**Answer:**

| 80 ÷ 2.5 | |
|---|---|
| 80 → 800<br>2.5 → 25 | The divisor is 2.5. Move the decimal one place to the right (multiply 2.5 by 10) so that the divisor is a whole number. Since the decimal point of the divisor was moved one place to the right, the decimal point in the dividend must be moved one place right (multiplying it by 10 as well). |

| | |
|---|---|
| $800 \div 25 = 32$ | Divide normally. |

## FRACTIONS

A **fraction** is a number that can be written in the form $\frac{a}{b}$, where $b$ is not equal to 0. The $a$ part of the fraction is the **numerator** (top number) and the $b$ part of the fraction is the **denominator** (bottom number).

If the denominator of a fraction is greater than the numerator, the value of the fraction is less than 1 and it is called a **proper fraction** (for example, $\frac{3}{5}$ is a proper fraction). In an **improper fraction**, the denominator is less than the numerator and the value of the fraction is greater than 1 (example: $\frac{8}{3}$ is an improper fraction). An improper fraction can be written as a mixed number. A **mixed number** has a whole number part and a proper fraction part. Improper fractions can be converted to mixed numbers by dividing the numerator by the denominator, which gives the whole number part, and the remainder becomes the numerator of the proper fraction part. (For example, the improper fraction $\frac{25}{9}$ is equal to mixed number $2\frac{7}{9}$ because 9 divides into 25 two times, with a remainder of 7.)

Conversely, mixed numbers can be converted to improper fractions. To do so, determine the numerator of the improper fraction by multiplying the denominator by the whole number, and then adding the numerator. The final number is written as the (now larger) numerator over the original denominator.

**HELPFUL HINT**

To convert mixed numbers to improper fractions:
$$a\frac{m}{n} = \frac{n \times a + m}{n}$$

Fractions with the same denominator can be added or subtracted by simply adding or subtracting the numerators; the denominator will remain unchanged. To add or subtract fractions with different denominators, find the **least common denominator (LCD)** of all the fractions. The LCD is the smallest number exactly divisible by each denominator. (For example, the least common denominator of the numbers 2, 3, and 8 is 24.) Once the LCD has been found, each fraction should be written in an equivalent form with the LCD as the denominator. To do this, each fraction can be multiplied by 1 in the form $\frac{a}{a}$, where $a$ is the value necessary to convert the denominator to the LCD. Once all fractions have the same denominator, the numerators can be added and the fractions reduced if necessary.

**HELPFUL HINT**

$$\frac{a}{b} \pm \frac{c}{b} = \frac{a \pm c}{b}$$

$$\frac{a}{b} \times \frac{c}{d} = \frac{ac}{bd}$$

$$\frac{a}{b} \div \frac{c}{d} = \left(\frac{a}{b}\right)\left(\frac{d}{c}\right) = \frac{ad}{bc}$$

To multiply fractions, the numerators are multiplied together and denominators are multiplied together. If there are any mixed numbers, they should first be changed to improper fractions. Then, the numerators are multiplied together and the denominators are multiplied together. The fraction can then be reduced if necessary. To divide fractions, multiply the first fraction by the reciprocal of the second.

Any common denominator can be used to add or subtract fractions. The quickest way to find a common denominator of a set of values is simply to multiply all the values together. The result might not be the least common denominator, but it will get the job done.

### SAMPLE QUESTIONS

19) Simplify: $2\frac{3}{5} + 3\frac{1}{4} - 1\frac{1}{2}$

**Answer:**

| | |
|---|---|
| $2\frac{3}{5} + 3\frac{1}{4} - 1\frac{1}{2}$ | |
| $= 2\frac{12}{20} + 3\frac{5}{20} - 1\frac{10}{20}$ | Change each fraction so it has a denominator of 20, which is the LCD of 5, 4, and 2. |
| $2 + 3 - 1 = 4$<br>$\frac{12}{20} + \frac{5}{20} - \frac{10}{20} = \frac{7}{20}$ | Add and subtract the whole numbers together and the fractions together. |
| $4\frac{7}{20}$ | Combine to get the final answer (a mixed number). |

20) Simplify: $\frac{7}{8} \times 3\frac{1}{3}$

**Answer:**

| | |
|---|---|
| $\frac{7}{8} \times 3\frac{1}{3}$ | |
| $3\frac{1}{3} = \frac{10}{3}$ | Change the mixed number to an improper fraction. |
| $\frac{7}{8}\left(\frac{10}{3}\right) = \frac{7 \times 10}{8 \times 3}$<br>$= \frac{70}{24}$ | Multiply the numerators together and the denominators together. |
| $= \frac{35}{12}$<br>$= 2\frac{11}{12}$ | Reduce the fraction. |

21) Simplify: $4\frac{1}{2} \div \frac{2}{3}$

**Answer:**

| | |
|---|---|
| $4\frac{1}{2} \div \frac{2}{3}$ | |
| $4\frac{1}{2} = \frac{9}{2}$ | Change the mixed number to an improper fraction. |

| | |
|---|---|
| $\frac{9}{2} \div \frac{2}{3}$ <br> $= \frac{9}{2} \times \frac{3}{2}$ <br> $= \frac{27}{4}$ | Multiply the first fraction by the reciprocal of the second fraction. |
| $= 6\frac{3}{4}$ | Simplify. |

## CONVERTING BETWEEN FRACTIONS AND DECIMALS

A fraction is converted to a decimal by using long division until there is no remainder and no pattern of repeating numbers occurs.

A decimal is converted to a fraction using the following steps:

▶ Place the decimal value as the numerator in a fraction with a denominator of 1.

▶ Multiply the fraction by $\frac{10}{10}$ for every digit in the decimal value, so that there is no longer a decimal in the numerator.

▶ Reduce the fraction.

### SAMPLE QUESTIONS

22) Write the fraction $\frac{7}{8}$ as a decimal.

**Answer:**

Divide the denominator into the numerator using long division.

23) Write the fraction 5/11 as a decimal.

**Answer:**

Dividing using long division yields a repeating decimal.

24) Write the decimal 0.125 as a fraction.

**Answer:**

| 0.125 | |
|---|---|
| $= \dfrac{0.125}{1}$ | Create a fraction with 0.125 as the numerator and 1 as the denominator. |
| $\dfrac{0.125}{1} \times \dfrac{10}{10} \times \dfrac{10}{10} \times \dfrac{10}{10} = \dfrac{125}{1000}$ | Multiple by 1 in the form 10/10 three times (one for each numeral after the decimal). |
| $= \dfrac{1}{8}$ | Simplify. |

Alternatively, recognize that 0.125 is read "one hundred twenty-five thousandths" and can therefore be written in fraction form as 125/1000.

# Rounding and Estimation

**Rounding** is a way of simplifying a complicated number. The result of rounding will be a less precise value with which it is easier to write or perform operations. Rounding is performed to a specific place value, for example the thousands or tenths place.

The rules for rounding are as follows:

1. Underline the place value being rounded to.
2. Locate the digit one place value to the right of the underlined value. If this value is less than 5, then keep the underlined value and replace all digits to the right of the underlined value with 0. If the value to the right of the underlined digit is greater than 5, then increase the underlined digit by one and replace all digits to the right of it with 0.

> **HELPFUL HINT**
>
> Estimation can often be used to eliminate answer choices on multiple-choice tests without having to work the problem to completion.

**Estimation** is when numbers are rounded and then an operation is performed. This process can be used when working with large numbers to find a close, but not exact, answer.

**SAMPLE QUESTIONS**

25) Round the number 138,472 to the nearest thousands.

**Answer:**

138,472

| 138,472 ≈ **138,000** | The 8 is in the thousands place, and the number to its right is 4. Because 4 is less than 5, the 8 remains and all numbers to the right become 0. |

26) The populations of five local towns are 12,341, 8975, 9431, 10,521, and 11,427. Estimate the total population to the nearest 1000 people.

**Answer:**

| 12,341 ≈ 12,000<br>8975 ≈ 9000<br>9431 ≈ 9000<br>10,521 ≈ 11,000<br>11,427 ≈ 11,000 | Round each value to the thousands place. |
| 12,000 + 9000 + 9000 + 11,000 + 11,000 = **52,000** | Add. |

# Ratios

A **ratio** is a comparison of two numbers and can be represented as $\frac{a}{b}$, $a{:}b$, or $a$ to $b$. The two numbers represent a constant relationship, not a specific value: for every $a$ number of items in the first group, there will be $b$ number of items in the second. For example, if the ratio of blue to red candies in a bag is 3:5, the bag will contain 3 blue candies for every 5 red candies. So, the bag might contain 3 blue candies and 5 red candies, or it might contain 30 blue candies and 50 red candies, or 36 blue candies and 60 red candies. All of these values are representative of the ratio 3:5 (which is the ratio in its lowest, or simplest, terms).

To find the *whole* when working with ratios, simply add the values in the ratio. For example, if the ratio of boys to girls in a class is 2:3, the *whole* is five: 2 out of every 5 students are boys, and 3 out of every 5 students are girls.

## SAMPLE QUESTIONS

27) There are 10 boys and 12 girls in a first-grade class. What is the ratio of boys to the total number of students? What is the ratio of girls to boys?

**Answer:**

| | |
|---|---|
| number of boys: 10<br>number of girls: 12<br>number of students: 22 | Identify the variables. |
| number of boys : number of students<br>$= 10 : 22$<br>$= \frac{10}{22}$<br>$= \frac{5}{11}$ | Write out and simplify the ratio of boys to total students. |
| number of girls : number of boys<br>$= 12 : 10$<br>$= \frac{12}{10}$<br>$= \frac{6}{5}$ | Write out and simplify the ratio of girls to boys. |

28) **A family spends $600 a month on rent, $400 on utilities, $750 on groceries, and $550 on miscellaneous expenses. What is the ratio of the family's rent to their total expenses?**

**Answer:**

| | |
|---|---|
| rent $= 600$<br>utilities $= 400$<br>groceries $= 750$<br>miscellaneous $= 550$<br>total expenses $= 600 + 400 + 750 + 550 = 2300$ | Identify the variables. |
| rent : total expenses<br>$= 600 : 2300$<br>$= \frac{600}{2300}$<br>$= \frac{6}{23}$ | Write out and simplify the ratio of rent to total expenses. |

## PROPORTIONS

A **proportion** is an equation which states that two ratios are equal. A proportion is given in the form $\frac{a}{b} = \frac{c}{d}$, where the $a$ and $d$ terms are the extremes and the $b$ and $c$ terms are the means. A proportion is solved using cross-multiplication ($ad = bc$) to create an equation with no fractional components. A proportion must have the same units in both numerators and both denominators.

## SAMPLE QUESTIONS

29) **Solve the proportion for $x$: $\frac{3x-5}{2} = \frac{x-8}{3}$.**

**Answer:**

| | |
|---|---|
| $\frac{(3x-5)}{2} = \frac{(x-8)}{3}$ | |
| $3(3x-5) = 2(x-8)$ | Cross-multiply. |
| $9x - 15 = 2x - 16$ | |
| $7x - 15 = -16$ | Solve the equation for $x$. |
| $7x = -1$ | |
| $x = -\frac{1}{7}$ | |

30) **A map is drawn such that 2.5 inches on the map equates to an actual distance of 40 miles. If the distance measured on the map between two cities is 17.25 inches, what is the actual distance between them in miles?**

**Answer:**

| | |
|---|---|
| $\frac{2.5}{40} = \frac{17.25}{x}$ | Write a proportion where $x$ equals the actual distance and each ratio is written as inches : miles. |
| $2.5x = 690$ | Cross-multiply and divide to solve for $x$. |
| $x = 276$ | |
| The two cities are **276 miles apart**. | |

31) **A factory knows that every 4 out of 1000 parts made will be defective. If in a month there are 125,000 parts made, how many of these parts will be defective?**

**Answer:**

| | |
|---|---|
| $\frac{4}{1000} = \frac{x}{125,000}$ | Write a proportion where $x$ is the number of defective parts made and both ratios are written as defective : total. |
| $1000x = 500,000$ | Cross-multiply and divide to solve for $x$. |
| $x = 500$ | |
| There are **500 defective parts** for the month. | |

# Percentages

A **percent** (or percentage) means per hundred and is expressed with a percent symbol (%). For example, 54% means 54 out of every 100. A percent can be converted to a decimal by removing the % symbol and moving the decimal point two places to the left, while a decimal can be converted to a percent by moving the decimal point two places to the right and attaching the % sign. A percent can be converted to a fraction by writing the percent as a fraction with 100 as the denominator and reducing. A fraction can be converted to a percent by performing the indicated division, multiplying the result by 100, and attaching the % sign.

The equation for finding percentages has three variables: the part, the whole, and the percent (which is expressed in the equation as a decimal). The equation, as shown below, can be rearranged to solve for any of these variables.

▶ $part = whole \times percent$

▶ $percent = \dfrac{part}{whole}$

▶ $whole = \dfrac{part}{percent}$

This set of equations can be used to solve percent word problems. All that's needed is to identify the part, whole, and/or percent, and then to plug those values into the appropriate equation and solve.

## SAMPLE QUESTIONS

32) **Change the following values to the indicated form:**

   A.   18% to a fraction

   B.   $\frac{3}{5}$ to a percent

   C.   1.125 to a percent

   D.   84% to a decimal

   **Answers:**

   A.   The percent is written as a fraction over 100 and reduced: $\frac{18}{100} = \frac{9}{50}$.

   B.   Dividing 3 by 5 gives the value 0.6, which is then multiplied by 100: **60%**.

   C.   The decimal point is moved two places to the right: $1.125 \times 100 =$ **112.5%**.

   D.   The decimal point is moved two places to the left: $84 \div 100 =$ **0.84**.

33) **In a school of 650 students, 54% of the students are boys. How many students are girls?**

**Answer:**

| | |
|---|---|
| Percent of students who are girls = 100% − 54% = 46% <br><br> percent = 46% = 0.46 <br><br> whole = 650 students <br><br> part = ? | Identify the variables. |
| part = whole × percent <br><br> = 650 x 0.46 = 299 <br><br> **There are 299 girls.** | Plug the variables into the appropriate equation. |

## Percent Change

**Percent change** problems involve a change from an original amount. Often percent change problems appear as word problems that include discounts, growth, or markups. In order to solve percent change problems, it's necessary to identify the percent change (as a decimal), the amount of change, and the original amount. (Keep in mind that one of these will be the value being solved for.) These values can then be plugged into the equations below:

▶  amount of change = original amount × percent change

▶  percent change = $\dfrac{\text{amount of change}}{\text{original amount}}$

▶  original amount = $\dfrac{\text{amount of change}}{\text{percent change}}$

### SAMPLE QUESTIONS

34)  **An HDTV that originally cost $1,500 is on sale for 45% off. What is the sale price for the item?**

**Answer:**

| | |
|---|---|
| original amount =$1,500 <br><br> percent change = 45% = 0.45 <br><br> amount of change =  ? | Identify the variables. |
| amount of change = original amount × percent change <br><br> = 1500 × 0.45 = 675 | Plug the variables into the appropriate equation. |
| 1500 − 675 = 825 <br><br> **The final price is $825.** | To find the new price, subtract the amount of change from the original price. |

35) **A house was bought in 2000 for $100,000 and sold in 2015 for $120,000. What was the percent growth in the value of the house from 2000 to 2015?**

**Answer:**

| | |
|---|---|
| original amount = $100,000 <br><br> amount of change = 120,000 − 100,000 = 20,000 <br><br> percent change = ? | Identify the variables. |
| percent change = $\dfrac{\text{amount of change}}{\text{original amount}}$ <br><br> $= \dfrac{20{,}000}{100{,}000}$ <br><br> $= 0.20$ | Plug the variables into the appropriate equation. |
| $0.20 \times 100 =$ **20%** | To find the percent growth, multiply by 100. |

# Exponents and Radicals

## EXPONENTS

An expression in the form $b^n$ is in an exponential notation where $b$ is the **base** and $n$ is an **exponent**. To perform the operation, multiply the base by itself the number of times indicated by the exponent. For example, $2^3$ is equal to $2 \times 2 \times 2$ or 8.

### Table 4.6. Operations with Exponents

| Rule | Example | Explanation |
|---|---|---|
| $a^0 = 1$ | $5^0 = 1$ | Any base (except 0) to the 0 power is 1. |
| $a^{-n} = \dfrac{1}{a^n}$ | $5^{-3} = \dfrac{1}{5^3}$ | A negative exponent becomes positive when moved from numerator to denominator (or vice versa). |
| $a^m a^n = a^{m+n}$ | $5^3 5^4 = 5^{3+4} = 5^7$ | Add the exponents to multiply two powers with the same base. |
| $(a^m)^n = a^{m \times n}$ | $(5^3)^4 = 5^{3(4)} = 5^{12}$ | Multiply the exponents to raise a power to a power. |
| $\dfrac{a^m}{a^n} = a^{m-n}$ | $\dfrac{5^4}{5^3} = 5^{4-3} = 5^1$ | Subtract the exponents to divide two powers with the same base. |
| $(ab)^n = a^n b^n$ | $(5 \times 6)^3 = 5^3 6^3$ | Apply the exponent to each base to raise a product to a power. |
| $\left(\dfrac{a}{b}\right)^n = \dfrac{a^n}{b^n}$ | $\left(\dfrac{5}{6}\right)^3 = \dfrac{5^3}{6^3}$ | Apply the exponent to each base to raise a quotient to a power. |

### Table 4.6. Operations with Exponents (continued)

| Rule | Example | Explanation |
|---|---|---|
| $\left(\frac{a}{b}\right)^{-n} = \left(\frac{b}{a}\right)^{n}$ | $\left(\frac{5}{6}\right)^{-3} = \left(\frac{6}{5}\right)^{3}$ | Invert the fraction and change the sign of the exponent to raise a fraction to a negative power. |
| $\frac{a^m}{b^n} = \frac{b^{-n}}{a^{-m}}$ | $\frac{5^3}{6^4} = \frac{6^{-4}}{5^{-3}}$ | Change the sign of the exponent when moving a number from the numerator to denominator (or vice versa). |

### SAMPLE QUESTIONS

36) Simplify: $\frac{(10^2)^3}{(10^2)^{-2}}$

**Answer:**

| | |
|---|---|
| $\frac{(10^2)^3}{(10^2)^{-2}}$ | |
| $= \frac{10^6}{10^{-4}}$ | Multiply the exponents raised to a power. |
| $= 10^{6-(-4)}$ | Subtract the exponent in the denominator from the one in the numerator. |
| $= 10^{10}$ <br> $= \mathbf{10{,}000{,}000{,}000}$ | Simplify. |

37) Simplify: $\frac{(x^{-2}y^2)^2}{x^3 y}$

**Answer:**

| | |
|---|---|
| $\frac{(x^{-2}y^2)^2}{x^3 y}$ | |
| $= \frac{x^{-4}y^4}{x^3 y}$ | Multiply the exponents raised to a power. |
| $= x^{-4-3}y^{4-1}$ <br> $= x^{-7}y^3$ | Subtract the exponent in the denominator from the one in the numerator. |
| $= \frac{y^3}{x^7}$ | Move negative exponents to the denominator. |

## RADICALS

**Radicals** are expressed as $\sqrt[b]{a}$, where $b$ is called the **index** and $a$ is the **radicand**. A radical is used to indicate the inverse operation of an exponent: finding the base which can be raised to $b$ to yield $a$. For example, $\sqrt[3]{125}$ is equal to 5 because $5 \times 5 \times 5$ equals 125. The same operation can be expressed using a fraction exponent, so $\sqrt[b]{a} = a^{\frac{1}{b}}$. Note that when no value is indicated for $b$, it is assumed to be 2 (square root).

When $b$ is even and $a$ is positive, $\sqrt[b]{a}$ is defined to be the positive real value $n$ such that $n^b = a$ (example: $\sqrt{16} = 4$ only, and not $-4$, even though $(-4)(-4) = 16$). If $b$ is even and $a$ is negative, $\sqrt[b]{a}$ will be a complex number (example: $\sqrt{-9} = 3i$). Finally if $b$ is odd, $\sqrt[b]{a}$ will always be a real number regardless of the sign of $a$. If $a$ is negative, $\sqrt[b]{a}$ will be negative since a number to an odd power is negative (example: $\sqrt[5]{-32} = -2$ since $(-2)^5 = -32$).

$\sqrt[n]{x}$ is referred to as the $n$th root of $x$.

▶   $n = 2$ is the square root

▶   $n = 3$ is the cube root

▶   $n = 4$ is the fourth root

▶   $n = 5$ is the fifth root

The following table of operations with radicals holds for all cases EXCEPT the case where $b$ is even and $a$ is negative (the complex case).

### Table 4.7. Operations with Radicals

| Rule | Example | Explanation |
|---|---|---|
| $\sqrt[b]{ac} = \sqrt[b]{a}\,\sqrt[b]{c}$ | $\sqrt[3]{81} = \sqrt[3]{27}\,\sqrt[3]{3} = 3\sqrt[3]{3}$ | The values under the radical sign can be separated into values that multiply to the original value. |
| $\sqrt[b]{\dfrac{a}{c}} = \dfrac{\sqrt[b]{a}}{\sqrt[b]{c}}$ | $\sqrt{\dfrac{4}{81}} = \dfrac{\sqrt{4}}{\sqrt{81}} = \dfrac{2}{9}$ | The $b$-root of the numerator and denominator can be calculated when there is a fraction under a radical sign. |
| $\sqrt[b]{a^c} = (\sqrt[b]{a})^c = a^{\frac{c}{b}}$ | $\sqrt[3]{6^2} = (\sqrt[3]{6})^2 = 6^{\frac{2}{3}}$ | The $b$-root can be written as a fractional exponent. If there is a power under the radical sign, it will be the numerator of the fraction. |
| $\dfrac{c}{\sqrt[b]{a}}\dfrac{\sqrt[b]{a^{b-1}}}{\sqrt[b]{a^{b-1}}} = \dfrac{c\sqrt[b]{a^{b-1}}}{a}$ | $\dfrac{5}{\sqrt{2}}\dfrac{\sqrt{2}}{\sqrt{2}} = \dfrac{5\sqrt{2}}{2}$ | To rationalize the denominator, multiply the numerator and denominator by the radical in the denominator until the radical has been canceled out. |
| $\dfrac{c}{b - \sqrt{a}} \times \dfrac{b + \sqrt{a}}{b + \sqrt{a}}$ $= \dfrac{c(b + \sqrt{a})}{b^2 - a}$ | $\dfrac{4}{3 - \sqrt{2}} \times \dfrac{3 + \sqrt{2}}{3 + \sqrt{2}}$ $= \dfrac{12 + 4\sqrt{2}}{7}$ | To rationalize the denominator, the numerator and denominator are multiplied by the conjugate of the denominator. |

## SAMPLE QUESTIONS

38) **Simplify:** $\sqrt{48}$

**Answer:**

| $\sqrt{48}$ | |
|---|---|
| $= \sqrt{16 \times 3}$ | Determine the largest square number that is a factor of the radicand (48) and write the radicand as a product using that square number as a factor. |
| $= \sqrt{16}\,\sqrt{3}$ <br> $= \mathbf{4\sqrt{3}}$ | Apply the rules of radicals to simplify. |

39) **Simplify:** $\dfrac{6}{\sqrt{8}}$

**Answer:**

| $\dfrac{6}{\sqrt{8}}$ | |
|---|---|
| $= \dfrac{6}{\sqrt{4}\,\sqrt{2}}$ <br> $= \dfrac{6}{2\sqrt{2}}$ | Apply the rules of radicals to simplify. |
| $= \dfrac{6}{2\sqrt{2}}\left(\dfrac{\sqrt{2}}{\sqrt{2}}\right)$ <br> $= \dfrac{\mathbf{3\sqrt{2}}}{\mathbf{2}}$ | Multiply by $\dfrac{\sqrt{2}}{\sqrt{2}}$ to rationalize the denominator. |

# Algebra

lgebra, meaning "restoration" in Arabic, is the mathematical method of finding the unknown. The first algebraic book in Egypt was used to figure out complex inheritances that were to be split among many individuals. Today, algebra is just as necessary when dealing with unknown amounts.

## Algebraic Expressions

The foundation of algebra is the **variable**, an unknown number represented by a symbol (usually a letter such as $x$ or $a$). Variables can be preceded by a **coefficient**, which is a constant (i.e., a real number) in front of the variable, such as $4x$ or $-2a$. An **algebraic expression** is any sum, difference, product, or quotient of variables and numbers (for example $3x^2$, $2x + 7y - 1$, and $\frac{5}{x}$ are algebraic expressions). **Terms** are any quantities that are added or subtracted (for example, the terms of the expression $x^2 - 3x + 5$ are $x^2$, $3x$, and 5). A **polynomial expression** is an algebraic expression where all the exponents on the variables are whole numbers. A polynomial with only two terms is known as a **binomial**, and one with three terms is a **trinomial**. A **monomial** has only one term.

**Figure 5.1. Polynomial Expression**

> **HELPFUL HINT**
>
> Simplified expressions are ordered by variable terms alphabetically with highest exponent first then down to constants.

**Evaluating expressions** is another way of saying "find the numeric value of an expression if the variable is equal to a certain number." To evaluate the expression, simply plug the given value(s) for the variable(s) into the equation and simplify. Remember to use the order of operations when simplifying:

- ▶ Parentheses
- ▶ Exponents
- ▶ Multiplication
- ▶ Division
- ▶ Addition
- ▶ Subtraction

## SAMPLE QUESTION

1) If $m = 4$, find the value of the following expression:
$5(m - 2)^3 + 3m^2 - \frac{m}{4} - 1$

**Answer:**

| $5(m - 2)^3 + 3m^2 - \frac{m}{4} - 1$ | |
|---|---|
| $= 5(4 - 2)^3 + 3(4)^2 - \frac{4}{4} - 1$ | Plug the value 4 in for $m$ in the expression. |
| $= 5(2)^3 + 3(4)^2 - \frac{4}{4} - 1$ | Calculate all the expressions inside the parentheses. |
| $= 5(8) + 3(16) - \frac{4}{4} - 1$ | Simplify all exponents. |
| $= 40 + 48 - 1 - 1$ | Perform multiplication and division from left to right. |
| $= \mathbf{86}$ | Perform addition and subtraction from left to right. |

# Operations with Expressions

## ADDING AND SUBTRACTING

Expressions can be added or subtracted by simply adding and subtracting **like terms**, which are terms with the same variable part (the variables must be the same, with the same exponents on each variable). For example, in the expressions $2x + 3xy - 2z$ and $6y + 2xy$, the like terms are $3xy$ and $2xy$. Adding the two expressions yields the new expression $2x + 5xy - 2z + 6y$. Note that the other terms did not change; they cannot combine because they have different variables.

## SAMPLE QUESTION

2) If $a = 12x + 7xy - 9y$ and $b = 8x - 9xz + 7z$, what is $a + b$?

**Answer:**

| | |
|---|---|
| $a + b = (12x + 8x) + 7xy - 9y - 9xz + 7z$ <br> $= \mathbf{20x + 7xy - 9y - 9xz + 7z}$ | The only like terms in both expressions are $12x$ and $8x$, so these two terms will be added, and all other terms will remain the same. |

## DISTRIBUTING AND FACTORING

Often simplifying expressions requires distributing and factoring. Distributing and factoring can be seen as two sides of the same coin. **Distribution** multiplies each term in the first factor by each term in the second factor to clear off parentheses. **Factoring** reverses this process, taking a polynomial in standard form and writing it as a product of two or more factors.

When distributing a monomial through a polynomial, the expression outside the parentheses is multiplied by each term inside the parentheses. (coefficients are multiplied, exponents are added, following the rules of exponents). The first step in factoring a polynomial is always to "undistribute" or factor out the **greatest common factor (GCF)** among the terms. The GCF is multiplied by, in parentheses, the expression that remains of each term when the GCF is divided out of each term. Factoring can be checked by multiplying the GCF factor through the parentheses again.

When simplifying two polynomials, each term in the first polynomial must multiply each term in the second polynomial. A binomial (two terms) multiplied by a binomial, will require $2 \times 2$ or 4 multiplications. For the binomial $\times$ binomial case, this process is sometimes called **FOIL**, which stands for *first, outer, inner,* and *last*. These terms refer to the placement of each term of the expression: multiply the first term in each expression, then the outside terms, then the inside terms, and finally the last terms. A binomial (two terms) multiplied by a trinomial (three terms), will require $2 \times 3$ or 6 products to simplify. The first term in the first polynomial multiplies each of the three terms in the second polynomial, then the second term in the first polynomial multiplies each of the three terms in the second polynomial. A trinomial (three terms) by a trinomial will require $3 \times 3$ or 9 products, etc.

**Figure 5.2. Distribution and Factoring**

Factoring is the reverse of distributing: the first step is always to remove ("undistribute") the GCF of all the terms, if there is a GCF (besides 1). The GCF is the product of any constants and/or variables that EVERY term shares. (For example, the GCF of $12x^3$, $15x^2$ and $6xy^2$ is $3x$ because $3x$ evenly divides all three terms). This shared factor can be taken out of each term and moved to the outside of the parentheses, leaving behind a polynomial where each term is the original term divided by the GCF. (The remaining terms for the terms in the example would be $4x^2$, $5x$, and $2xy$.) It may be possible to factor the polynomial in the parentheses further, depending on the problem.

## FACTORING TRINOMIALS

If the leading coefficient is $a = 1$, the trinomial is in the form $x^2 + bx + c$ and can often be rewritten in the factored form, as a product of two binomials: $(x + m)(x + n)$. Recall that the product of two binomials can be written in expanded form $x^2 + mx + nx + mn$. Equating this expression with $x^2 + bx + c$, the constant term $c$ would have to equal the product $mn$. Thus, to work backward from the trinomial to the factored form, consider all the numbers $m$ and $n$ that multiply to make $c$. For example, to factor $x^2 + 8x + 12$, consider all the pairs that multiply to be 12 ($12 = 1 \times 12$ or $2 \times 6$ or $3 \times 4$). Choose the pair that will make the coefficient of the middle term (8) when added. In this example 2 and 6 add to 8, so making $m = 2$ and $n = 6$ in the expanded form gives:

| $x^2 + 8x + 12 = x^2 + 2x + 6x + 12$ | |
|---|---|
| $= (x^2 + 2x) + (6x + 12)$ | Group the first two terms and the last two terms. |
| $= x(x + 6) + 2(x + 6)$ | Factor the GCF out of each set of parentheses. |
| $= (x + 6)(x + 2)$ | The two terms now have the common factor $(x + 6)$, which can be removed, leaving $(x + 2)$ and the original polynomial is factored. |

In general:

| $x^2 + bx + c = x^2 + mx + nx + mn$, where $c = mn$ and $b = m + n$ | |
|---|---|
| $= (x^2 + mx) + (nx + mn)$ | Group. |
| $= x(x + m) + n(x + m)$ | Factor each group. |
| $= (x + m)(x + n)$ | Factor out the common binomial. |

Note that if none of the factors of $c$ add to the value $b$, then the trinomial cannot be factored, and is called **prime**.

If the leading coefficient is not 1 ($a \neq 1$), first make sure that any common factors among the three terms are factored out. If the $a$-value is negative, factor out $-1$ first as well. If the $a$-value of the new polynomial in the parentheses is still not 1, follow this rule: Identify two values $r$ and $s$ that multiply to be $ac$ and add to be $b$. Then write the polynomial in this form: $ax^2 + bx + c = ax^2 + rx + sx + c$, and proceed by grouping, factoring, and removing the common binomial as above.

There are a few special factoring cases worth memorizing: difference of squares, binomial squared, and the sum and difference of cubes.

▶ **Difference of squares** (each term is a square and they are subtracted):

▷ $a^2 - b^2 = (a + b)(a - b)$

▷ Note that a sum of squares is never factorable.

► **Binomial squared:**

▷ $a^2 + 2ab + b^2 = (a + b)(a + b) = (a + b)^2$

► **Sum and difference of cubes:**

▷ $a^3 + b^3 = (a + b)(a^2 - ab + b^2)$

▷ $a^3 - b^3 = (a - b)(a^2 + ab + b^2)$

▷ Note that the second factor in these factorizations will never be able to be factored further.

## SAMPLE QUESTIONS

3) **Factor: $16x^2 + 52x + 30$**

**Answer:**

| $16x^2 + 52x + 30$ | |
|---|---|
| $= 2(8x^2 + 26x + 15)$ | Remove the GCF of 2. |
| $= 2(8x^2 + 6x + 20x + 15)$ | To factor the polynomial in the parentheses, calculate $ac = (8)(15) = 120$, and consider all the pairs of numbers that multiply to be 120: $1 \times 120$, $2 \times 60$, $3 \times 40$, $4 \times 30$, $5 \times 24$, $6 \times 20$, $8 \times 15$, and $10 \times 12$. Of these pairs, choose the pair that adds to be the $b$-value 26 (6 and 20). |
| $= 2[(8x^2 + 6x) + (20x + 15)]$ | Group. |
| $= 2[(2x(4x + 3) + 5(4x + 3)]$ | Factor out the GCF of each group. |
| $= 2[(4x + 3)(2x + 5)]$ | Factor out the common binomial. |
| $\mathbf{2(4x + 3)(2x + 5)}$ | |

If there are no values $r$ and $s$ that multiply to be $ac$ and add to be $b$, then the polynomial is prime and cannot be factored.

4) **Expand the following expression: $5x(x^2 - 2c + 10)$**

**Answer:**

| $5x(x^2 - 2c + 10)$ | |
|---|---|
| $(5x)(x^2) = 5x^3$ | Distribute and multiply the term outside the parentheses to all three terms inside the parentheses. |
| $(5x)(-2c) = -10xc$ | |
| $(5x)(10) = 50x$ | |
| $\mathbf{= 5x^3 - 10xc + 50x}$ | |

5) **Expand the following expression:** $x(5 + z) - z(4x - z^2)$

**Answer:**

| $x(5 + z) - z(4x - z^2)$ | |
|---|---|
| $= 5x + zx - 4zx + z^3$ | Distribute for each set of parentheses. Note that $-z$ is distributed and that $(-z)(-z^2) = +z^3$. <u>Not distributing the negative is a very common error.</u> Note that the $xz$ is a like term with $zx$ (commutative property) and the terms can therefore be combined. |
| $= z^3 - 3xz + 5x$ | Combine like terms and place terms in the appropriate order (highest exponents first). |

6) **Expand the following expression:** $(x^2 - 5)(2x - x^3)$

**Answer:**

| $(x^2 - 5)(2x - x^3)$ | |
|---|---|
| $(x^2)(2x) = 2x^3$ $(x^2)(-x^3) = -x^5$ $(-5)(2x) = -10x$ $(-5)(-x^3) = 5x^3$ | Apply FOIL: first, outside, inside, and last. |
| $= 2x^3 - x^5 - 10x + 5x^3$ | Combine like terms and put them in order. |
| $= -x^5 + 7x^3 - 10x$ | |

7) **Factor the expression** $16z^2 + 48z$

**Answer:**

| $16z^2 + 48z$ $= 16z(z + 3)$ | Both terms have a $z$, and 16 is a common factor of both 16 and 48. So the greatest common factor is $16z$. Factor out the GCF. |
|---|---|

8) **Factor the expression** $6m^3 + 12m^3n - 9m^2$

**Answer:**

| $6m^3 + 12m^3n - 9m^2$ $= 3m^2(2m + 4mn - 3)$ | All the terms share the factor $m^2$, and 3 is the greatest common factor of 6, 12, and 9. So, the GCF is $3m^2$. |
|---|---|

9)  Factor the expression $3b^2 - 30b - 72$

**Answer:**

| $3b^2 - 30b - 72$ | |
|---|---|
| $= 3(b^2 - 10b - 24)$ | Factor out 3, since all the terms share the factor 3. |
| $= 3(b^2 - 12b + 2b - 24)$ | Factor the remaining trinomial in the parentheses. Identify all the values that can be multiplied to make $-24$ ($-24 = 1 \times -24, -1 \times 24, 2 \times -12, -2 \times 12, 3 \times -8, -3 \times 8, 4 \times -6, -4 \times 6$). Choose the factors 2 and $-12$ because these values add up to the $b$-value $-10$. Rewrite $-10b$ as $-12b + 2b$. |
| $= 3[(b^2 - 12b) + (2b - 24)]$ | Group the terms. |
| $= 3[b(b - 12) + 2(b - 12)]$ | Factor each group. |
| $= 3(b - 12)(b + 2)$ | Factor the binomial $(b - 12)$ out of each term. |

# Linear Equations

An **equation** states that two expressions are equal to each other. Polynomial equations are categorized by the highest power of the variables they contain: the highest power of any exponent of a linear equation is 1, a quadratic equation has a variable raised to the second power, a cubic equation has a variable raised to the third power, and so on.

## SAMPLE QUESTION

10)  **Which of the following is a linear equation?**

A.  $x + 5$

B.  $x = x^2$

C.  $\frac{x}{x} = 1$

D.  $2y = 3$

**Answer:**

A.  Incorrect. This is an expression, not an equation.

B.  Incorrect. This is a quadratic equation (the variable is raised to the second power).

C.   Incorrect. It looks like the highest power is 1. However, the $x$s in the fraction cancel, meaning the equation has no variable; it simply states that $1 = 1$.

**D.   Correct.** This is the only answer that has a highest power of one and includes an equal sign.

## Solving Linear Equations

Solving an equation means finding the value or values of the variable that make the equation true. To solve a linear equation, it is necessary to manipulate the terms so that the variable being solved for appears alone on one side of the equal sign while everything else in the equation is on the other side.

The way to solve linear equations is to "undo" all the operations that connect numbers to the variable of interest. Follow these steps:

1.   Eliminate fractions by multiplying each side by the least common multiple of any denominators.
2.   Distribute to eliminate parentheses, braces, and brackets.
3.   Combine like terms.
4.   Use addition or subtraction to collect all terms containing the variable of interest to one side, and all terms not containing the variable to the other side.
5.   Use multiplication or division to remove coefficients from the variable of interest.

Sometimes there are no numeric values in the equation or there are a mix of numerous variables and constants. The goal is to solve the equation for one of the variables in terms of the other variables. In this case, the answer will be an expression involving numbers and letters instead of a numeric value.

### SAMPLE QUESTIONS

11)   **Solve for $x$:** $\dfrac{100(x + 5)}{20} = 1$

**Answer:**

| | |
|---|---|
| $\dfrac{100(x + 5)}{20} = 1$ | |
| $(20)\left(\dfrac{100(x + 5)}{20}\right) = (1)(20)$ | Multiply both sides by 20 to cancel |
| $100(x + 5) = 20$ | out the denominator. |

| | |
|---|---|
| $100x + 500 = 20$ | Distribute 100 through the parentheses. |
| $100x = -480$ | "Undo" the +500 by subtracting 500 on both sides of the equation to isolate the variable term. |
| $x = \frac{-480}{100}$ | "Undo" the multiplication by 100 by dividing by 100 on both sides to solve for x. |
| $= -4.8$ | |

12)  Solve for $x$: $2(x + 2)^2 - 2x^2 + 10 = 42$

**Answer:**

| | |
|---|---|
| $2(x + 2)^2 - 2x^2 + 10 = 42$ | |
| $2(x + 2)(x + 2) - 2x^2 + 10 = 42$ | Simplify the left-hand side of the equation using the order of operations and combining like terms. Begin with the exponent. |
| $2(x^2 + 4x + 4) - 2x^2 + 10 = 42$ | Apply FOIL. |
| $2x^2 + 8x + 8 - 2x^2 + 10 = 42$ | Distribute the 2. |
| $8x + 18 = 42$ | Combine like terms on the left-hand side. |
| $8x = 24$ | Isolate the variable. "Undo" + 18 by subtracting 18 on both sides. |
| $x = 3$ | "Undo" multiplication by 8 by dividing both sides by 8. |

13)  Solve the equation for $D$: $\frac{A(3B + 2D)}{2N} = 5M - 6$

**Answer:**

| | |
|---|---|
| $\frac{A(3B + 2D)}{2N} = 5M - 6$ | |
| $3AB + 2AD = 10MN - 12N$ | Multiply both sides by 2N to clear the fraction, and distribute the A through the parentheses. |
| $2AD = 10MN - 12N - 3AB$ | Isolate the term with the D in it by moving 3AB to the other side of the equation. |
| $D = \frac{(10MN - 12N - 3AB)}{2A}$ | Divide both sides by 2A to get D alone on the right-hand side. |

## GRAPHS OF LINEAR EQUATIONS

The most common way to write a linear equation is **slope-intercept form**, $y = mx + b$. In this equation, $m$ is the slope, which describes how steep the line is,

and $b$ is the $y$-intercept. Slope is often described as "rise over run" because it is calculated as the difference in $y$-values (rise) over the difference in $x$-values (run). The slope of the line is also the rate of change of the dependent variable $y$ with respect to the independent variable $x$. The $y$-intercept is the point where the line crosses the $y$-axis, or where $x$ equals zero.

To graph a linear equation, identify the $y$-intercept and place that point on the $y$-axis. If the slope is not written as a fraction, make it a fraction by writing it over 1 $\left(\frac{m}{1}\right)$. Then use the slope to count up (or down, if negative) the "rise" part of the slope and over the "run" part of the slope to find a second point. These points can then be connected to draw the line. To find the equation of a line, identify the $y$-intercept, if possible, on the graph and use two easily identifiable points to find the slope. If the $y$-intercept is not easily identified, identify the slope by choosing easily identifiable points; then choose one point on the graph, plug the point and the slope values into the equation, and solve for the missing value $b$.

▶  slope: $m = \frac{y_2 - y_1}{x_2 - x_1}$

▶  standard form: $Ax + By = C$

▶  $m = -\frac{A}{B}$

▶  $x\text{-intercept} = \frac{C}{A}$

▶  $y\text{-intercept} = \frac{C}{B}$

Another way to express a linear equation is standard form: $Ax + By = C$. In order to graph equations in this form, it is often easiest to convert them to point-slope form. Alternately, it is easy to find the $x$- or $y$-intercept from this form, and once these two points are known, a line can be drawn through them. To find the $x$-intercept, simply make $y = 0$ and solve for $x$. Similarly, to find the $y$-intercept, make $x = 0$ and solve for $y$.

## SAMPLE QUESTIONS

14) **What is the equation of the following line?**

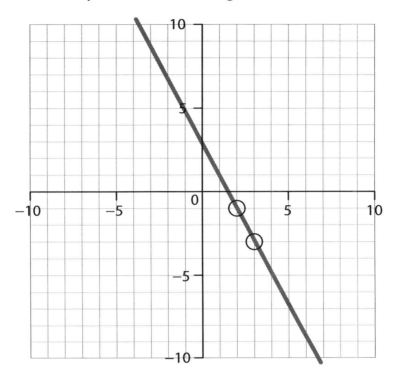

**Answer:**

| | |
|---|---|
| $b = 3$ | The $y$-intercept can be identified on the graph as $(0, 3)$. |
| $m = \dfrac{(-3) - (-1)}{3 - 2} = \dfrac{-2}{1} = -2$ | To find the slope, choose any two points and plug the values into the slope equation. The two points chosen here are $(2, -1)$ and $(3, -3)$. |
| $y = -2x + 3$ | Counting squares and verifying the line goes down 2 and over 1 to get from one point on the line to another point on the line gives the same result. Replace $m$ with $-2$ and $b$ with 3 in $y = mx + b$ |

15) **What is the slope of the line whose equation is $6x - 2y - 8 = 0$?**

**Answer:**

$$6x - 2y - 8 = 0$$

| | |
|---|---|
| $-2y = -6x + 8$ | Rearrange the equation into slope-intercept form by solving the equation for *x*. |
| | "Undo" 6*x* by subtracting 6*x* on both sides of the equation. |
| $y = \frac{-6x + 8}{-2}$ | "Undo" multiplication of −2 by *y* by dividing both sides by −2. |
| $y = 3x - 4$ | Simplify the fractions. |
| **= 3** | The slope is 3, the value attached to *x*. |

16) **What is the equation of the following graph?**

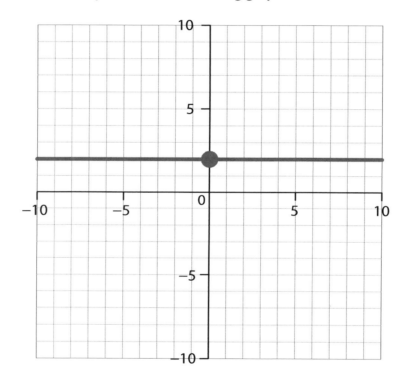

**Answer:**

| | |
|---|---|
| $y = 0x + 2$, **or** $y = 2$ | The line has a rise of 0 and a run of 1, so the slope is $\frac{0}{1} = 0$. There is no *x*-intercept. The *y*-intercept is (0, 2), meaning that the *b*-value in the slope-intercept form is 2. |

17) **Write the equation of the line going through the points (−2, 5) and (−5, 3).**

**Answer:**

| $(-2, 5)$ and $(-5, 3)$ | |
|---|---|
| $m = \dfrac{3 - 5}{(-5) - (-2)}$ $= \dfrac{-2}{-3}$ $= \dfrac{2}{3}$ | Calculate the slope. |
| $5 = \dfrac{2}{3}(-2) + b$ $5 = \dfrac{-4}{3} + b$ $b = \dfrac{19}{3}$ | To find $b$, plug into the equation $y = mx + b$ the slope for $m$ and a set of points for $x$ and $y$. |
| $y = \dfrac{2}{3}x + \dfrac{19}{3}$ | Replace $m$ and $b$ to find the equation of the line. |

18) The revenue of a company in the year 2010 was $50,000. The revenue five years later was $125,000. Assuming that the revenue grew in a linear manner, what was the rate of change of revenue per year?

**Answer:**

| rate of change = slope $= \dfrac{125,000 - 50,000}{5 - 0} = \dfrac{75,000}{5} = 15,000$ | The rate of change is just the slope. It is helpful to represent year 2010 as $t = 0$. Then the two points given are $(0, 50000)$ and $(5, 125000)$. |
|---|---|
| **The rate of change of revenue is $15,000 per year.** | |

## BUILDING EQUATIONS

In word problems, it is often necessary to translate a verbal description of a relationship into a mathematical equation. No matter the problem, this process can be done using the same steps:

1. Read the problem carefully and identify what value needs to be solved for.
2. Identify the known and unknown quantities in the problem, and assign the unknown quantities a variable.
3. Create equations using the variables and known quantities.
4. Solve the equations.
5. Check the solution: Does it answer the question asked in the problem? Does it make sense?

> **HELPFUL HINT**
>
> Use the acronym STAR to remember word-problem strategies: Search the problem, Translate into an expression or equation, Answer, and Review.

## SAMPLE QUESTIONS

19) **A school is holding a raffle to raise money. There is a $3 entry fee, and each ticket costs $5. If a student paid $28, how many tickets did he buy?**

**Answer:**

| | |
|---|---|
| Number of tickets $= x$ <br> Cost per ticket $= 5$ <br> Cost for $x$ tickets $= 5x$ <br> Total cost $= 28$ <br> Entry fee $= 3$ | Identify the quantities. |
| $5x + 3 = 28$ | Set up equations. The total cost for $x$ tickets will be equal to the cost for $x$ tickets plus the $3 flat fee. |
| $5x + 3 = 28$ <br> $5x = 25$ <br> $x = 5$ <br> The student bought **5 tickets**. | Solve for the equation. |

20) **Kelly is selling shirts for her school swim team. There are two prices: a student price and a nonstudent price. During the first week of the sale, Kelly raised $84 by selling 10 shirts to students and 4 shirts to nonstudents. She earned $185 in the second week by selling 20 shirts to students and 10 shirts to nonstudents. What is the student price for a shirt?**

**Answer:**

| | |
|---|---|
| Student price $= s$ <br> Nonstudent price $= n$ | Assign variables. |
| $10s + 4n = 84$ <br> $20s + 10n = 185$ | Create two equations using the number of shirts Kelly sold and the money she earned. |
| $10s + 4n = 84$ <br> $10n = -20s + 185$ <br> $n = -2s + 18.5$ <br> $10s + 4(-2s + 18.5) = 84$ <br> $10s - 8s + 74 = 84$ <br> $2s + 74 = 84$ <br> $2s = 10$ <br> $s = 5$ <br> The student cost for shirts is **$5**. | Solve the system of equations using substitution. Since the question asks for the student price, the goal is to solve for $s$. Therefore, solve one of the equations for $n$, so that when the expression is substituted for $n$, $n$ will be eliminated and $s$ will remain. |

# LINEAR INEQUALITIES

An **inequality** shows the relationship between two expressions, much like an equation. However, the equal sign is replaced with an inequality symbol that expresses the following relationships:

- ► < less than
- ► > greater than
- ► ≤ less than or equal to
- ► ≥ greater than or equal to

Inequalities are read from left to right. For example, the inequality $x \leq 8$ would be read as "$x$ is less than or equal to 8," meaning $x$ has a value smaller than or equal to 8. The set of solutions of an inequality can be expressed using a number line.

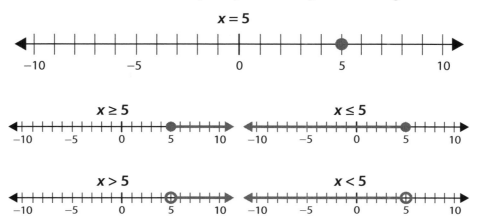

**Figure 5.3. Inequalities on a Number Line**

The shaded region on the number line represents the set of all the numbers that make an inequality true. One major difference between equations and inequalities is that equations generally have one or two solutions, while inequalities generally have infinitely many solutions (an entire interval on the number line containing infinitely many values).

## SOLVING LINEAR INEQUALITIES

Linear inequalities can be solved in the same way as linear equations, with one exception. When multiplying or dividing both sides of an inequality by a negative number, the direction of the inequality sign must reverse—"greater than" becomes "less than" and "less than" becomes "greater than."

**SAMPLE QUESTIONS**

21) Solve for $z$: $3z + 10 < -z$

**Answer:**

Solve the inequality using the same steps used to solve equations.

| $3z + 10 < -z$ | |
|---|---|
| $3z < -z - 10$ | Collect nonvariable terms to one side. |
| $4z < -10$ | Collect variable terms to the other side. |
| $z < -2.5$ | Isolate the variable. |

22) Solve for $x$: $2x - 3 > 5(x - 4) - (x - 4)$

**Answer:**

| $2x - 3 > 5(x - 4) - (x - 4)$ | |
|---|---|
| $2x - 3 > 5x - 20 - x + 4$ | Distribute 5 through the parentheses and −1 through the parentheses. |
| $2x - 3 > 4x - 16$ | Combine like terms. |
| $-2x > -13$ | Collect $x$-terms to one side, and constant terms to the other side. |
| $x < 6.5$ | Divide both sides by −2; since dividing by a negative, reverse the direction of the inequality. |

## GRAPHING LINEAR INEQUALITIES IN TWO VARIABLES

Linear inequalities in two variables can be graphed in much the same way as linear equations. Start by graphing the corresponding equation of a line (temporarily replace the inequality with an equal sign, and then graph). This line creates a boundary line of two half-planes. If the inequality is a "greater/less than," the boundary should not be included and a dotted line is used. A solid line is used to indicate that the boundary should be included in the solution when the inequality is "greater/less than or equal to."

One side of the boundary is the set of all points $(x,y)$ that make the inequality true. This side is shaded to indicate that all these values are solutions. The simplest method to determine which side should be shaded is to choose a point (*x*,*y*) on one side of the boundary and evaluate the inequality, plugging in this *x*- and *y*- value. If the point makes the inequality true, that side should be shaded; if it does not, it is not a solution, so the other side should be shaded. A second point can be tested as a check. Any point on the shaded side should make the inequality true.

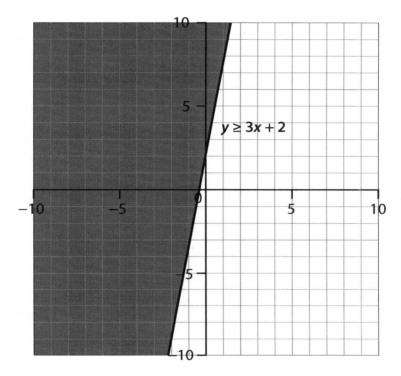

**Figure 5.4. Graphing Inequalities**

A set of two or more linear inequalities is a **system of inequalities**. Solutions to the system are all the values of the variables that make every inequality in the system true. Systems of inequalities are solved graphically by graphing all the inequalities in the same plane. The region where all the shaded solutions overlap is the solution to the system.

## SAMPLE QUESTIONS

23) **Graph the following inequality: $3x + 6y \leq 12$**

**Answer:**

The easiest way to graph this line is to find the *x*- and *y*-intercepts. Find the *y*-intercept by making $x = 0$ and solving for *y*. This gives $(0, 2)$ as the *y*-intercept. Find the *x*-intercept by making $y = 0$ and solving for *x*. This give $(4, 0)$ as the *x*-intercept. Knowing these two points, the line can be drawn. Because the inequality says "or equal to," the boundary line is included and is represented by a solid line. To determine which side to shade, choose a value on one side of the boundary, plug it in, and determine if it is a solution. For example, choosing the origin $(0, 0)$ and plugging it into the inequality gives $3(0) + 6(0)$, which gives 0, which is less than 12, so it must be a solution. Therefore, ALL the solutions lie on the same side as $(0, 0)$. Shade the side that includes $(0, 0)$.

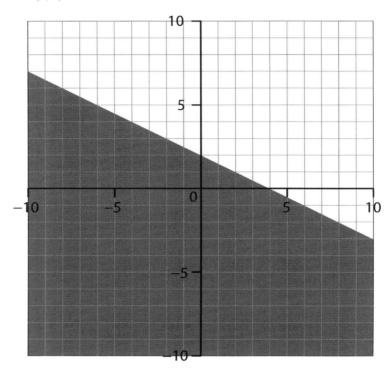

24)   **What is the inequality represented on the graph below?**

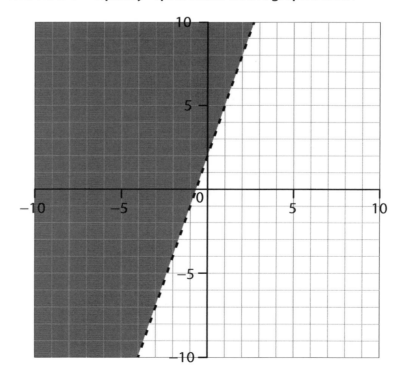

**Answer:**

| | |
|---|---|
| *y*-intercept: (0,2)<br><br>slope: 3<br><br>$y = 3x + 2$ | The line crosses the *y*-axis at $y = 2$.<br><br>To arrive at another point on the line, go up 3 (rise) and right 1 (run).<br><br>Determine the equation of the boundary line. |
| $y > 3x + 2$ | Replace the equal sign with the appropriate inequality: the line is dotted and the shading is above the line, indicating that the symbol should be "greater than." Check a point: for example (1, 5) is a solution since $5 > 3(-1) + 2$. |

25)  **Graph the system of inequalities:** $-x + y \le 1, x \ge 1, y > 2x - 4$

**Answer:**

To solve the system, graph all three inequalities in the same plane; then identify the area where the three solutions overlap. All points $(x, y)$ in this area will be solutions to the system since they satisfy all three inequalities. The first inequality is a solid line with slope 1, and the area below that line is shaded. The second inequality is a vertical line and the area to the right of that line is shaded. The third inequality is the dashed line with slope 2 and the area above that line is shaded. The overlapping area is the shaded triangle in the middle. To check the solution, choose one point in that area. It looks like (0, 0) is a solution and plugging that point into each inequality confirms that it is a solution.

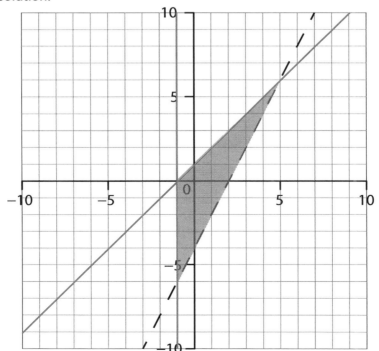

# FUNCTIONS

## WORKING WITH FUNCTIONS

Functions can be thought of as a process: when something is put in, an action (or operation) is performed, and something different comes out. A **function** is a relationship between two quantities (for example $x$ and $y$) in which, for every value of the independent variable (usually $x$), there is exactly one value of the dependent variable (usually $y$). Briefly, each input has *exactly one* output. Graphically this means the graph passes the **vertical line test**: anywhere a vertical line is drawn on the graph, the line hits the curve at exactly one point. The notation $f(x)$ or $g(t)$, etc., is often used when a function is being considered. This is **function notation.** The

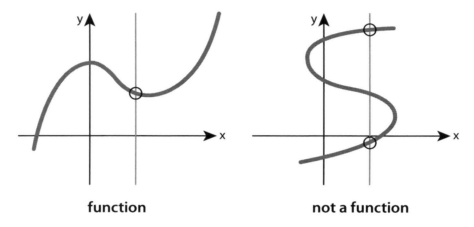

function                    not a function

**Figure 5.5. Vertical Line Test**

input value is $x$ and the output value $y$ are written as $y = f(x)$. Thus, $f(2)$ represents the output value (or $y$ value) when $x = 2$, and $f(2) = 5$ means that when $x = 2$ is plugged into the $f(x)$ function, the output ($y$ value) is 5. In other words, $f(2) = 5$ represents the point (2,5) on the graph of $f(x)$.

Every function has an **input domain** and **output range**. The domain is the set of all the possible $x$ values that can be used as input values (these are found along the horizontal axis on the graph), and the range includes all the $y$ values or output values that result from applying $f(x)$ (these are found along the vertical axis on the graph). Domain and range are usually intervals of numbers and are often expressed as inequalities.

A function $f(x)$ is **even** if $f(-x) = f(x)$. Even functions have symmetry across the $y$-axis. An example of an even function is the parent quadratic $y = x^2$, because any value of $x$ (for example, 3) and its opposite $-x$ (for example, $-3$) have the same $y$ value (for example, $3^2 = 9$ and $(-3)^2 = 9$). A function is **odd** if $f(-x) = -f(x)$. Odd functions have symmetry about the origin. For example, $f(x) = x^3$ is an odd function because $f(3) = 27$, and $f(-3) = -27$. A function may be even, odd, or neither.

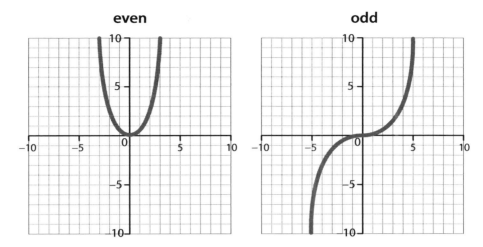

**Figure 5.6. Even and Odd Function**

## SAMPLE QUESTIONS

26) **What is the domain and range of the following function?**

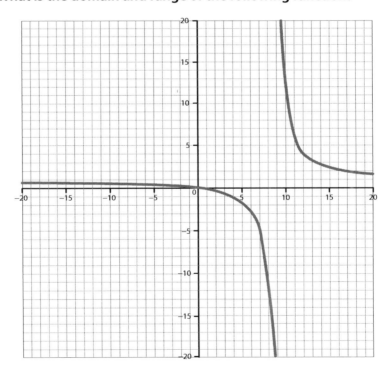

**Answer:**

This function has an asymptote at $x = 8$, so is not defined there. Exclude 8 from the domain. Otherwise, the function is defined for all other values of $x$. The proper way to write the domain is:

**D:** $-\infty < x < 8$ or $8 < x < \infty$

Another way to state the domain is "all real numbers except 8." Sometimes interval notations are used: $(-\infty, 8)$ U $(8, \infty)$. The round brackets indicate that 8 is not included; square brackets [ ] would indicate that the value is included in the domain. The U symbol simply means *or*.

Since the function has a horizontal asymptote at $y = 1$ that it never crosses, the function never takes the value 1, so the range is all real numbers except 1, or **R:** $-\infty < y < 1$ *or* $1 < y < \infty$.

27)  **Evaluate:** $f(4)$ *if* $f(x) = x^3 - 2x + \sqrt{x}$

**Answer:**

| $f(4)$ if $f(x) = x^3 - 2x + \sqrt{x}$ | |
| --- | --- |
| $f(4) = (4)^3 - 2(4) + \sqrt{(4)}$ | Plug in 4. |
| $= 64 - 8 + 2$ <br> $= 58$ | Follow the PEMDAS order of operations. |

28)  **Which of the following represents a function?**

| A. | | | B. | | |
| --- | --- | --- | --- | --- | --- |
| $x$ | $g(x)$ | | $x$ | $f(x)$ | |
| 0 | 0 | | 0 | 1 | |
| 1 | 1 | | 0 | 2 | |
| 2 | 2 | | 0 | 3 | |
| 1 | 3 | | 0 | 4 | |

| C. | | | D. | | |
| --- | --- | --- | --- | --- | --- |
| $t$ | $f(t)$ | | $x$ | $f(x)$ | |
| 1 | 1 | | 0 | 0 | |
| 2 | 2 | | 5 | 1 | |
| 3 | 3 | | 0 | 2 | |
| 4 | 4 | | 5 | 3 | |

**Answer:**

For a set of numbers to represent a function, every input must generate a unique output. Therefore, if the same input ($x$) appears more than once in the table, determine if that input has two different outputs. If so, then the table does not represent a function.

A.    Incorrect. This table is not a function because input value 1 has two different outputs (1 and 3).

B. Incorrect. Table B is not function because 0 is the only input and results in four different values.

C. **Correct.** Each input has one output.

D. Incorrect. This table also has one input going to two different values.

29) **What is the domain and the range of the following graph?**

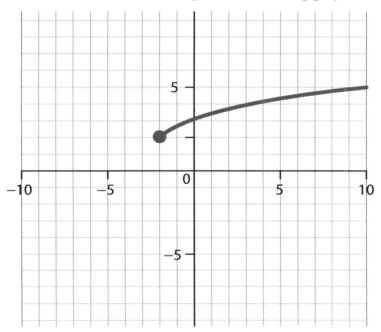

**Answer:**

For the domain, this graph goes on to the right to positive infinity. Its leftmost point, however, is $x = -2$. Therefore, its domain is all real numbers equal to or greater than –2, **D: – 2 ≤ x < ∞.** In interval notation, write **[–2, ∞).**

The lowest range value is $y = 2$. Although it has a decreasing slope, this function continues to rise and there is no reason to think it will stop rising. Therefore, the domain is all real numbers greater than 2, **R: 2 ≤ y < ∞.**

Also notice that this is indeed a graph of a function, since there is no $x$-value that has more than one $y$-value. It passes the vertical line test, since any vertical line drawn anywhere in the domain of the function results in hitting the curve only once.

# Geometry

Geometry is the study of shapes, angles, volumes, areas, lines, points, and the relationships among them. It is normally approached as an axiomatic system; that is, a small number of entities are taken for granted as true, and everything else is derived logically from them.

## Properties of Shapes

### BASIC DEFINITIONS

The basic figures from which many other geometric shapes are built are points, lines, and planes. A point is a location in a plane. It has no size or shape, but is represented by a dot. It is labeled using a capital letter.

Two points may be connected by a **line** that extends indefinitely in both directions. There are infinitely many points on a line. A line is a one-dimensional figure. Lines are represented by any two points (say, $A$ and $B$) on the line and the line symbol: ($\overleftrightarrow{AB}$). For any two points, a line can be defined that goes through the points. Any points on the same line are co-linear. If two lines are parallel, they will never touch. Parallel lines have the exact same slopes. Two lines with different slopes intersect at a point. If two lines are perpendicular, they intersect at 90° angles.

A **line segment** has two endpoints and a finite length. The length of a segment, called the measure of the segment, is the distance from $A$ to $B$. A line segment is a subset of a line, and is also denoted with two points, but with a segment symbol: ($\overline{AB}$). The midpoint of a line segment is the point at which the segment is divided into two equal parts. A line, segment, or plane that passes through the midpoint of a segment is called a bisector of the segment, since it cuts the segment into two equal segments.

A **ray** has one endpoint and extends indefinitely in one direction. It is defined by its endpoint, followed by any other point on the ray: ($\overrightarrow{AB}$). It is important that the first letter represents the endpoint. A ray is sometimes called a half line.

### Table 6.1. Basic Geometric Figures

| Term | Dimensions | Graphic | Symbol |
|------|-----------|---------|--------|
| point | zero | ● | ·A |
| line segment | one | A——B | $\overline{AB}$ |
| ray | one | A—B→ | $\overrightarrow{AB}$ |
| line | one | ←—→ | $\overleftrightarrow{AB}$ |
| plane | two | ▱ | Plane M |

A **plane** is a flat sheet that extends indefinitely in two directions (like an infinite sheet of paper). A plane is a two-dimensional (2D) figure. A plane can ALWAYS be defined through any three noncollinear points in three-dimensional (3D) space. A plane is named using any three points that are in the plane (for example, plane **ABC**). Any points lying in the same plane are said to be coplanar. When two planes intersect, the intersection is a line.

### SAMPLE QUESTION

1)  **Which points and lines are not contained in plane *M* in the diagram below?**

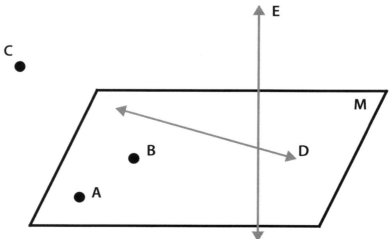

**Answer:**

Points *A* and *B* and line *D* are all on the same plane, as is the ray beginning at *D*. Point *C* is above the plane, and line *E* cuts through the plane and thus is on a more vertical plane. The point at which line *E* intersects plane *M* is on plane *M* but the line as a whole is not.

## ANGLES

Angles are formed when two rays share a common endpoint. They are named using three letters, with the vertex point in the middle (for example ∠*ABC*, where *B* is the vertex). They can also be labeled with a number or named by their vertex alone (if it is clear to do so). Angles are commonly measured in degrees or radians. They are also classified based on their angle measure. A **right angle** has a measure of exactly 90°. **Acute angles** have measures that are less than 90°, whereas **obtuse angles** have measures that are greater than 90°.

Any two angles that add to make 90° are called **complementary angles**. A 30° angle would be complementary to a 60° angle. **Supplementary angles** add up to 180°. A supplementary angle to a 60° angle would be a 120° angle; likewise, 60° is the **supplement** of 120°. The complement and supplement of any angle must always be positive. For example, a 140 degree has no complement. Angles that are next to each other and share a common ray are called **adjacent angles**. Angles that are adjacent and supplementary are called a **linear pair** of angles. Their nonshared rays form a line (thus the *linear* pair). Note that angles that are supplementary do not need to be adjacent; their measures simply need to add to 180°.

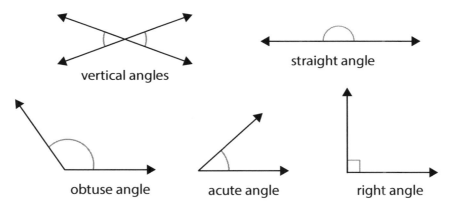

**Figure 6.1. Types of Angles**

**Vertical angles** are formed when two lines intersect. Four angles will be formed; the vertex of each angle is at the intersection point of the lines. The vertical angles across from each other will be equal in measure. The angles adjacent to each other will be linear pairs and therefore supplementary.

A ray, line, or segment that divides an angle into two equal angles is called an **angle bisector**.

## SAMPLE QUESTIONS

2) **How many pairs of supplementary angles are there in the following figure?**

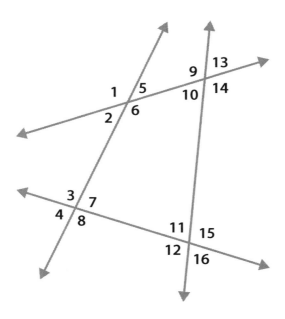

**Answers:**

Any two angles that are adjacent to one another on a line are supplementary. Therefore, there are **sixteen supplementary pairs** here (∠1 and ∠5, ∠2 and ∠6, ∠5 and ∠6, ∠2 and ∠1, and so on).

3) **If angles *M* and *N* are supplementary and ∠*M* is 30° less than twice ∠*N*, what is the degree measurement of each angle?**

**Answer:**

This problem requires a system of equations to solve:

$\angle M + \angle N = 180°$

$\angle M = 2\angle N - 30°$

Replacing ∠*M* with 2∠*N* − 30° gives:

| | |
|---|---|
| $2\angle N - 30° + \angle N = 180°$ | Substitute. |
| $3\angle N - 30° = 180°$ | Combine like terms. |
| $3\angle N = 210°$ | Add 30 to both sides. |
| $\angle N = 70°$ | Divide by 3. |

Since ∠*N* and ∠*M* are supplementary, ∠*M* must be 110°. Work can be checked by using the second equation: 110 = 2(70) − 30 verifies the answers.

## CIRCLES

Circles are a fundamental shape in geometry. A **circle** is the set of all the points in a plane that are the same distance from a fixed point (called the **center**). The distance from the center to any point on the circle is the **radius** of the circle. The distance around the circle (the perimeter) is called the **circumference**.

The ratio of a circle's circumference to its diameter is a constant value called pi ($\pi$), an irrational number which is commonly rounded to 3.14. The formula to find a circle's circumference is $C = 2\pi r$. The formula to find the enclosed area of a circle is $A = \pi r^2$.

Circles have a number of unique parts and properties:

▶ The **diameter** is the largest measurement across a circle. It passes through the circle's center, extending from one side of the circle to the other. The measure of the diameter is twice the measure of the radius.

▶ A line that cuts across a circle and touches it twice is called a **secant** line.

▶ A line that touches a circle or any curve at one point is **tangent** to the circle or the curve. These lines are always exterior to the circle. A line tangent to a circle and a radius drawn to the point of tangency meet at a right angle (90°).

▶ An **arc** is any portion of a circle between two points on the circle. The **measure** of an arc is in degrees, whereas the **length of the arc** will be in linear measurement (such as centimeters or inches). A **minor arc** is the small arc between the two points (it measures less than 180°), whereas a **major arc** is the large arc between the two points (it measures greater than 180°).

▶ An angle with its vertex at the center of a circle is called a **central angle**. For a central angle, the measure of the arc intercepted by the sides of the angle (in degrees) is the same as the measure of the angle.

▶ The part of a secant line that lies within a circle is called a **chord**.

▶ A **sector** is the part of a circle *and* its interior that is inside the rays of a central angle (its shape is like a slice of pie). The formula for area of a sector using $\theta$ in degrees is *sector area* $= \dfrac{\theta}{360}\pi r^2$ (note that this formula is simply the total area of the circle multiplied by $\dfrac{\theta}{360}$, the fraction of the complete circle area that the sector contains). If $\theta$ is in radians, then *sector area* $= \dfrac{r^2\theta}{2}$.

▶ The formula to find the **arc length** (measured in linear units like centimeters, inches, or feet) is *arc length* $= s = \dfrac{\theta}{360}(2\pi\alpha) = \dfrac{\theta}{180}(\pi\alpha)$, where

$\alpha$ is the central angle forming the arc, measured in degrees. Again, this is just the fraction of the total circumference. The formula to find the length of the arc if $\alpha$ is measured in radians is *arc length $s = r\alpha$*.

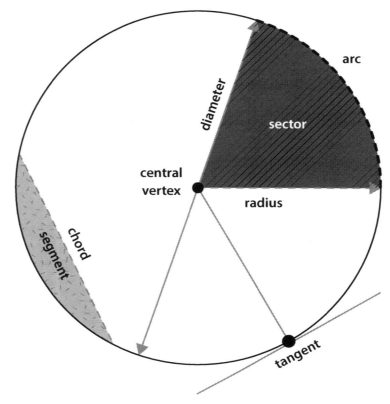

**Figure 6.2. Parts of a Circle**

▶ An **inscribed angle** has a vertex on the circle and is formed by two chords that share that vertex point. The angle measure of an inscribed angle is one-half the angle measure of the central angle with the same endpoints on the circle (in the diagram below right, $\theta = \frac{\alpha}{2}$).

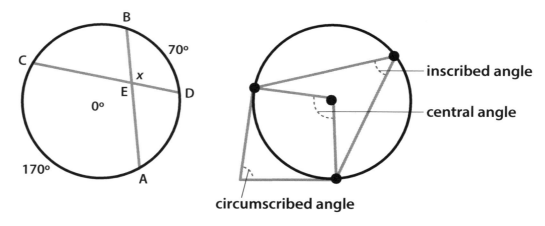

**Figure 6.3. Angles in a Circle**

▶ A **circumscribed angle** has rays tangent to the circle. The angle lies outside of the circle.

▶ Any angle outside the circle, whether formed by two tangent lines, two secant lines, or a tangent line and a secant line, is equal to half the difference of the intercepted arcs.

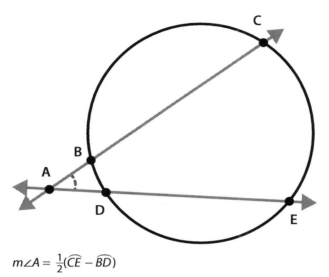

$$m\angle A = \tfrac{1}{2}(\overset{\frown}{CE} - \overset{\frown}{BD})$$

**Figure 6.4. Angles Outside a Circle**

▶ Angles are formed within a circle when two chords intersect in the circle. The measure of the smaller angle formed is half the sum of the two smaller arc measures (in degrees). Likewise, the larger angle is half the sum of the two larger arc measures (think: average the arc measures).

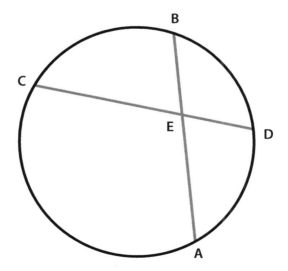

$$m\angle E = \tfrac{1}{2}(\overset{\frown}{AC} + \overset{\frown}{BD})$$

**Figure 6.5. Intersecting Chords**

▶ If a chord intersects a line tangent to the circle, the angle formed by this intersection measures one half the measurement of the intercepted arc (in degrees).

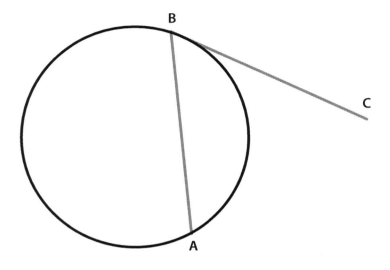

$m\angle ABC = \frac{1}{2}m\widehat{AB}$

**Figure 6.6. Intersecting Chord and Tangent**

## SAMPLE QUESTIONS

4)   **Find the area of the sector *NHS* of the circle below with center at *H*:**

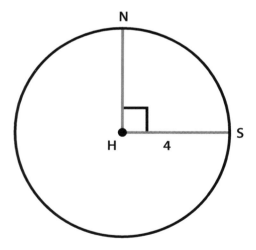

**Answer:**

| | |
|---|---|
| $A = \pi 4^2 = 16\pi$ | First, determine the area of the entire circle. |
| $\dfrac{x}{16\pi} = \dfrac{90°}{360°}$ | Next, write a proportion. |
| $x = 4\pi$ | Solve. |

This answer makes sense because the sector in question is a quarter of the circle, and the area is one quarter of the total area.

5)   **In the circle below with center *O*, the minor arc *ACB* measures 5 feet. What is the measurement of *m∠AOB*?**

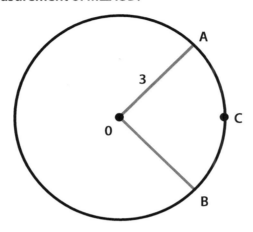

**Answer:**

The circumference of this circle is $C = 2\pi r = 2\pi(3) = 6\pi$ or 18.84. Now a proportion can be set up, equating the ratio of the arc lengths to the ratio of the angle measures:

| | |
|---|---|
| $\dfrac{5}{18.84} = \dfrac{x}{360°}$ | |
| $x = 95.54°$ | Multiply both sides by 360 to solve. |

6)   **In the circle below with center *A*, there are two congruent chords. Solve for *x*.**

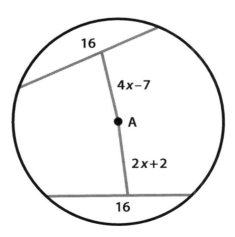

**Answer:**

A circle's chords are equal only if they are the same distance from the circle. This means that the two segments expressed in terms of *x* are equal. The equation that must be solved is:

$$4x - 7 = 2x + 2$$
$$2x = 9$$
$$x = 4.5$$

## TRIANGLES

Much of geometry is concerned with **triangles** as they are commonly used shapes. A good understanding of triangles allows decomposition of other shapes (specifically polygons) into triangles for study.

Triangles have three sides, and the three interior angles always sum to 180°. The formula for the area of a triangle is $A = \frac{1}{2}bh$ or one-half the product of the base and height (or altitude) of the triangle.

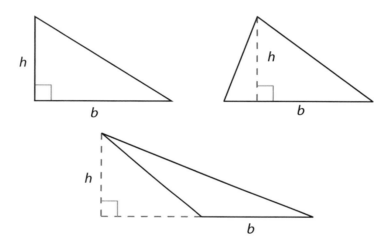

**Figure 6.7. Finding the Base and Height of Triangles**

Some important segments in a triangle include the angle bisector, the altitude, and the median. The **angle bisector** extends from the side opposite an angle to bisect that angle. The **altitude** is the shortest distance from a vertex of the triangle to the line containing the **base side** opposite that vertex. It is perpendicular to that line and can occur on the outside of the triangle. The **median** extends from an angle to bisect the opposite side.

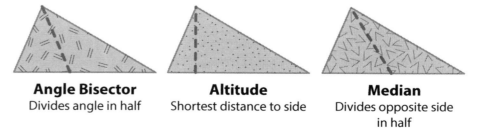

| **Angle Bisector** | **Altitude** | **Median** |
| Divides angle in half | Shortest distance to side | Divides opposite side in half |

**Figure 6.8. Important Segments in a Triangle**

Triangles have two "centers." The **orthocenter** is formed by the intersection of a triangle's three altitudes. The **centroid** is where a triangle's three medians meet.

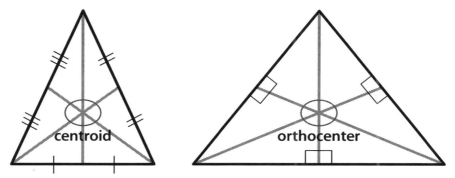

**Figure 6.9. Centroid and Orthocenter of a Triangle**

Triangles can be classified in two ways: by sides and by angles.

A **scalene triangle** has no equal sides or angles. An **isosceles triangle** has two equal sides and two equal angles, often called **base angles**. In an **equilateral triangle**, all three sides are equal as are all three angles. Moreover, because the sum of the angles of a triangle is always 180°, each angle of an equilateral triangle must be 60°.

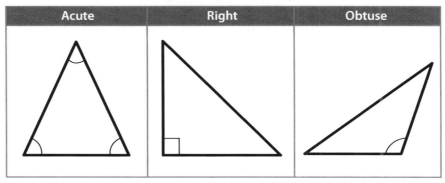

**Figure 6.10. Types of Triangles**

A **right triangle** has one right angle (90°) and two acute angles. An **acute triangle** has three acute angles (all angles are less than 90°). An **obtuse triangle** has one obtuse angle (more than 90°) and two acute angles.

For any triangle, the side opposite the largest angle will have the longest length, while the side opposite the smallest angle will have the shortest length. The **triangle inequality theorem** states that the sum of any two sides of a triangle must be greater than the third side. If this inequality does not hold, then a triangle cannot be formed. A consequence of this theorem is the **third-side rule**: if $b$ and $c$ are two sides of a triangle, then the measure of the third side $a$ must be between the sum of the other two sides and the difference of the other two sides: $c - b < a < c + b$.

Solving for missing angles or sides of a triangle is a common type of triangle problem. Often a right triangle will come up on its own or within another triangle. The relationship among a right triangle's sides is known as the **Pythagorean theorem**: $a^2 + b^2 = c^2$, where $c$ is the hypotenuse and is across from the 90° angle. Right triangles with angle measurements of 90° – 45° – 45° and 90° – 60° – 30° are known as *special* right triangles and always have the following relationship between legs and hypotenuse:

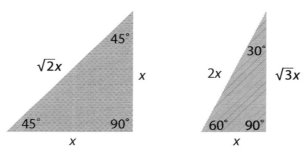

Figure 6.11. Special Right Triangles

## SAMPLE QUESTIONS

7) What are the minimum and maximum values of the third side of the triangle, x, to the nearest hundredth?

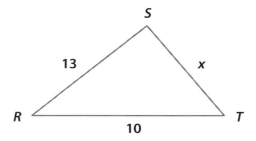

Answers:

The sum of two sides is 23 and their difference is 3. To connect the two other sides and enclose a space, $x$ must be less than the sum and greater than the difference (that is, $3 < x < 23$). Therefore, **$x$'s minimum value to the nearest hundredth is 3.01 and its maximum value is 22.99.**

8) Examine and classify each of the following triangles:

**1.**

**2.**

**3.**

**4.**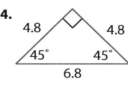

Answers:

**Triangle 1 is an equilateral triangle** (since all 3 sides are equal, and all 3 angles are equal)

**Triangle 2 is a scalene, right triangle** (since all 3 sides are different, and there is a 90° angle)

**Triangle 3 is an obtuse isosceles triangle** (since there are 2 equal sides and, consequently, 2 equal angles)

**Triangle 4 is a right, isosceles triangle** (since there are 2 equal sides and a 90° angle)

9) Given the diagram, if $XZ = 100$, $WZ = 80$, and $XU = 70$, then $WY = ?$

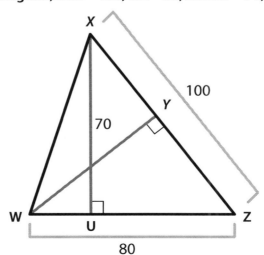

**Answer:**

*WY* can be seen as one of the legs of a right triangle, but from the given information it is unclear how that segment divides *XZ* (we cannot assume that it splits in exactly in two since the triangle is not necessarily isosceles). Another approach is required. Since altitude *XU* and base *WZ* are given values, the area of the triangle can be written in two different ways and equated.

| | |
|---|---|
| $A = \frac{1}{2}(80)(70) = 2800$ | The height *XU* = 70 and base *WZ* = 80 give the area of triangle *XWZ*. |
| $A = \frac{1}{2}(100)(WY)$ | The area of triangle *XWZ* can also be written using *XZ* = 100 and height *WY*. |
| $2800 = \frac{1}{2}(100)(WY)$ | Since both these represent the same area, these may be equated, and *WY* can be solved for. |

*WY* = 56

## QUADRILATERALS

All closed, four-sided shapes are **quadrilaterals**. The sum of all internal angles in a quadrilateral is always 360°. (Think of drawing a diagonal to create two triangles. Since each triangle contains 180°, two triangles, and therefore the quadrilateral, must contain 360°.) The **area of any quadrilateral** is $A = bh$, where *b* is the base and *h* is the height (or altitude).

A **parallelogram** is a quadrilateral with two pairs of parallel sides. A rectangle is a parallelogram with two pairs of equal sides and four right angles. A **kite** also has two pairs of equal sides, but its equal sides are consecutive. Both a **square** and a **rhombus** have four equal sides. A square has four right angles, while a rhombus has a pair of acute opposite angles and a pair of obtuse opposite angles. A **trapezoid** has exactly one pair of parallel sides.

## Table 6.2 Properties of Parallelograms

| Term | Shape | Properties |
|---|---|---|
| Parallelogram | | Opposite sides are parallel. |
| | | Consecutive angles are supplementary. |
| | | Opposite angles are equal. |
| | | Opposite sides are equal. |
| | | Diagonals bisect each other. |

| Term | Shape | Properties |
|------|-------|-----------|
| Rectangle | | All parallelogram properties hold.<br>Diagonals are congruent *and* bisect each other.<br>All angles are right angles. |
| Square | | All rectangle properties hold.<br>All four sides are equal.<br>Diagonals bisect angles.<br>Diagonals intersect at right angles and bisect each other. |
| Kite | | Kites have exactly one pair of opposite equal angles and two pairs of equal consecutive sides.<br>Diagonals meet at right angles. |
| Rhombus | | All four sides are equal.<br>Diagonals bisect angles.<br>Diagonals intersect at right angles and bisect each other. |
| Trapezoid | | Trapezoids have exactly one pair of parallel sides (called bases).<br>Bases have different lengths.<br>Isosceles trapezoids have a pair of equal sides (and base angles). |

## SAMPLE QUESTIONS

10) **Figure *WEST* is a parallelogram. Determine each of the following:**

$\overline{TW} = $ _____

$\overline{EM} \cong $ _____

$\overline{TM} = \frac{1}{2}$ _____

$\angle STW \cong \angle$ _____

$\angle EST + \angle$ _____ $= 180°$.

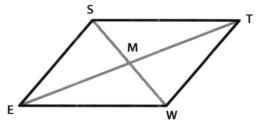

**Answer:**

Line $\overline{TW}$ is parallel to $\overline{SE}$ (opposite sides are equal); $\overline{EM}$ is congruent to $\overline{TM}$; $\overline{TM}$ is one half of $\overline{TE}$ (since diagonals bisect each other); $\angle STW$ is congruent to $\angle SEW$ (opposite sides are equal); and the sum of angles $\angle EST$ and $\angle STW$ is 180° (consecutive angles are supplementary); $\angle SEW$ would also work.

11) In parallelogram *ABCD*, the measure of the exterior angle at *C* is *m*° = 260°. What is the measure of *n*°?

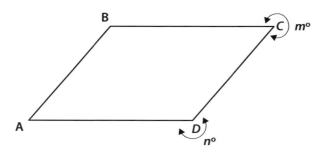

**Answers:**

The two variables are exterior angles. If these two angles were to be added to the interior angles (*A* and *D*) the sum of each pair would be 360°. Since *ABCD* is a parallelogram, these two consecutive interior angles are supplementary. The problem can be solved with this information:

$260° + m\angle C = 360°$

$m\angle C + m\angle D = 180°$

$m\angle D + n = 360°$

It follows from the first equation that $m\angle C = 100°$. Substituting that value in for $\angle C$ in the second equation yields $m\angle D = 80°$. Substituting 80° in for $m\angle D$ in the third equation gives **n = 280°**.

12) A rectangular section of a football field has dimensions of *x* and *y* and an area of 1000 square feet. Three additional lines drawn vertically divide the section into four smaller rectangular areas as seen in the diagram below. If all the lines shown need to be painted, calculate the total number of linear feet, in terms *x*, to be painted.

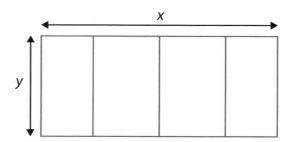

**Answer:**

Since the area is 1000 square feet, $xy = 1000$. The total perimeter of the larger rectangle is $2x + 2y$. In addition, the three interior lines, each of length *y*, need to be painted for a total of $2x + 2y + 3y$ or $2x + 5y$. To express the total in terms of *x*, solve $xy = 1000$ for *y*, and substitute:

| | |
|---|---|
| $y = \frac{1000}{x}$ | Solve for $y$. |
| $P = 2x + 5y$ | |
| $= 2x + 5\left(\frac{1000}{x}\right)$ | Solve for the perimeter. |
| $= 2x + \frac{5000}{x}$ | |

## POLYGONS

Any closed shape made up of three or more line segments is a polygon. In addition to triangles and quadrilaterals, **hexagons** and **octagons** are two common polygons:

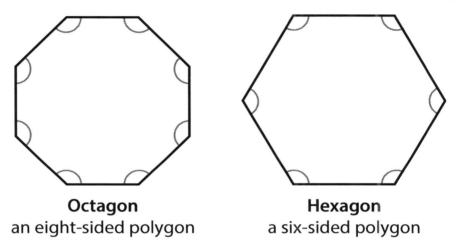

**Octagon**
an eight-sided polygon

**Hexagon**
a six-sided polygon

**Figure 6.12. Common Polygons**

The two polygons depicted above are **regular polygons**, meaning that they are equilateral (all sides having equal lengths) and equiangular (all angles having equal measurements). Angles inside a polygon are **interior angles**, whereas those formed by one side of the polygon and a line extending outside the polygon are **exterior angles**:

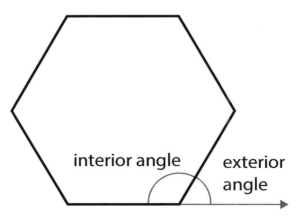

interior angle     exterior angle

**Figure 6.13. Interior and Exterior Angles**

The sum of the all the exterior angles of a polygon is always 360°. Dividing 360° by the number of a polygon's sides finds the measure of the polygon's exterior angles.

To determine the sum of a polygon's interior angles, choose one vertex and draw diagonals from that vertex to each of the other vertices, decomposing the polygon into multiple triangles. For example, an octagon has six triangles within it, and therefore the sum of the interior angles is 6 × 180° = 1080°. In general, the formula for finding the sum of the angles in a polygon is sum of angles = $(n - 2) \times 180°$, where $n$ is the number of sides of the polygon.

To find the measure of a single interior angle in a regular polygon, simply divide the sum of the interior angles by the number of angles (which is the same as the number of sides). So, in the octagon example, each angle is $\frac{1080}{8} = 135°$.

In general, the formula to find the measure of a regular polygon's interior angles is: *interior angle* $= \frac{(n - 2)}{n} \times 180°$ where $n$ is the number of sides of the polygon.

To find the area of a polygon, it is helpful to know the perimeter of the polygon ($p$), and the **apothem** ($a$). The apothem is the shortest (perpendicular) distance from the polygon's center to one of the sides of the polygon. The formula for the area is: *regular polygon area* $= \frac{ap}{2}$.

Finally, there is no universal way to find the perimeter of a polygon (when the side length is not given). Often, breaking the polygon down into triangles and adding the base of each triangle all the way around the polygon is the surest way to calculate the perimeter.

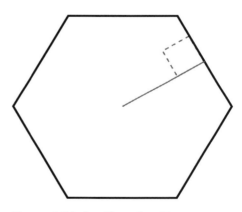

**Figure 6.14. Apothem in a Hexagon**

**SAMPLE QUESTIONS**

13) **What is the measure of an exterior angle and an interior angle of a regular 400-gon?**

**Answer:**

The sum of the exterior angles is 360°. Dividing this sum by 400 gives $\frac{360°}{400} = $ **0.9°**. Since an interior angle is supplementary to an exterior angle, all the interior angles have measure 180 – 0.9 = **179.1°**. Alternately, using the formula for calculating the interior angle gives the same result:

*interior angle* $= \frac{400 - 2}{400} \times 180° = 179.1°$

14) The circle and hexagon below both share center point T. The hexagon is entirely inscribed in the circle. The circle's radius is 5. What is the area of the shaded area?

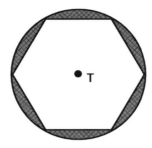

**Answer:**

The area of the circle (with radius $r = 5$) is:

$A = 5^2\pi = 25\pi = 78.54$

To find the hexagon's area, the perimeter must be calculated. The key is using the interior angle formula to find the measure of the interior angles: $\frac{(6-2)}{6}(180°) = 120°$. Six triangles can be drawn by drawing segments from the center of the hexagon to each vertex. Since these triangles are all the same (congruent), and isosceles, they divide each 120° angle exactly in half. Thus, each of the three angles of each triangle is 60°. Moreover the triangles are, in fact, equilateral. The side length of the hexagon is therefore 5 units, and the perimeter is 30. Drawing a perpendicular to the side and using special triangles to find the side opposite the 60° angle calculates the apothem:

The apothem is $2.5\sqrt{3}$, and the area can now be calculated as $area = \frac{ap}{2}$ $= \frac{(2.5\sqrt{3})(30)}{2} = \frac{75\sqrt{3}}{2} = 64.95$.

The shaded area constitutes only parts of the circle that are not in the polygon. The difference between the circle's area and the polygon's area is $78.54 - 64.95 = \textbf{13.59}$.

## THREE-DIMENSIONAL SHAPES

**Three-dimensional shapes** have depth in addition to width and length. The sides of three-dimensional shapes exist on a flat plane, so questions concerning these shapes require the use of the properties discussed above.

Volume is expressed as the number of cubic units any solid can hold—that is, what it takes to fill it up. Surface area is the sum of the areas of the two-dimensional figures that are found on its surface. Three-dimensional shapes have unique formulas:

## Table 6.3. Three-Dimensional Shapes and Formulas

| Term | Shape | Formula | |
|------|-------|---------|--|
| Prism | | $V = Bh$  $SA = 2lw + 2wh + 2lh$  $SA = 2B + lateral\ area$ | $B$ = area of base  $h$ = height  $l$ = length  $w$ = width  $d$ = longest diagonal |
| Cube | | $V = s^3$  $SA = 6s^2$  $d^2 = a^2 + b^2 + c^2$ | $s$ = cube edge |
| Sphere | | $V = \frac{4}{3}\pi r^3$  $SA = 4\pi r^2$ | $r$ = radius |
| Cylinder | | $V = Bh = \pi r^2 h$  $SA = 2\pi r^2 + 2\pi rh$ | $B$ = area of base  $h$ = height  $r$ = radius |
| Cone | | $V = \frac{1}{3}\pi r^2 h$  $SA = \pi r^2 + \pi rl$ | $r$ = radius  $h$ = height  $l$ = slant height |
| Pyramid | | $V = \frac{1}{3}Bh$  $SA = B + \frac{1}{2}(p)l$ | $B$ = area of base  $h$ = height  $p$ = perimeter  $l$ = slant height |

## SAMPLE QUESTIONS

15) A sphere has a radius $z$. If that radius is increased by $t$, by how much is the surface area increased? Write the answer in terms of $z$ and $t$.

Answer:

| | |
|---|---|
| $SA_1 = 4\pi z^2$ | The original surface area is: |
| $SA_2 = 4\pi(z + t)^2$ | The increased surface area is: |
| $= 4\pi(z^2 + 2zt + t^2)$ | |
| $= 4\pi z^2 + 8\pi zt + 4\pi t^2$ | |

| $4\pi z^2 + 8\pi zt + 4\pi t^2 - 4\pi z^2$ | To find the difference between the two, subtract the original from the increased surface area: |
| --- | --- |
| $= 4\pi t^2 + 8\pi zt$ | The surface area increased by $4\pi t^2 + 8\pi zt$. |

16) **The length of the base of a rectangular pyramid measures 4 feet, and the width of the base is half of the pyramid's height. What is the pyramid's volume in terms of height?**

**Answer:**

The length of the base is $l = 4$. The width of the base is $w = \frac{1}{2}h$.

The base of the pyramid is rectangular and thus has area:

$B = lw = 4\left(\frac{1}{2}h\right) = 2h$

Plugging this information into a pyramid's volume equation provides the answer:

$V = \frac{1}{3}Bh = \frac{1}{3}(2h)h = \frac{2h^2}{3}$

17) **A cube with volume 27 cubic meters is inscribed within a sphere and all of the cube's vertices touch the sphere. What is the length of the sphere's radius?**

**Answer:**

Since the cube's volume is 27, each side length is equal to $\sqrt[3]{27} = 3$. The long diagonal distance from one of the cube's vertices to its opposite vertex will provide the sphere's diameter. Using the super Pythagorean theorem, it is found that:

$d = \sqrt{3^2 + 3^2 + 3^2} = \sqrt{27} = 5.2$

This is the diameter of the sphere. Half of this length is the radius, which is **2.6 meters**.

# Transformations of Geometric Figures

## TRANSLATIONS, ROTATIONS, REFLECTIONS, AND CONGRUENCE

Geometric figures are often drawn in the coordinate $xy$-plane, with the vertices or centers of the figures indicated by ordered pairs. Important understandings about the nature of a figure can be examined by performing **transformations**, which are manipulations of the shape in the plane. The original shape is called the **pre-image**, and the shape after a transformation is applied is called the **image**.

A **translation** transforms a shape by moving it right or left, or up or down. Translations are sometimes called slides. The image under this transformation is identical in size and shape to the pre-image. In other words, the image is **congruent**, or identical in size, to the pre-image. All corresponding pairs of angles are congruent, and all corresponding side lengths are congruent.

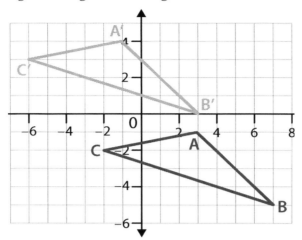

The translation moved triangle ABC left 4 units
and up 6 units to produce triangle A'B'C'.

**Figure 6.15. Translation**

Translations are often written with pointy brackets: {−x, y}. The first number represents the change in the x direction (left/right), while the second number shows the change in the y direction (up/down). The symbol ≅ is read "congruent."

Similarly, rotations and reflections preserve the size and shape of the figure, so congruency is preserved. A **rotation** takes a pre-image and rotates it about a fixed point (often the origin) in the plane. Although the position or orientation of the shape changes, the angles and side lengths remain the same.

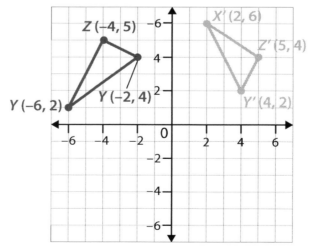

The triangle XYZ is rotated 90 in the clockwise
direction about the origin (0, 0).

**Figure 6.16. Rotation**

A **reflection** takes each point in the pre-image and flips it over a point or line in the plane (often the *x*- or *y*-axis, but not necessarily). The image is congruent to the pre-image. When a figure is flipped across the *y*-axis, the signs of all *x*-coordinates will change. The *y*-coordinates change sign when a figure is reflected across the *x*-axis.

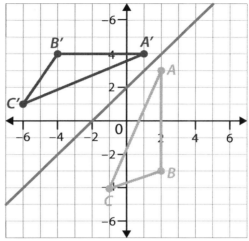

The triangle ABC is reflected over the line to produce the triangle A'B'C'.

**Figure 6.17. Reflection**

### SAMPLE QUESTIONS

18) If quadrilateral *ABCD* has vertices *A* (−6, 4), *B* (−6, 8), *C* (2, 8), and *D* (4, −4), what are the new vertices if *ABCD* is translated 2 units down and 3 units right?

**Answer:**

Translating two units down decreases each *y*-value by 2, and moving 3 units to the right increases the *x*-value by 3. The new vertices are *A* (−3, 2), *B* (−3, 6), *C* (5, 6), and *D* (7, −6).

19) If quadrilateral *ABCD* has vertices *A* (−6, 4), *B* (−6, 8), *C* (2, 8), and *D* (4, −4), what are the new vertices if *ABCD* is rotated 270° and then reflected across the *x*-axis?

**Answer:**

When a figure is rotated 270°, the coordinates change: $(a, b) \rightarrow (b, -a)$ (see the summary of rotation coordinate changes in the next section). After the rotation, the new coordinates are (4, 6), (8, 6), (8, −2), and (−4, −4). Reflecting across the *x*-axis requires that every *y*-value is multiplied by −1 to arrive at the completely transformed quadrilateral with vertices of (4, −6), (8, −6), (8, 2), and (−4, 4).

## DILATIONS AND SIMILARITY

The last transformations of interest are dilations. A **dilation** increases (or decreases) the size of a figure by some **scale factor**. Each coordinate of the points that make up the figure is multiplied by the same factor. If the factor is greater than 1, multiplying all the factors enlarges the shape; if the factor is less than 1 (but greater than 0), the shape is reduced in size.

In addition to the scale factor, a dilation needs a **center of dilation**, which is a fixed point in the plane about which the points are multiplied. Usually, but not always, the center of dilation is the origin (0,0). For dilations about the origin, the image coordinates are calculated by multiplying each coordinate by the scale factor **k**. Thus, point **(x, y) → (kx, ky)**. Although dilations do not result in congruent figures, the orientation of the figure is preserved; consequently, corresponding line segments will be parallel.

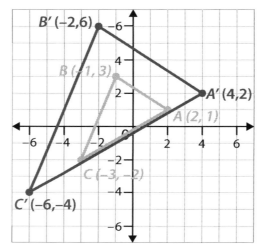

The triangle ABC is dilated by the scale
factor 2 to produce triangle A'B'C'.

**Fiure 6.18. Dilation**

Importantly, dilations do NOT create images that are congruent to the original because the size of each dimension is increased or decreased (the only exception being if the scale factor is exactly 1). However, the shape of the figure is maintained. The corresponding angle measures will be congruent, but the corresponding side lengths will be **proportional**. In other words, the image and pre-image will be **similar** shapes.

Considering congruent and similar shapes as a consequence of transformations is helpful in understanding what is meant by congruence and similarity. Often, however, the fact that two shapes are congruent or similar is given as a fact, unrelated to a transformation. In that case, much information is being given in a single statement. For example, given that $\triangle ABC \sim \triangle PQR$ (~ is read *is similar to*) tells the reader that $\angle A \cong \angle P$, $\angle B \cong \angle Q$, $\angle C \cong \angle R$, and $\frac{AB}{PQ} = \frac{BC}{QR} = \frac{AC}{PR} = k$ (where $k$ is the constant of proportionality).

## TRANSFORMING COORDINATES

Transformations in a plane can actually be thought of as functions. An input pair of coordinates, when acted upon by a transformation, results in a pair of output coordinates. Each point is moved to a unique new point (a one-to-one correspondence).

| Table 6.4. How Coordinates Change for Transformations in a Plane | |
| --- | --- |
| **Type of Transformation** | **Coordinate Changes** |
| Translation right $m$ units and up $n$ units | $(x, y) \rightarrow (x + m, y + n)$ |
| Rotations about the origin in positive (counterclockwise) direction | |
| **Rotation 90°** | $(x, y) \rightarrow (-y, x)$ |
| **Rotation 180°** | $(x, y) \rightarrow (-x, -y)$ |
| **Rotation 270°** | $(x, y) \rightarrow (y, -x)$ |
| Reflections about the | |
| **$x$-axis** | $(x, y) \rightarrow (x, -y)$ |
| **$y$-axis** | $(x, y) \rightarrow (-x, y)$ |
| line **$y = x$** | $(x, y) \rightarrow (y, x)$ |
| Dilations about the origin by a factor of $k$ | |
| **$0 < k < 1 \rightarrow$ size reduced** | |
| **$k > 1 \rightarrow$ size enlarged** | $(x, y) \rightarrow (kx, ky)$ |

20) Triangle *ABC* with coordinates $(2, 8)$, $(10, 2)$, and $(6, 8)$ is transformed in the plane as shown in the diagram. What transformations result in the image triangle *A'B'C'*?

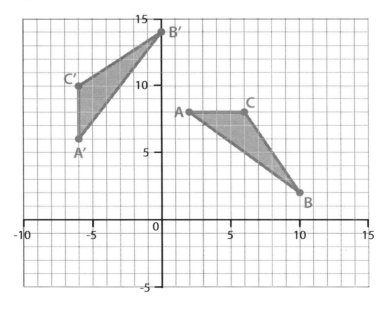

**Answer:**

Since the orientation of the triangle is different from the original, it must have been rotated. A counterclockwise rotation of 90° about the point A (2, 8) results in a triangle with the same orientation. Then the triangle must be translated to move it to the image location. Pick one point, say A, and determine the translation necessary to move it to point A'. In this case, each point on the pre-image must be translated 8 units left and 2 units down. **This could be written {−8, −2}.** Note that other transformations could also result in the same image. For example, triangle ABC could be rotated clockwise 270° and then translated.

21) **If quadrilateral *ABCD* has vertices *A* (−6, 4), *B* (−6, 8), *C* (2, 8), and *D* (4, −4), what are the new vertices if *ABCD* is increased by a factor of 5 about the origin?**

**Answer:**

Changing coordinates to account for a dilation transformation requires that all the coordinates be multiplied by the scale factor. The new vertices are *A* (−30, 20), *B* (−30, 40), *C* (10, 40), and *D* (20, −20).

## TRANSFORMATIONS AND COORDINATE GEOMETRY PROOF

Using transformation and coordinates can be a powerful method of proving geometric theorems. For example, the image of a line in a plane that has been translated within the plane is clearly parallel to its pre-image. This can be proven using transformations.

Consider any line with slope $m = \frac{\Delta y}{\Delta x} = \frac{\text{rise}}{\text{run}}$, as shown in Figure 6.19. The $\Delta y$ can be represented with a vertical segment, and the $\Delta x$ with a horizontal segment, which forms a triangle as shown. When the line is shifted vertically down 4 units (or in any direction, really), the triangle representing slope will be congruent to the original slope triangle. Thus, the rise and run are equivalent, and the slopes must be equal. This proves that lines are parallel if and only if they have equal slopes.

Similarly, a rotation transformation can prove that two lines are perpendicular if and only if they have opposite, reciprocal slopes. This is facilitated by using a line that goes through (0,0) and rotating about that point.

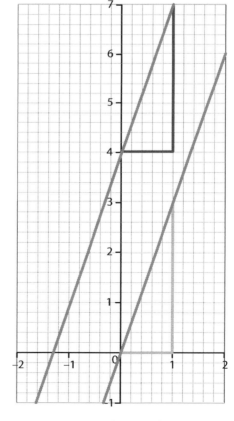

**Figure 6.19. Translation of a Line in a Plane**

This can be assumed since any line can be translated to the origin without changing its slope, as seen in the previous example.

If the line with positive slope in this diagram contains points (0,0) and (*a*,*b*), then the slope of this line is $\frac{b}{a}$. When the line is rotated 90° about the origin, point (*a*,*b*) → (–*b*,*a*), according to the rules of rotations. Thus, the image line passes through (0,0) and (–*b*,*a*) and has slope $\frac{a}{-b} = -\frac{a}{b}$. Notice that the slope of the image line is the opposite, reciprocal (flip) of the pre-image line. This proves the theorem.

In the Figure 3.20, the slope of the pre-image line is 3, whereas the slope of the perpendicular image line is $-\frac{1}{3}$.

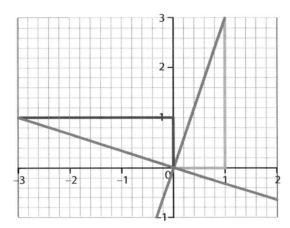

Figure 6.20. Rotation of a Line in a Plane

Another theorem that can be proven using coordinate geometry is that **all circles are similar to one another**. Suppose that circle 1 has radius $r_1$ and center (*h*,*k*), and circle 2 has radius $r_2$ ($r_2 > r_1$) and center (*a*,*b*). Circle 2 can be re-centered to (*h*,*k*) by doing a horizontal translation of $h - a$ and a vertical translation $k - b$. Then a dilation can be performed about the center with a scale factor of $\frac{r_1}{r_2}$. This results in the image of circle 2 landing right on top of circle 1, showing that the circles are similar.

All equations for two-dimensional lines have a slope, a zero slope, or an undefined slope. A horizontal line has zero slope and a vertical line has undefined slope (since its slope would be the opposite, reciprocal of a horizontal line, which would require division by 0).

## SAMPLE QUESTIONS

22) **Identify three lines perpendicular to *y* = 3*x* + 3.**

**Answer:**

There are an infinite number of lines perpendicular to this line since the line does not stop. Three possibilities are $y = -\frac{1}{3}x + 3$, $y = -\frac{1}{3}x$, and $y = -\frac{1}{3}x - 3$. These four equations are depicted below. The original equation is the only line with a positive slope. Note that all of the lines perpendicular to $y = 3x$ + 3 are parallel to one another. Any

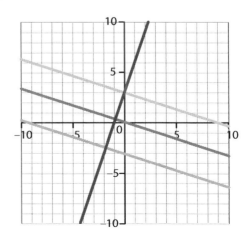

line with the form $y = -\frac{1}{3}x + b$, where $b$ is any real number, is perpendicular to the original line.

23) **If one line has a slope of $\frac{k}{6}$ and a line parallel to that line has a slope of $\frac{k-10}{12}$, what is the slope of a line perpendicular to both these lines?**

**Answer:**

Since the slopes of the two given lines are equal, $x$ can be solved for by setting these two equations equal to one another:

$\frac{k}{6} = \frac{k-10}{12}$

$12k = 6k - 60$

$6k = -60$

$k = -10$

If $k$ is equal to $-10$, then the slope of these parallel lines is $-\frac{5}{3}$. **A line perpendicular to both of these lines would have a slope of $\frac{3}{5}$.**

# Statistics and Probability

The statistics and probability sections below will provide multiple ways to collect, interpret, and display data. **Data** is simply the result of an observation or measurement. Data is often collected when an experiment or survey is performed. Conclusions are drawn from this data using various mathematical formulas.

To collect data, investigators run experiments or observe behavior. In an **experiment**, a treatment is applied to a group (of people, animals, plants, etc.), and the effect of that treatment is observed. In a **randomized experiment**, the subjects are randomly split into two groups (by a flip of a coin or a random number generator, for example). One group is a **control** group and does not receive the treatment, and the other group does receive the treatment. Then measurements are conducted on each group, and results are compared. In an **observational study** no treatment is applied, but researchers observe and measure some variable of interest. An example of an observational study is studying the relationship between left- or right-handedness and industrial accidents. No treatment would be applied to either group in this situation.

Information is frequently used to make statements about an entire population. In these cases, because collecting data from every member of the population is impossible, statisticians collect data from a small, random, but specific subset of the entire population. This random **sample** enables inferences to be made about the entire population. There are a variety of methods of creating a representative sample that are beyond the scope of this text, but it is important to note that statistics are only as good as the experiment and sampling methods used. Too small a sample will not represent the larger population, and a sample that is not representative of the population introduces **bias** into the experiment. For example, if a survey was to be conducted about Americans' feelings on race relations, bias could occur if the sample did not include people of different races, sexes, and geographical locations (including urban, suburban, and rural locations).

# Describing Sets of Data

## MEASURES OF CENTRAL TENDENCY

If there are more than two measurements of a certain event or phenomenon, central values help identify trends in the entirety of measurements. There are three such **central tendencies** that describe the "center" of the data in different ways. The **mean** is the arithmetic average and is found by dividing the sum of all measurements by the number of measurements. The equation for the mean, can be written as follows:

$$\text{population mean} = \mu = \frac{x_1 + x_2 + ...x_N}{N} = \frac{\Sigma x}{N} \qquad \text{sample mean} = \overline{x} = \frac{x_1 + x_2 + ...x_n}{n} = \frac{\Sigma x}{n}$$

The data points are represented by $x$s with subscripts; the sum is denoted using the Greek letter sigma $(\Sigma)x$; $N$ is the number of data points in the entire population; and $n$ is the number of data points in a sample set.

The **median** divides the measurements into two equal halves. The median is the measurement right in the middle of an odd set of measurements (the fifth-largest in nine measurements) or the average of the two middle numbers in an even data set (the average of the fifth- and sixth-largest measurements of ten total measurements). When calculating the median, it is important to order the data values from least to greatest before attempting to locate the middle value. The **mode** is simply the measurement that occurs most often. There can be many modes in a data set, or no mode. Since measures of central tendency describe a *center* of the data, all three of these measures will be between the lowest and highest data values (inclusive).

Unlike the mean, the median is not affected by very large or very small unusual measurements (**outliers**). Notice that in the following sample questions, both have the same data points, but the median is not skewed by the single large value. That is, the median is much closer to the terms in the data set than the mean is. If there is a high outlier, the mean will be greater than the median; if there is a low or negative outlier, the mean will be lower than the median. When outliers are present, the median is a better measure of the center of the data than the mean is.

### SAMPLE QUESTIONS

1) **What is the mean of the following data set? {1000, 0.1, 10, 1}**

   **Answer:**

   The mean to the nearest hundredth is found as follows:

   $\frac{1000 + 0.1 + 10 + 1}{4} =$ **252.78**

2) **What is the median of the following data set? {1000, 10, 1, 0.1}**

   **Answer:**

   Since there are an even number of data points in the set, the median will be the mean of the two middle numbers. Order the numbers from least to greatest: 0.1, 1, 10, and 1000. The two middle numbers are 1 and 10, and their mean is:

$$\frac{1 + 10}{2} = \textbf{5.5}$$

**3)**  **Josey has an average of 81 on four equally weighted tests she has taken in her statistics class. She wants to determine what grade she must receive on her fifth test so that her mean is 83, which will give her a B in the course, but she does not remember her other scores. What grade must she receive on her fifth test?**

**Answer:**

Even though Josey does not know her test scores, she knows her average. Therefore it can be assumed that each test score was 81, since four scores of 81 would average to 81. To find the score, $x$, that she needs:

$$\frac{4(81) + x}{5} = 83$$

$$324 + x = 415$$

$$x = 91$$

Josey must score a 91 on the last test to have a mean score of 83.

## MEASURES OF VARIATION

The values in a data set can be very close together (close to the mean), or very spread out. This is called the **spread** or **dispersion** of the data. Sometimes most of the data is close to the mean, but there are one or more values far from the mean. These are called **outliers**. There are a few **measures of variation** (or **measures of dispersion**) that quantify the spread within a data set. **Range** is the difference between the largest and smallest data points in a set:

*R = largest data point – smallest data point*

Notice range depends on only two data points, the two extremes. Sometimes these data points are outliers; regardless, for a large data set, relying on only two data points is not an exact tool. The understanding of the data set can be improved by calculating **quartiles**. To calculate quartiles, first arrange the data in ascending order and find the set's median (also called quartile 2 or Q2). Then find the median of the lower half of the data, called quartile 1 (Q1), and the median of the upper half of the data, called quartile 3 (Q3). These three points divide the data into four equal groups of data (thus the word *quartile*). Each quartile contains 25% of the data.

**Interquartile range (IQR)** provides a more reliable range that is not as affected by extremes. IQR is the difference between the third quartile data point and the first quartile data point:

$$IQR = Q_3 - Q_1$$

The interquartile range gives the spread of the middle 50% of the data.

A measure of variation that depends on the mean is **standard deviation**, which uses every data point in a set and basically calculates the average distance of each data point from the mean of the data. Standard deviation can be computed for an entire population, if the data set is not too large, or for a sample of the population. The formula for standard deviation is slightly different based on whether it is a population standard deviation (denoted by $\sigma$ or lowercase sigma) or a sample standard deviation (denoted by the letter $s$):

$$\sigma = \sqrt{\frac{\Sigma(x_i - \mu)^2}{N}} \qquad\qquad s = \sqrt{\frac{\Sigma(x_i - \bar{x})^2}{n-1}}$$

Thus, to calculate standard deviation, the difference between the mean $\mu$ or $\bar{x}$ or and each data point $x_i$ is calculated. Each of these differences is squared (this is done mostly to make all the differences positive). The average of the squared values is computed by summing the squares and dividing by $N$ or $(n - 1)$. (The reason for dividing by $n - 1$ and not just $n$ is beyond the scope of this text.) Then the square root is taken, to "undo" the previous squaring.

The **variance** of a data set is simply the square of the standard variation:

$$V = \sigma^2 = \frac{1}{N} \sum_{i=1}^{N} (x_i - \mu)^2$$

Variance measures how narrowly or widely the data points are distributed. A variance of zero means every data point is the same; a large variance means the data is widely spread out.

## SAMPLE QUESTIONS

4) **What are the range and interquartile range of the following set? {3, 9, 49, 64, 81, 100, 121, 144, 169}**

   Answer:

   The range is the difference between the largest and smallest data points:

   $R = 169 - 3 = 166$

   The set's median is 81, which is $Q_2$. The median of the bottom half of the data is midway between 9 and 49, which, averaging those two numbers, is 29. This is $Q_1$. The median of the upper half of the data is midway between 121 and 144, which, averaging those two numbers, is 132.5. This is $Q_3$. Thus, the $IQR = Q_3 - Q_1 = 132.5 - 29 = $ **103.5.**

5) **In a group of 7 people, 1 person has no children, 2 people have 1 child, 2 people have 2 children, 1 person has 5 children, and 1 person has 17 children. To the nearest hundredth of a child, what is the standard deviation in this group? What is the variance?**

**Answer:**

| | |
|---|---|
| {0, 1, 1, 2, 2, 5, 17} | Create a data set out of this scenario. |
| $\mu = \dfrac{0 + 1 + 1 + 2 + 2 + 5 + 17}{7} = 4$ | Calculate the population mean. |
| $(0 - 4)^2 = (-4)^2 = 16$<br>$(1 - 4)^2 = (-3)^2 = 9$<br>$(1 - 4)^2 = (-3)^2 = 9$<br>$(2 - 4)^2 = (-2)^2 = 4$<br>$(2 - 4)^2 = (-2)^2 = 4$<br>$(5 - 4)^2 = (1)^2 = 1$<br>$(17 - 4)^2 = (13)^2 = 169$ | Find the square of the difference of each term and the mean $(x_i - \mu)^2$. |
| $\sigma = \sqrt{\dfrac{212}{7}} = \sqrt{30.28} = 5.50$ | Plug the sum ($\Sigma$) of these squares, 212, into the standard deviation formula. |

**The standard deviation is 5.50 and the variance is 30.28.** Notice that both the mean and the standard deviation are greatly skewed by the outlier value 17. Of the 7 people, 5 have fewer than 3 children, but the mean number of children is 4. Most of the people have within 1 or 2 children of one another, but the deviation is more than 5 children. An outlier seriously skews statistics, especially in a small data set.

6) **What happens to the mean and the standard deviation of a data set if all *n* values of the data set are increased by the same amount? What if each data value is multiplied by the same value?**

**Answer:**

When all the members of a data set are increased by the same amount, the sum of the data is increased by the product of that number times the number of values *n*. For example, if each member of a data set with ten values were increased by 4, the sum would be increased by 40. To calculate the new mean:

$$new\ mean = \frac{3a + 3b + 3c + 3d}{4} = \frac{3(a + b + c + d)}{4} = 3\left(\frac{a + b + c + d}{4}\right) = 3\ (old\ mean)$$

The new mean is just shifted up by the amount each data value is increased. Since each data value is shifted up the same amount, and the mean is also shifted up by that amount, the deviation between each value and the mean will be unchanged.

Thus, when the same value is added to each element of a data set, the mean increases by the same value and the standard deviation is unchanged.

When all the members of a data set are multiplied by the same amount, the sum of the values will be multiplied by that amount due to the distributive property, and the mean will also be multiplied by the same value. Say there are four values, a, b, c, and d, and each is multiplied by 3:

In the standard deviation formula, since each of the differences will also be multiplied by 3, the squares of the difference will be multiplied by 9, so the variance is multiplied by 9. But after the square root of the variance is taken to calculate the standard deviation, standard deviation is changed by a factor of 3.

Thus both the mean and the standard deviation of a data set is changed by the same factor (*k*) when each value of the data set is multiplied by some factor *k*.

# Box Plots

A **box plot** depicts the median and quartiles along a scaled number line. A box plot is meant to summarize the data in a visual manner and emphasize central trends while decreasing the pull of outlier data. To construct a box plot:

1. Create a number line that begins at the lowest data point and terminates at the highest data point.

2. Find the quartiles of the data: $Q_1$, the median ($Q_2$), and $Q_3$. Create a horizontal rectangle (the "box") whose left border is $Q_1$ and right border is $Q_3$.

3. Draw a vertical line within the box to mark the median.

4. Draw a horizontal line going from the left edge of the box to the smallest data value.

5. Draw a horizontal line going from the right edge of the box to the largest data value.

Figure 7.1. Box Plot

When reading a box plot, the following stands out:

▶ The length of the box is the IQR, $Q_3 - Q_1$, hence the middle 50% of the data.

▶ Each of the four pieces (the whiskers and two pieces in the box) represent 25% of the data.

▸ The horizontal lines (whiskers) show by their length whether the data higher or lower than the middle 50% is more or less prominent.

▸ Reading from left to right: the horizontal line (whisker) shows the spread of the first quarter; the box's left compartment shows the spread of the second quarter; the box's right compartment shows the spread of the third quarter; and the right horizontal line (whisker) shows the spread of the fourth quarter.

> **HELPFUL HINT**
>
> Box plots are also known as box-and-whisker plots, because if they are drawn correctly the two horizontal lines look like whiskers.

### SAMPLE QUESTION

7) **A recent survey asked 8 people how many pairs of shoes they wear per week. Their answers are in the following data set: {1, 3, 5, 5, 7, 8, 12}. Construct a box plot from this data.**

**Answer:**

Create a number line that begins at 1 and ends at 12. $Q_1$ is 3, the median ($Q_2$) is 5, and $Q_3$ is 8. A rectangle must be drawn whose length is 5 and that borders on $Q_1$ and $Q_3$. Mark the median of 5 within the rectangle. Draw a horizontal line going left to 1. Draw a horizontal line going right to 12.

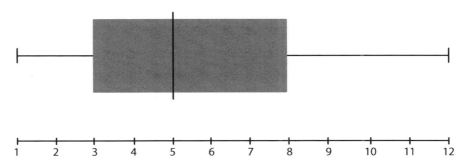

# Graphs, Charts, and Tables

## PIE CHARTS

**Pie charts** summarize the prominence of categories in a data set. Appropriate uses of pie charts may include budgets, production breakdowns, population analyses, and data that is best expressed as percentages. A pie chart simply states the proportion of each category within the whole. To construct a pie chart, the categories of a data set must be determined. The frequency of each category must be found and that frequency converted to a percent of the total. To draw the pie chart, determine the angle of each slice by multiplying the percentage by 360°.

### SAMPLE QUESTION

8) **A firm is screening applicants for a job by education-level attainment. There are 125 individuals in the pool. By the highest level of education attained in the pool, 5 have a doctorate, 20 have a master's degree, 40 have a bachelor's degree, 30 have an associate degree, and the remaining only have a high school degree. Construct a pie chart showing the highest level of education attained by the applicants.**

**Answer:**

The total given to us is 125, meaning there are 30 applicants with just a high school degree. Next, a frequency table must be created. The percent is found by dividing the frequency of a specific category by the total (125). Multiply that percent by 360° to get the angle measure:

| Category | Frequency | Percent | Angle Measure |
|---|---|---|---|
| High School | 30 | 24% | 86.4 |
| Associate | 30 | 24% | 86.4 |
| Bachelor's | 40 | 32% | 115.2 |
| Master's | 20 | 16% | 57.6 |
| Doctorate | 5 | 4% | 14.4 |

The pie chart below expresses the table's data.

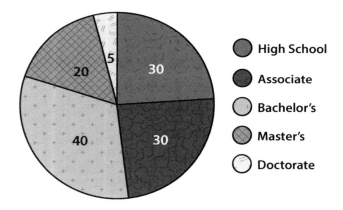

## SCATTER PLOTS

A scatter plot is displayed in the first quadrant of the *xy*-plane where all numbers are positive. A scatter plot is an easy way to tell if there is a correlation between two variables in a data set. Data points are plotted as ordered pairs, with one variable along the horizontal axis and the other along the vertical axis. Constructing a scatter plot requires the plotting of every point on a domain and range that includes every data outcome. Often, but not always, the data points will show a linear tendency. There is a **positive correlation** (expressed as a positive slope) if increasing one variable appears to result in an increase in the other variable. A **negative correlation** (expressed as a negative slope) occurs when an increase in one variable causes a decrease in the other. If the scatter plot shows no discernible pattern, then there is no correlation (a zero, mixed, or indiscernible slope). Scatter plots are often used for lab experiments and any attempt to establish a causal link.

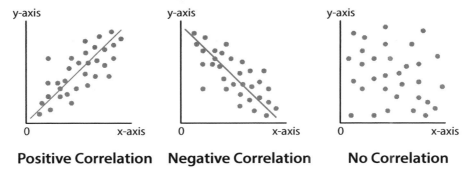

**Figure 7.2. Scatter Plots and Correlation**

Working from data points, or using the regression feature of a calculator, a regression equation can be created that encapsulates the directionality of the scatter plot. If the regression equation is graphed, the resulting line (or curve) is known as a regression line (or curve). This is also known as the "line of best fit." To figure out how well the regression line (or curve) fits every data point on a scatter plot, the equation's **correlation coefficient** ($r$) can be considered. The formula for computing the correlation coefficient is complex, but the calculator will provide this number along with the regression line if the diagnostics feature is on. The value of $r$ is between –1 and 1. The closer $r$ is to 1 (if the line has a positive slope) or –1 (if the line has a negative slope), the better the regression line fits the data. The closer the $r$ value is to 0, the weaker the correlation between the line and the data. Generally, if the absolute value of the correlation coefficient is 0.8 or higher, then it is considered to be a strong correlation, while an $|r|$ value of less than 0.5 is considered a weak correlation.

To determine which curve is the "best fit" for a set of data, **residuals** are calculated. The calculator automatically calculates and saves these values to a list called RESID. These values are all the differences between the actual $y$-value of data points and the $y$-value calculated by the best-fit line or curve for that $x$-value. These values can be plotted on an $xy$-plane with the $x$-values along the $x$-axis and the residuals along the $y$-axis. This is called a **residual plot**. The residual plot helps determine if a line is the best model for the data. Residual points that are randomly dispersed above and below the horizontal indicate that a linear model is appropriate, while a $u$ shape or upside-down $u$ shape indicate a nonlinear model would be more appropriate.

Once a best-fit line (or curve) is established, it can be used to estimate output values given an input value within the domain of the data. For a short extension outside that domain, reasonable predictions may be possible. However, the further from the domain of the data the line is extended, the greater the reduction in the accuracy of the prediction. For example, a model is created from the growth data of a city over a twenty-year period; that model will not be a good predictor of the population of the city in one hundred years.

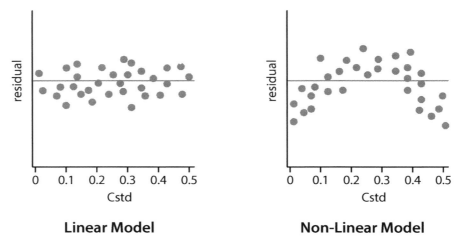

**Figure 7.3. Residual Plots**

It is important to note here that just because two variables have a strong positive or negative correlation, it cannot necessarily be inferred that those two quantities have a **causal** relationship—that is, that one variable changing *causes* the other quantity to change. There are often other factors that play into their relationship. For example, a positive correlation can be found between the number of ice cream sales and the number of shark attacks at a beach. It would be incorrect to say that selling more ice cream *causes* an increase in shark attacks. It is much more likely that on hot days more ice cream is sold, and many more people are swimming, so one of them is more likely to get attacked by a shark. Confusing correlation and causation is one of the most common statistical errors people make.

**HELPFUL HINT**

A graphing calculator can provide the regression line, *r* value, and residuals list.

**SAMPLE QUESTION**

9) Based on the scatter plot, where the *x*-axis represents hours spent studying per week and the *y*-axis represents the average percent grade on exams during the school year, is there a correlation between the amount of studying for a test and test results?

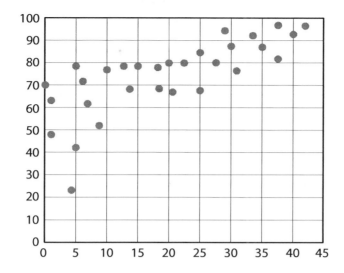

Answer:

**There is a somewhat weak positive correlation.** As the number of hours spent studying increases, the average percent grade also generally increases.

# LINE GRAPHS

**Line graphs** are used to display a relationship between two variables, such as change over time. Like scatter plots, line graphs exist in quadrant I of the *xy*-plane. Line graphs are constructed by graphing each point and connecting each point to the next consecutive point by a line. To create a line graph, it may be necessary to consolidate data into single bivariate data points. Thus, a line graph is a function, with each *x*-value having exactly one *y*-value, whereas a scatter plot may have multiple *y*-values for one *x*-value.

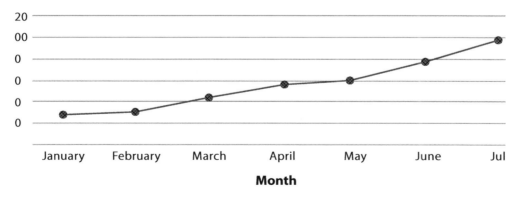

**Figure 7.4. Line Graph**

## SAMPLE QUESTION

10) Create a line graph based on the following survey values, where the first column represents an individual's age and the other represents that individual's reported happiness level on a 20-point scale (0 being the least happy that person has been and 20 being the happiest). Then interpret the resulting graph to determine whether the following statement is true or false: *On average, middle-aged people are less happy than young or older people are.*

| Age | Happiness |
| --- | --- |
| 12 | 16 |
| 13 | 15 |
| 20 | 18 |
| 15 | 12 |
| 40 | 5 |
| 17 | 17 |
| 18 | 18 |
| 19 | 15 |
| 42 | 7 |
| 70 | 17 |
| 45 | 10 |
| 60 | 12 |
| 63 | 15 |
| 22 | 14 |
| 27 | 15 |
| 36 | 12 |
| 33 | 10 |
| 44 | 8 |
| 55 | 10 |
| 80 | 10 |
| 15 | 13 |
| 40 | 8 |
| 17 | 15 |
| 18 | 17 |
| 19 | 20 |
| 22 | 16 |
| 27 | 15 |
| 36 | 9 |
| 33 | 10 |
| 44 | 6 |

**Answer:**

To construct a line graph, the data must be ordered into consolidated categories by averaging the data of people who have the same age so that the data is one-to-one. For example, there are two twenty-two-year-olds who are reporting. Their average happiness level is 15. When all the data has been consolidated and ordered from least to greatest, the table and graph below can be presented.

| Age | Happiness |
| --- | --- |
| 12 | 16 |
| 13 | 15 |
| 15 | 12.5 |
| 17 | 16 |
| 18 | 17.5 |
| 19 | 17.5 |
| 20 | 18 |
| 22 | 15 |
| 27 | 15 |
| 33 | 10 |
| 36 | 10.5 |
| 40 | 6.5 |
| 42 | 7 |
| 44 | 7 |
| 45 | 10 |
| 55 | 10 |
| 60 | 12 |
| 63 | 15 |
| 70 | 17 |
| 80 | 10 |

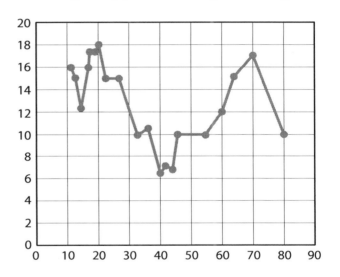

**Average Happiness Rating Versus Age**

**The statement that, on average, middle-aged people are less happy than young or older people appears to be true.** According to the graph, people in their thirties, forties, and fifties are less happy than people in their teens, twenties, sixties, and seventies.

# BAR GRAPHS

Like line graphs, **bar graphs** compare changes between groups or over time. The data here is grouped into certain ranges and represented by rectangles (a bar graph's rectangles can be vertical or horizontal, depending on whether the dependent variable is placed on the *x*- or *y*-axis). Instead of the *xy*-plane, however, one axis is made up of types of categories. Bar graphs are useful because the differences between categories are easy to see. Reading a bar graph requires understanding that the width or height (depending on vertical or horizontal orientation) of each rectangle indicates the total within that category, and the difference among the rectangles shows the difference year to year.

**Figure 7.5. Bar Graph**

11) **A company X had a profit of $10,000 in 2010, $12,000 in 2011, and each of the following two years saw a 30% increase in profits. Create a bar graph displaying the profit from each of these four years.**

**Answer:**

If 2012 saw a 30% increase from 2011, that year's profit is 1.3($12,000) = $15,600; by the same method, the profit in 2013 was $20,280. The bar graph below captures this data:

## STEM-AND-LEAF PLOTS

**Stem-and-leaf plots** are ways of organizing large amounts of data by grouping it into classes. All data points are broken into two parts: a stem and a leaf. For instance, the number 512 might be broken into a stem of 5 and a leaf of 12. All data in the

500 range would appear in the same row (this group of data is a class). Usually a simple key is provided to explain how the data is being represented. For instance, 5|12 = 512 would show that the stems are representing hundreds. The advantage of this display is that it shows general density and shape of the data in a compact display, yet all original data points are preserved and available. It is also easy to find medians and quartiles from this display.

| Stem | Leaf |
|---|---|
| 0 | 5 |
| 1 | 6, 7 |
| 2 | 8, 3, 6 |
| 3 | 4, 5, 9, 5, 5, 8, 5 |
| 4 | 7, 7, 7, 8 |
| 5 | 5, 4 |
| 6 | 0 |

Figure 7.6. Stem and Leaf Plot

## SAMPLE QUESTION

12)  The table gives the weights of wrestlers (in pounds) for a certain competition. What is the mean, median, and IQR of the data?

| | |
|---|---|
| 2 | 05, 22, 53, 40 |
| 3 | 07, 22, 29, 45, 89, 96, 98 |
| 4 | 10, 25, 34 |
| 6 | 21 |

Key: 2|05 = 205 pounds

**Answer:**

| | |
|---|---|
| $\mu = \frac{\Sigma x}{N}$ <br> $= \frac{5281}{15}$ <br> $= \textbf{353.1 lbs.}$ | Find the mean using the equation for the population mean. |
| Q1 = 253 <br> Q2 = 345 <br> Q3 = 410 <br> IQR = 410 − 253 <br> = 157 <br> **The median is 345 lbs.** <br> **The IQR is 157 lbs.** | Find the median and IQR by counting the leaves and identifying Q1, Q2, and Q3. |

## FREQUENCY TABLES AND HISTOGRAMS

The frequency of a particular data point is the number of times that data point occurs. Constructing a frequency table requires that the data or data classes be arranged in ascending order in one column and the frequency in another column.

A histogram is used to compare the frequency of specified ranges of data. It is a graphical representation of a frequency table. A histogram is constructed in quadrant I of the *xy*-plane, with data in each equal-width class presented as a bar and the height of each bar representing the frequency of that class. Unlike bar graphs, histograms cannot have gaps between bars. A histogram is used to determine the distribution of data among the classes. Examples of histograms include population statistics, arrivals and departures at airports, and ecological studies such as the average temperature over a year.

Histograms can be symmetrical, skewed left or right, or multimodal (data spread around). Note that **skewed left** means the peak of the data is on the *right*, with a tail to the left, while **skewed right** means the peak is on the *left*, with a tail to the right. This seems counterintuitive to many; the "left" or "right" always refers to the tail of the data. This is because a long tail to the right, for example, means there are high outlier values that are skewing the data to the right.

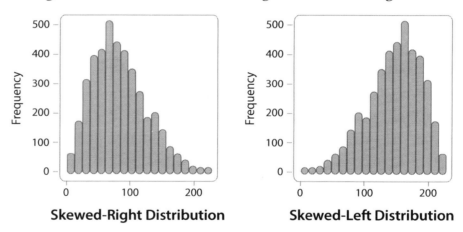

**Figure 7.7. Histograms**

A **two-way frequency table** compares **categorical data** (data in more than one category) of two related variables (bivariate data). Two-way frequency tables are also called **contingency tables** and are often used to analyze survey results. One category is displayed along the top of the table and the other category down along the side. Rows and columns are added and the sums appear at the end of the row or column. The sum of all the row data must equal the sum of all the column data. From a two-way frequency table, the **joint relative frequency** of a particular category can be calculated by taking the number in the row and column of the categories in question and dividing by the total number surveyed. This gives the percent of the total in that particular category. Sometimes the **conditional relative frequency** is of interest. In this case, calculate the relative frequency confined to a single row or column, because a condition was given that restricts the data examined.

### Students by Grade and Gender

| | 9th grade | 10th grade | 11th grade | 12th grade | Total |
|---|---|---|---|---|---|
| Male | 57 | 63 | 75 | 61 | 256 |
| Female | 54 | 42 | 71 | 60 | 227 |
| Total | 111 | 105 | 146 | 121 | 483 |

**Figure 7.8. Two-Way Frequency Table**

## SAMPLE QUESTIONS

13) **A café owner tracked the number of customers he had over a twelve-hour period one day in the frequency table below. Display the data in a histogram and determine what kind of distribution there is in the data.**

| Time | Number of Customers |
|---|---|
| 6 a.m. – 8 a.m. | 5 |
| 8 a.m. – 9 a.m. | 6 |
| 9 a.m. – 10 a.m. | 5 |
| 10 a.m. – 12 p.m. | 23 |
| 12 p.m. – 2 p.m. | 24 |
| 2 p.m. – 4 p.m. | 9 |
| 4 p.m. – 6 p.m. | 4 |

**Answer:**

Since time is the independent variable, it is on the *x*-axis and the number of customers is on the *y*-axis. For the histogram to correctly display data continuously, categories on the *x*-axis must be equal 2-hour segments. The 8 a.m. – 9 a.m. and 9 a.m. – 10 a.m. categories must be combined for a total

**Customers per Hour**

of 11 customers in that time period. The correct graph is displayed below. Although not perfectly symmetrical, the amount of customers peaks in the middle and is therefore considered symmetrical.

14) **In a class of 30 students, 10% got an A, 30% got a B, 30% received a C, 10% received a D, and the remainder received an F on a recent exam (the minimum possible grade recorded was a 50). Create a frequency table summarizing this data. Estimate the average (mean) grade on the exam by using the midpoint of each class of grade.**

**Answer:**

Frequency tables deal with total frequency. Every percent then must be multiplied by 30 students to figure out the total number of students in each grade category. Additionally, the number of students with an F can be found by multiplying the remaining percent by 30: $(1 - 0.10 - 0.30 - 0.30 - 0.10)$ $(30) = 6$.

| Grade | Number of Students |
|---|---|
| A (90 – 100) | 3 |
| B (80 – 89) | 9 |
| C (70 – 79) | 9 |
| D (60 – 69) | 3 |
| F (50 – 59) | 6 |

An estimate of the class average using approximate midpoints of each class and computing the weighted average:

$$\frac{3(95) + 9(85) + 9(75) + 3(65)\ 6(55)}{30} = \frac{2250}{3.0} = \mathbf{75}.$$

15) **Cineflix movie theater polled its moviegoers on a weeknight to determine their favorite type of movie. The results are in the two-way frequency table below.**

| Moviegoers | Comedy | Action | Horror | Totals |
|---|---|---|---|---|
| Male | 15 | 25 | 21 | 61 |
| Female | 8 | 18 | 17 | 43 |
| Totals | 23 | 43 | 38 | 104 |

**Determine whether each of the following statements is true or false.**

A. Action films are the most popular type of movie

B. About 1 in 5 moviegoers prefers comedy films

C. Men choose the horror genre more frequently than women do

**Answers:**

A.    **True**. More people (42) chose action movies than comedy (23) or horror (38).

B.    **True**. Find the ratio of total number of people who prefer comedy to total number of people. $\frac{23}{103} = 0.22$; 1 in 5 is 20%, so 22% is about the same.

C.    **False**. The percentage of men who choose horror is less than the percentage of women who do.

*part = number of men who prefer horror = 21*

*whole = number of men surveyed = 60*

$percent = \frac{part}{whole}$

$= \frac{21}{60} = 0.35 = 35\%$

*part = number of women who prefer horror = 17*

*whole = number of women surveyed = 43*

$percent = \frac{part}{whole}$

$= \frac{17}{43} = 0.40 = 40\%$

# Counting Principles

## THE FUNDAMENTAL COUNTING PRINCIPLE

An **outcome** is any possible result of an experiment, such as the outcome "heads" in a coin toss. The set of all possible outcomes for a specific experiment is called the **sample space**. The sample space for tossing a single coin is {H = heads, T = tails}. Any outcome's probability is based on all the unique possibilities that could occur, so being able to calculate all the possible outcomes is critical to finding probabilities. The number of unique possible outcomes for any sequence of events is often calculated by the **fundamental counting principle**. This principle states that the total number of possible outcomes is the product of the total possible number of outcomes in each trial. Suppose a coin is tossed three times. Each toss of the coin is a trial. Each trial has two possible outcomes. By the fundamental counting principle, the total number of possibilities (the number of elements in the sample space) when a coin is tossed three times is $2 \times 2 \times 2 = 8$. They are {HHH, HHT, HTT, HTH, TTH, THH, THT, TTT}.

## SAMPLE QUESTIONS

16)    **A personal assistant is struggling to pick a shirt, tie, and cufflink set that go together. If his client has 70 shirts, 2 ties, and 5 cufflinks, how many possible combinations does he have to consider?**

**Answer:**

The formula is always the same. The total number of combinations is (70)(2)(5) = 700. **There are 700 shirt, tie, and cufflink combinations.**

17) **A bank requires a four-digit personal identification number (PIN) for access to an automated teller machine. If only numbers 1 – 9 are allowed, how many different four-digit PIN numbers are there?**

**Answer:**

Assuming repeat digits are allowed, there are 9 possible numbers for each of the 4 digits (each digit is a "trial"). Thus, there are $9 \times 9 \times 9 \times 9 =$ **6561 possible PIN codes.**

18) **How many ways can four distinct books be arranged on the shelf?**

**Answer:**

As in the previous problem, there are four slots to be filled. Unlike the previous problem, however, each slot does not have the same number of choices. For the first slot, there are four book choices. Once one book is chosen to be put on the shelf, there are only three book choices for the second slot, two for the third slot, and one for the last. The total number of ways to arrange the four books is $4 \times 3 \times 2 \times 1 =$ **24.**

## COMBINATIONS AND PERMUTATIONS

Combinations and permutations are arrangements of a set of objects. In **combinations**, the order of the arrangement or selection does not matter. For **permutations**, the order of the arrangement or selection is important. A "combination lock" is therefore *misnamed*—it really should be a *permutation lock*, since the order in which the numbers are dialed is important. An example of a question calling for a combination would be, "How many ways can a committee of three people be chosen from twelve people?" The order in which the people are chosen is not relevant if all the positions on the committee are exactly the same.

The formulas for calculating the number of permutations or combinations both use factorials. Factorials are expressed by an integer, followed by an exclamation point (!). Recall that a factorial $n!$ is the product of $n$ times $(n - 1)$, times $(n - 2)$, etc., until $n$ is multiplied by 1. For example, $3! = 3 \times 2 \times 1 = 6$. Zero factorial is defined to 1, that is $0! = 1$.

Also recall that factorial expressions, when divided, can be simplified. For example,

$$10! \div 8! = \frac{10 \times 9 \times 8 \times 7 \times 6 \times 5 \times 4 \times 3 \times 2 \times 1}{8 \times 7 \times 6 \times 5 \times 4 \times 3 \times 2 \times 1} = 10 \times 9 = 90$$

since all the number from 8 down to 1 cancel. In the following two formulas, represents the total amount of items or actions and represents the total number of these items that are to be selected or ordered.

| Permutation Formula $P(n, k) = \frac{n!}{(n - k)!}$ | Combination Formula $C(n, k) = \frac{n!}{(n - k)! \, k!}$ |
| --- | --- |

**Figure 7.9. Permutation and Combination Formulas**

*The only difference between the two formulas is the k! in the combination denominator. This is to account for redundancy of data with the same values just in a different order. Dividing by this k! reduces the number of possibilities.*

The example from the previous section about ordering four books on a shelf is actually a permutation problem. Since each book is unique, when arranging them, the order matters. Using the permutation formula with $n = 4$ items, all $k = 4$ of which are being ordered, yields $P(4,4) = \frac{4!}{(4 - 4)!} = \frac{4!}{0!} = \frac{4 \times 3 \times 2 \times 1}{1} = 24$, which is the same answer arrived at before.

## SAMPLE QUESTIONS

19) **If there are twenty applicants for three open positions, in how many different ways can a team of three be hired?**

**Answer:**

In this problem, $n = 20$ and $k = 3$. Since the three positions are presumably identical, the order of hiring is not important, so this is a combination problem. Using the combination formula:

$C(20, 3) = \frac{20!}{(20 - 3)! \, 3!} = \frac{20!}{17! \, 3!} = \frac{(20)(19)(18)}{3!} = 1140$

There are **1140 different three-person teams** that can be hired.

Another way to think about this problem is to calculate all the ways that a three-spot team can be created and then divide by how many ways that team of three can be arranged. For the first spot, 20 people can be chosen; for the second, 19; for the third, 18. This gives (20)(19)(18) = 6840 teams of three. But this is too many since the order of those three chosen does not matter, so it is necessary to divide by the number of ways possible to order three people = 3 × 2 × 1 = 6. Dividing, 6840 by 6 gives 1140.

20) **At a sandwich shop, a customer has a choice of ten toppings he can add to his sandwich. If three distinct toppings are added, how many three-topping sandwiches are possible?**

**Answer:**

This question is a combination problem—the order does not matter, only that each item added be distinct. Plugging the appropriate values into the equation, it is found that:

$$C(10, 3) = \frac{10!}{(10-3)!\,3!} = 120$$

There are **120 possible sandwiches** with three toppings added out of ten possible ingredients to add.

21) **Calculate the number of unique permutations that can be made out of all the letters in the word** *pickle*, **the number of unique permutations that can be made out of all the letters in the word** *cheese*, **and the number of unique permutations that can be made out of all the letters in the word** *blueberry*.

**Answer:**

To find the number of unique permutations of the letters of *pickle*, use the permutation formula with the total number of letters $n = 6$, and the number to be arranged $k = 6$.

$$P(6, 6) = \frac{6!}{(6-6)!} = \frac{720}{1} = 720$$

(Or think of it as six slots that need to be filled; in the first there are six choices, the second five choices, etc., giving 6! as the answer.)

**There are 720 distinct arrangements of the letters in the word** *pickle*.

The word *cheese* has the letter *e* that repeats three times. Thus, some permutations of the six letters will be indistinguishable from others, as the reader will be unable to tell one *e* from another. The number of permutations must be divided by the number of ways the three *e*s can be arranged, 3! = 6. The formula is:

*total number of permutations = number of ways to arrange 6 letters/number of ways to arrange 3 letters* $= \frac{6!}{3!} = 6 \times 5 \times 4 = 120$

**There are 120 distinct arrangements of the letters in the word** *cheese*.

The word *blueberry* repeats *b* two times, *e* two times, and *r* two times. To calculate the number of unique arrangements of all nine letters, calculate the number of ways to arrange nine items, and divide by the number of ways the *b*s can be arranged (2!), the *e*s can be arranged (2!), and the *r*s can be arranged (2!):

*total number of permutations* $= \frac{9!}{2!\,2!\,2!} = \frac{9!}{8} = 45{,}360.$

**There are 45,360 distinct arrangements of all the letters in the word** *blueberry*.

22) **Suppose 7 runners are lining up for a race. 3 runners are women and 4 are men. How many ways can they line up if they can line up in any order? How many ways can they line up if the women must be beside each other, and the men must be grouped together?**

**Answer:**

If all 7 can be arranged in any order, there are 7! = **5040 arrangements**. If the women must stay together, and the men must stay together, there are 2 groups that can be arranged in exactly 2 ways (women on the left and men on the right, or vice-versa). Within these groups, the women can be arranged 3! ways and the men 4! ways. Using the fundamental counting principle:

*total number of arrangements with men grouped and women grouped =*
$2 \times 3! \times 4! = 2 \times 6 \times 24 =$ **288**.

# Probability

## PROBABILITY OF A SINGLE EVENT

**Probability** is the likelihood of one or a certain number of specific events occurring. The probability of a single event occurring is the number of outcomes in which that event occurs (called **favorable events**) divided by the number of items in the sample space (total possible outcomes):

$$P \text{ (an event)} = \frac{number\ of\ favorable\ outcomes}{total\ number\ of\ possible\ outcomes}$$

The probability of any event occurring will always be a fraction or decimal between 0 and 1. It may also be expressed as a percent. An event with 0 probability will never occur and an event with a probability of 1 is certain to occur. The probability of an event not occurring is referred to as that event's **complement**. The sum of an event's probability and the probability of that event's complement will always be 1.

### SAMPLE QUESTIONS

23) **In an experiment to see if a certain drug works correctly, it is determined that there are 10 distinct equally likely outcomes that would show the drug works incorrectly and 1 that it does work correctly. All else being equal, what is the probability that the experiment shows the drug in question works correctly?**

**Answer:**

The problem specified there are 11 equally likely possible outcomes: 10 negatives and 1 positive. Therefore, the probability of the 1 positive occurring is:

$P \text{ (drug working correctly)} = \frac{1}{11}$

24) **What is the difference between the probability that when a six-sided die is rolled an even number outcome results and the probability that the die lands on the number 5?**

**Answer:**

In both of these probabilities, the denominator is 6. There are 3 even numbers possible in the first event. There is just 1 possible favorable outcome in the other. The two probabilities are:

$P$ (rolling even) $= \frac{3}{6}$

$P$ (rolling 5) $= \frac{1}{6}$

The difference then is $\frac{2}{6}$ or $\frac{1}{3}$.

25) **Only 20 tickets were issued in a raffle. If someone were to buy 6 tickets, what is the probability that person would not win the raffle?**

**Answer:**

If 6 tickets were purchased, that means 14 remain. Thus, the probability of not winning the raffle is:

$P$ (not winning) $= \frac{14}{20}$

Notice that the sum of the probability of winning, $\frac{6}{20}$, and the probability of losing, $\frac{14}{20}$, is **1**. Since these events are complements of each other, one of these must occur (the raffle participant either wins or loses).

## PROBABILITY OF MULTIPLE EVENTS

If events are **independent events**, the probability of one occurring does not affect the probability of the other event occurring. If events are **dependent events**, the probability of one occurring changes the probability of the other event occurring. Rolling a die and getting one number does not change the probability of getting any particular number on the next roll. The number of faces has not changed, so these are independent events. When drawing two cards from a deck of cards, it is important to pay attention to whether the card is *replaced* or not. If the cards are drawn *with replacement*, then the second draw of a card is independent of the first draw (assuming the cards are shuffled). If the cards are drawn *without replacement*, then the probability of the second draw is affected by the first draw, and the events are dependent.

The probability of two independent events occurring is the product of the two events' probabilities:

$$P (A \text{ and } B) = P(A) \times P(B)$$

The probability of one event *or* another occurring can be found using the following formula:

$$P (A \text{ or } B) = P(A) + P(B) - P (A \text{ and } B)$$

Notice this is exactly the same as finding in set theory. These topics are closely related. Two events that are **mutually exclusive** *cannot* happen at the same time. This is similar to disjoint sets in set theory. In that case, $P(A$ and $B) = 0$ and $P(A$ or $B) = P(A) + P(B)$. For example, if a single die is to be rolled one time, event $A$ represents getting an even number, and event $B$ represents getting the number 5, then these events are mutually exclusive and $P(A$ and $B) = 0$. Also, the probability of one or the other event occurring is $P(A$ or $B) = P(A) + P(B) = \frac{1}{2} + \frac{1}{6} = \frac{4}{6} = \frac{2}{3}$.

**Conditional probability** is the probability of an event ($A$) occurring given that another event ($B$) has occurred. Above, the formula did not specify that an event had already occurred. Conditional probability deals with a fact of past occurrence. The example of calculating the probability of drawing a second card from a deck when the first card was not replaced is an example of conditional probability.

The notation $P(B|A)$ represents the probability that event $B$ occurs, given that event $A$ has already occurred (it is read "probability of $B$, given $A$"). For example, suppose 2 cards are drawn from a deck of 10 cards, numbered 1 through 10, without replacement. Let event $A$ be drawing a 7 on the first draw; then $P(A) = \frac{1}{10}$. Let event $B$ be drawing a 5 on the second draw. The probability that a 5 is now drawn given that 7 was already drawn is $P(B|A) = \frac{1}{9}$, since there are now only 9 cards from which to draw. The probability of both events occurring is $P(A$ and $B) = \frac{1}{10} \times \frac{1}{9} = P(A) \times P(B|A)$. Note that the $P(B)$ just represents the probability of drawing a 7 out of 10 cards, so it is incorrect to say $P(A$ and $B) = P(A) \times P(B)$. The fact that the 7 has already been drawn prior to the second event must be taken into account. In general,

$$P(A \text{ and } B) = P(B|A)P(A) = P(A|B)P(B)$$

This formula can be rearranged to solve for any of the three quantities on the right side, if necessary. If $A$ and $B$ are independent events, then the left side becomes $P(A) \times P(B)$ and the above equation simplifies to:

$$P(B|A) = P(B) \text{ or } P(A|B) = P(A)$$

for $A$ and $B$ independent.

## SAMPLE QUESTIONS

26) **A group of ten individuals is drawing straws. There are 30 straws and 2 of them are short. If the straws are not replaced, what is the probability, as a percentage, that none of the first three individuals to draw straws will draw a short straw?**

**Answer:**

Drawing straws in this scenario is a sequence of dependent events. The total number of possible outcomes diminishes after each person draws. Therefore, the first person has a probability of 28 normal-sized straws out of 30 straws. The second person, however, only has 27 normal straws out of 29, since the first person took out, and did not replace, 1 straw. The third person's probability is even lower, at 26 out of the 28. Thus,

P (3 people not drawing short straws) $= \frac{28}{30} \times \frac{27}{29} \times \frac{26}{28} = \frac{117}{145} = 0.81$

There is an **81% chance** that none of the first three people to draw will get a short straw.

27) **A used car dealership is selling 30 cars, and 2 of these cars are defective. One individual buys a car that is defective. What is the probability of the next person at the dealership buying a car that is not defective?**

**Answer:**

These two events are dependent and conditional since one already occurred. The probability of the first event occurring was $\frac{2}{30}$. Since one of the defective cars was purchased, the probability that the next car purchased is not defective is 28 properly functioning cars over 29 defective and properly functioning cars. The conditional probability is:

$P$ (not defective car | defective car) $= \frac{P \text{ (defective AND 2nd not defective)}}{P \text{ (defective)}} =$

$\frac{\frac{2}{30} \times \frac{28}{29}}{\frac{2}{30}} = \frac{\textbf{28}}{\textbf{29}}$

28) **Alyssa has 2 blue blouses out of 13 total. The likelihood of her wearing blue slacks if she is wearing a blue blouse is $\frac{1}{10}$. What is the likelihood that she wears blue slacks and a blue blouse?**

**Answer:**

| | |
|---|---|
| $P(B) = \frac{2}{13}$ | Let $P(B)$ stand for the chance of wearing a blue blouse. |
| $P(S\|B) = \frac{1}{10}$ | Let $P(S\|B)$ the probability of her wearing blue slacks, given that she is wearing a blue blouse. |
| $P(S\|B) = \frac{P(B \text{ and } S)}{P(B)}$ $\frac{1}{10} = \frac{P(B \text{ and } S)}{\frac{2}{13}}$ $P(B \text{ and } S) = \frac{2}{130}$ $= \frac{1}{65}$ | Plug what is known into the conditional probability formula. |

Thus, the probability of Alyssa wearing blue slacks and a blue blouse is $\frac{1}{65}$.

# Part IV: Practice

# Practice Test

## Reading

After reading the passage, choose the best answer to each question.

Skin coloration and markings have an important role to play in the world of snakes. Those intricate diamonds, stripes, and swirls help the animals hide from predators, but perhaps most importantly (for us humans, anyway), the markings can also indicate whether the snake is venomous. While it might seem counterintuitive for a venomous snake to stand out in bright red or blue, that fancy costume tells any nearby predator that approaching him would be a bad idea.

If you see a flashy-looking snake in the woods, though, those markings don't necessarily mean it's venomous: some snakes have found a way to ward off predators without the actual venom. The scarlet kingsnake, for example, has very similar markings to the venomous coral snake with whom it frequently shares a habitat. However, the kingsnake is actually nonvenomous; it's merely pretending to be dangerous to eat. A predatory hawk or eagle, usually hunting from high in the sky, can't tell the difference between the two species, and so the kingsnake gets passed over and lives another day.

**1**

**According to information presented in the passage, what is the difference between kingsnakes and coral snakes?**

A.   Both kingsnakes and coral snakes are nonvenomous, but coral snakes have colorful markings.

B.   Both kingsnakes and coral snakes are venomous, but kingsnakes have colorful markings.

C.   Kingsnakes are nonvenomous while coral snakes are venomous.

D.   Coral snakes are nonvenomous while kingsnakes are venomous.

**2**

**In this passage, the author's primary purpose is to:**

A. explain how the markings on a snake are related to whether it's venomous.

B. teach readers the difference between coral snakes and kingsnakes.

C. illustrate why snakes are dangerous.

D. demonstrate how animals survive in difficult environments.

**3**

**The information in the passage best supports which of the following conclusions?**

A. The kingsnake is dangerous to humans.

B. The coral snake and the kingsnake are both hunted by the same predators.

C. It's safe to handle snakes in the woods because you can easily tell whether they're poisonous.

D. The kingsnake changes its markings when hawks or eagles are close by.

**4**

**Which of the following summaries of the passage is accurate?**

A. Humans can use coloration and markings on snakes to determine whether they're venomous.

B. Animals often use coloration to hide from predators.

C. The scarlet kingsnake and the coral snake have nearly identical markings.

D. Venomous snakes often have bright markings, although nonvenomous snakes can also mimic those colors.

**5**

**Which statement is NOT a detail from the passage?**

A. Predators will avoid eating kingsnakes because their markings are similar to those on coral snakes.

B. Kingsnakes and coral snakes live in the same habitats.

C. The coral snake uses its coloration to hide from predators.

D. The kingsnake is not venomous.

**6**

**Which of the following words is a synonym for <u>intricate</u> as it is used in Paragraph 1?**

A. complex

B. colorful

C. purposeful

D. changeable

In recent decades, jazz has been associated with New Orleans and festivals like Mardi Gras, but in the 1920s, jazz was a booming trend whose influence reached into many aspects of American culture. In fact, the years between World War I and the Great Depression were known as the Jazz Age, a term coined by A. Scott Fitzgerald in his famous novel The Great Gatsby. Sometimes also called the Roaring Twenties, this time period saw major urban centers experiencing new economic, cultural, and artistic vitality. In the United States, musicians flocked to cities like New York and Chicago, which would become famous hubs for jazz musicians. Ella Fitzgerald, for example, moved from Virginia to New York City to begin her much-lauded singing career, and jazz pioneer Louis Armstrong got his big break in Chicago.

Jazz music was played by and for a more expressive and freed populace than the United States had previously seen. Women gained the right to vote and were openly seen drinking and dancing to jazz music. This period marked the emergence of the flapper, a woman determined to make a statement about her new role in society. Jazz music also provided the soundtrack for the explosion of African American art and culture now known as the Harlem Renaissance. In addition to Fitzgerald and Armstrong, numerous musicians, including Duke Ellington, Fats Waller, and Bessie Smith, promoted their distinctive and complex music as an integral part of the emerging African American culture.

**7**

**Which of the following statements best expresses the main idea of the passage?**

A.  People should associate jazz music with the 1920s, not modern New Orleans.

B.  Jazz music played an important role in many cultural movements of the 1920s.

C.  Many famous jazz musicians began their careers in New York City and Chicago.

D.  African Americans were instrumental in launching jazz into mainstream culture.

**8**

**The information in the passage best supports which of the following conclusions?**

A.  Jazz music was important to minority groups struggling for social equality in the 1920s.

B.  Duke Ellington, Fats Waller, and Bessie Smith were the most important jazz musicians of the Harlem Renaissance.

C.  Women gained the right to vote with the help of jazz musicians.

D.  Duke Ellington, Fats Waller, and Bessie Smith all supported women's right to vote.

**9**

**In this passage, the author's primary purpose is to:**

A.  explain the role jazz musicians played in the Harlem Renaissance

B.  inform the reader about the many important musicians playing jazz in the 1920s

C.  discuss how jazz influenced important cultural movements in the 1920s

D.  provide a history of jazz music in the 20th century

**10**

**Which of the following is NOT a fact stated in the passage?**

A.  The years between World War I and the Great Depression were known as the Jazz Age.

B.  Ella Fitzgerald and Louis Armstrong both moved to New York City to start their music careers.

C.  Women danced to jazz music during the 1920s to make a statement about their role in society.

D.  Jazz music was an integral part of the emerging African American culture of the 1920s.

**11**

**The information in the passage best supports which of the following conclusions?**

A.  A. Scott Fitzgerald supported jazz musicians in New York and Chicago.

B.  Jazz music is no longer as popular as it once was.

C.  Both women and African Americans used jazz music as a way of expressing their newfound freedom.

D.  Flappers and African American musicians worked together to produce jazz music.

Alexis de Tocqueville, a young Frenchman from an aristocratic family, visited America in the early 1800s. He spent nine months travelling around America and talking to people. After observing American social life and politics, he returned to France and wrote Democracy in America, which was published in 1835. One of Tocqueville's observations is:

"Amongst the novel objects that attracted my attention during my stay in the United States, nothing struck me more forcibly than the general equality of conditions. I readily discovered the prodigious influence which this primary fact exercises on the whole course of society, by giving a certain direction to public opinion, and a certain tenor to the laws; by imparting new maxims to the governing powers, and peculiar habits to the governed. I speedily perceived that the influence of this fact extends far beyond the political character and the laws of the country, and that it has no less empire over civil society than over the Government; it creates opinions, engenders sentiments, suggests the ordinary practices of life, and modifies whatever it does not produce. The more I advanced in the study of American society, the more I perceived that the equality of conditions is the fundamental fact from which all others seem to be derived, and the central point at which all my observations constantly terminated."

**12**

**Which of the following statements best expresses the main idea of the passage?**

A.   Equality did not exist in the early years of America.

B.   Concern for equality of conditions has a central influence on both the political activity and the everyday life of America.

C.   The ordinary lives of Americans demonstrate that the American government is insisting that people are treated with equality.

D.   In American society, all people have rights that make them equal in terms of living conditions.

**13**

**The author's use of terms like "prodigious," "fundamental fact," and "central point" suggest which of the following purposes?**

A.   to convince readers that they need to believe in equality

B.   to engage and focus the reader's attention on the principles of Americans

C.   to contrast America and France

D.   to express his enthusiasm about equality in America

**14**

**The author would most likely agree with which of the following statements about America?**

A.   With a multitude of resources and possibilities, America offers everyone a chance to improve his or her status.

B.   Right from the beginning, at least three social classes emerged in America with most people falling in the middle.

C.   Americans have, right from the beginning, been eager to achieve and prosper.

D.   In the early decades when America had just become an independent country with a new government, people lived in equality.

The bacteria, fungi, insects, plants, and animals that live together in a habitat have evolved to share a pool of limited resources. They've competed for water, minerals, nutrients, sunlight, and space—sometimes for thousands or even millions of years.

As these communities have evolved, the species in them have developed complex, long-term interspecies interactions known as symbiotic relationships.

Ecologists characterize these interactions based on whether each party benefits. In mutualism, both individuals benefit, while in synnecrosis, both organisms are harmed. A relationship where one individual benefits and the other is harmed is known as parasitism. Examples of these relationships can easily be seen in any ecosystem. Pollination, for example, is mutualistic—pollinators get nutrients from the flower, and the plant is able to reproduce—while tapeworms, which steal nutrients from their host, are parasitic.

There's yet another class of symbiosis that is controversial among scientists. As it's long been defined, commensalism is a relationship where one species benefits and the other is unaffected. But is it possible for two species to interact and for one to remain completely unaffected? Often, relationships described as commensal include one species that feeds on another species' leftovers; remoras, for instance, will attach themselves to sharks and eat the food particles they leave behind. It might seem like the shark gets nothing from the relationship, but a closer look will show that sharks in fact benefit from remoras, which clean the sharks' skin and remove parasites. In fact, many scientists claim that relationships currently described as commensal are just mutualistic or parasitic in ways that haven't been discovered yet.

## 15

**Which of the following words is a synonym for <u>controversial</u> as it is used in Paragraph 3?**

A. debatable

B. objectionable

C. confusing

D. upsetting

## 16

**In this passage, the author's primary purpose is to:**

A. argue that commensalism isn't actually found in nature

B. describe the many types of symbiotic relationships

C. explain how competition for resources results in long-term interspecies relationships

D. provide examples of the many different ways individual organisms interact

## 17

**Which of the following is NOT a fact stated in the passage?**

A. Mutualism is an interspecies relationship where both species benefit.

B. Synnecrosis is an interspecies relationship where both species are harmed.

C. The relationship between plants and pollinators is mutualistic.

D. The relationship between remoras and sharks is parasitic.

**18**

Epiphytes are plants that attach themselves to trees and derive nutrients from the air and surrounding debris. Sometimes, the weight of epiphytes can damage the trees on which they're growing. The relationship between epiphytes and their hosts would be described as:

A.   mutualism

B.   commensalism

C.   parasitism

D.   synnecrosis

**19**

According to information presented in the passage, why is commensalism controversial among scientists?

A.   Many scientists believe that an interspecies interaction where one species is unaffected does not exist.

B.   Some scientists believe that relationships where one species feeds on the leftovers of another should be classified as parasitism.

C.   Because remoras and sharks have a mutualistic relationship, no interactions should be classified as commensalism.

D.   Only relationships among animal species should be classified as commensalism.

**20**

The information in the passage best supports which of the following conclusions about symbiotic relationships?

A.   Scientists cannot decide how to classify symbiotic relationships among species.

B.   The majority of interspecies interactions are parasitic because most species do not get along.

C.   If two species are involved in a parasitic relationship, one of the species will eventually become extinct.

D.   Symbiotic relationships evolve as the species that live in a community adapt to their environments and each other.

The social and political discourse of America continues to be permeated with idealism. An idealistic viewpoint asserts that the ideals of freedom, equality, justice, and human dignity are the truths that Americans must continue to aspire to. Idealists argue that truth is what should be, not necessarily what is. In general, they work to improve things and to make them as close to ideal as possible.

**21**

**In this passage, the author's primary purpose is to:**

A.  advocate for freedom, equality, justice, and human rights

B.  explain what an idealist believes in

C.  explain what's wrong with social and political discourse in America

D.  persuade readers to believe in certain truths

The greatest changes in sensory, motor, and perceptual development happen in the first two years of life. When babies are first born, most of their senses operate in a similar way to those of adults. For example, babies are able to hear before they are born; studies show that babies turn toward the sound of their mothers' voices just minutes after being born, indicating they recognize the mother's voice from their time in the womb.

The exception to this rule is vision. A baby's vision changes significantly in its first year of life; initially it has a range of vision of only 8 – 12 inches and no depth perception. As a result, infants rely primarily on hearing; vision does not become the dominant sense until around the age of 12 months. Babies also prefer faces to other objects. This preference, along with their limited vision range, means that their sight is initially focused on their caregiver.

**22**

**Which of the following summaries of the passage is accurate?**

A.  Babies have no depth perception until 12 months, which is why they focus only on their caregivers' faces.

B.  Babies can recognize their mothers' voices when born, so they initially rely primarily on their sense of hearing.

C.  Babies have senses similar to those of adults except for their sense of sight, which doesn't fully develop until 12 months.

D.  Babies' senses go through many changes in the first year of their lives.

**23**

**According to information presented in the passage, which of the following senses do babies primarily rely on?**

A.  vision

B.  hearing

C.  touch

D.  smell

**24**

**Which of the following best describes the purpose of the passage?**

A.   expository

B.   narrative

C.   persuasive

D.   descriptive

Popcorn is often associated with fun and festivities, both in and out of the home. It's eaten in theaters, usually after being salted and smothered in butter, and in homes, fresh from the microwave. But popcorn isn't just for fun—it's also a multimillion-dollar-a-year industry with a long and fascinating history.

While popcorn might seem like a modern invention, its history actually dates back thousands of years, making it one of the oldest snack foods enjoyed around the world. Popcorn is believed by food historians to be one of the earliest uses of cultivated corn. In 1948, Herbert Dick and Earle Smith discovered old popcorn dating back 4000 years in the New Mexico Bat Cave. For the Aztec Indians who called the caves home, popcorn (or *momochitl*) played an important role in society, both as a food staple and in ceremonies. The Aztecs cooked popcorn by heating sand in a fire; when it was heated, kernels were added and would pop when exposed to the heat of the sand.

The American love affair with popcorn began in 1912, when popcorn was first sold in theaters. The popcorn industry flourished during the Great Depression when it was advertised as a wholesome and economical food. Selling for five to ten cents a bag, it was a luxury that the downtrodden could afford. With the introduction of mobile popcorn machines at the World's Columbian Exposition, popcorn moved from the theater into fairs and parks. Popcorn continued to rule the snack food kingdom until the rise in popularity of home televisions during the 1950s.

The popcorn industry reacted to the decline in sales quickly by introducing pre-popped and unpopped popcorn for home consumption. However, it wasn't until microwave popcorn became commercially available in 1981 that at-home popcorn consumption began to grow exponentially. With the wide availability of microwaves in the United States, popcorn also began popping up in offices and hotel rooms. However, the home still remains the most popular popcorn eating spot: today, 70 percent of the 16 billion quarts of popcorn consumed annually in the United States are eaten at home.

**25**

**Which of the following words is a synonym for <u>staple</u> as it is used in Paragraph 2?**

A.   something produced only for special occasions

B.   something produced regularly in large quantities

C.   something produced by cooking

D.   something fastened together securely

**26**

**The information in the passage best supports which of the following conclusions?**

A.   People ate less popcorn in the 1950s than in previous decades because they went to the movies less.

B.   Without mobile popcorn machines, people would not have been able to eat popcorn during the Great Depression.

C.   People enjoyed popcorn during the Great Depression because it was a luxury food.

D.   During the 1800s, people began abandoning theaters to go to fairs and festivals.

**27**

**In this passage, the author's primary purpose is to:**

A.   explain how microwaves affected the popcorn industry

B.   show that popcorn is older than many people realize

C.   illustrate the history of popcorn from ancient cultures to modern times

D.   demonstrate the importance of popcorn in various cultures

**28**

**Which of the following does the author of the passage credit for the growth of the popcorn industry in the United States?**

A.   the use of popcorn in ancient Aztec ceremonies

B.   the growth of the home television industry

C.   the marketing of popcorn during the Great Depression

D.   the nutritional value of popcorn

**29**

**Which of the following summaries of the passage is accurate?**

A.   Popcorn is a popular snack food that dates back thousands of years. Its popularity in the United States has been tied to the growth of theaters and the availability of microwaves.

B.   Popcorn has been a popular snack food for thousands of years. Archaeologists have found evidence that many ancient cultures used popcorn as a food staple and in ceremonies.

C.   Popcorn was first introduced to America in 1912, and its popularity has grown exponentially since then. Today, over 16 billion quarts of popcorn are consumed in the United States annually.

D.   Popcorn is a versatile snack food that can be eaten with butter or other toppings. It can also be cooked in a number of different ways, including in microwaves.

**30**

**Which of the following is NOT a fact stated in the passage?**

A.    Archaeologists have found popcorn dating back 4000 years.

B.    Popcorn was first sold in theaters in 1912.

C.    Consumption of popcorn dropped in 1981 with the growing popularity of home televisions.

D.    70 percent of the popcorn consumed in the United States is eaten in homes.

The study showed that private tutoring is providing a significant advantage to those students who are able to afford it. Researchers looked at the grades of students who had received free tutoring through the school versus those whose parents had paid for private tutors. The study included 2500 students in three high schools across four grade levels. The study found that private tutoring corresponded with a rise in grade point average (GPA) of 0.5 compared to students who used the school's free tutor service and 0.7 compared to students who used no tutoring. After reviewing the study, the board is recommending that the school restructure its free tutor service to provide a more equitable education for all students.

**31**

**Which of the following would weaken the author's argument?**

A.    the fact that the cited study was funded by a company that provides discounted tutoring through schools

B.    a study showing differences in standardized test scores between students at schools in different neighborhoods

C.    a statement signed by local teachers stating that they do not provide preferential treatment in the classroom or when grading

D.    a study showing that GPA does not strongly correlate with success in college

**32**

**Which of the following types of arguments is used in the passage?**

A.    emotional argument

B.    appeal to authority

C.    specific evidence

D.    rhetorical questioning

AMERICAN COWSLIP: This plant grows spontaneously in Virginia and other parts of North America. It flowers the beginning of May, and the seeds ripen in July, soon after which the stalks and leaves decay, so that the roots remain inactive till the following spring. It is propagated by offsets, which the roots put out freely when they are in a loose moist soil and a shady situation; the best time to remove the roots, and take away the offsets, is in August, after the leaves and stalks are decayed, that they may be fixed well in their new situation before the frost comes on.

**33**

According to information presented in the passage, American Cowslip grows spontaneously because

A.    the seeds ripen quickly.

B.    the roots remain inactive.

C.    soil is moist most of the year.

D.    the roots put out offsets.

It could be said that the great battle between the North and South we call the Civil War was a battle for individual identity. The states of the South had their own culture, one based on farming, independence, and the rights of both man and state to determine their own paths. Similarly, the North had forged its own identity as a center of centralized commerce and manufacturing. This clash of lifestyles was bound to create tension, and this tension was bound to lead to war. But people who try to sell you this narrative are wrong. The Civil War was not a battle of cultural identities—it was a battle about slavery. All other explanations for the war are either a direct consequence of the South's desire for wealth at the expense of her fellow man or a fanciful invention to cover up this sad portion of our nation's history. And it cannot be denied that this time in our past was very sad indeed.

**34**

Which of the following words is a synonym for <u>fanciful</u> as it is used in the passage?

A.    complicated

B.    imaginative

C.    successful

D.    unfortunate

**35**

In this passage, the author's primary purpose is to:

A.    convince readers that slavery was the main cause of the Civil War

B.    illustrate the cultural differences between the North and the South before the Civil War

C.    persuade readers that the North deserved to win the Civil War

D.    demonstrate that the history of the Civil War is too complicated to be understood clearly

36

**Which of the following statements best expresses the main idea of the passage?**

A.   The Civil War was the result of cultural differences between the North and South.

B.   The Civil War was caused by the South's reliance on slave labor.

C.   The North's use of commerce and manufacturing allowed it to win the war.

D.   The South's belief in the rights of man and state cost the war.

# Writing

## MULTIPLE CHOICE

Use the writing sample below to answer the six questions that follow.

(1) For centuries, <u>artists and philosophers have long debated about the relationship between life and art.</u> (2) While some argue that art is an imitation of life, others believe that, just as often, life ends up imitating art. (3) In no other genre is the impact of art on our real lives more visible than in the realm of science fiction. (4) Great minds of science fiction such as Jules Verne, Gene Roddenberry, H. G. Wells, and Stanley Kubrick have introduced ideas that, though fantastical at the time of their inception, eventually became reality. (5) Many of these artists were dead before they ever saw their ideas come to life.

(6) Some of humanity's biggest accomplishments were achieved first in science fiction. (7) Jules Verne wrote about humanity traveling to the moon over a century before it happened. (8) Scientists Robert H. Goddard and Leo Szilard both credit his work—on liquid-fueled rockets and atomic power, respectively—to H. G. Wells and his futuristic novels. (9) Gene Roddenberry, the creator of *Star Trek*, dreamed up replicators long before 3-D printers were invented.

(10) Jules Verne's work, for example, was the inspiration for both the submarine and the modern-day helicopter. (11) H. G. Wells wrote about automatic doors long before they began to turn up in almost every grocery store in America. (12) Roddenberry's *Star Trek* is even credited as the inspiration for the creation of the mobile phone. (13) Kubrick's HAL from *2001: A Space Odyssey* represented voice control at its finest, long before virtual assistants were installed in all the new smartphone models.

**1**

In context, which revision to sentence 5 (reproduced below) is most needed?

*Many of these artists were dead before they ever saw their ideas come to life.*

A.   delete the sentence

B.   change *many* to *most*

C.   change *dead* to *deceased*

D.   change *saw* to *witnessed*

**2**

Which of the following introductory phrases should be inserted at the beginning of sentence 6 (reproduced below)?

*Some of humanity's biggest accomplishments were achieved first in science fiction.*

A.   Therefore,

B.   In fact,

C.   However,

D.   In addition,

**3**

In context, which is the best version of the underlined portion of sentence 1 (reproduced below)?

*artists and philosophers have long debated about the relationship between life and art.*

A. artists and philosophers have examined the facts and debated about the relationship between life and art.

B. artists and philosophers have hemmed, hawed, and debated about the relationship between life and art.

C. artists and philosophers have debated about the relationship between life and art.

D. artists and philosophers have hemmed and hawed about the relationship between life and art.

**4**

In context, which revision to sentence 8 (reproduced below) is most needed?

**Scientists Robert H. Goddard and Leo Szilard both credit his work—on liquid-fueled rockets and atomic power, respectively—to H. G. Wells and his futuristic novels.**

A. delete the sentence

B. insert always after the word both

C. change his to their

D. delete the phrase inside the dashes

**5**

In context, which of the following would provide the best introduction to the final paragraph?

A. Transportation was of particular concern to science fiction writers, who dreamed up new ways for humanity to get around the world.

B. These same authors had other interesting ideas as well.

C. Sometimes science fiction is so much like life it is incredible.

D. Many of the ideas life borrows from science fiction have infiltrated our everyday lives and our world to an even greater degree.

Go on

**6**

**In context, which of the following would provide the best conclusion to the essay?**

A.   Science fiction will, no doubt, continue to influence our technology and our world for many years to come.

B.   These men are important figures in history for their ideas, and they should be respected as such.

C.   It is unfair that these creative individuals did not receive any money or rewards in exchange for their ideas.

D.   Science fiction is really an interesting topic, with many ideas and influential people to study and understand.

Use the writing sample below to answer the six questions that follow.

(1) Since its birth, humanity has sought explanations for the unexplainable. (2) In ancient cultures, mythology explained the weather, the elements of nature, and even the creation of the universe. (3) More recently, as recently as the last two centuries, many cultures have turned to folklore and superstition to explain odd occurrences and behaviors. (4) In the folk traditions of European countries, <u>one creature in particular takes the blame when individuals, especially children, begin acting strangely, the changeling.</u>

(5) According to many folk traditions, <u>changelings were the children of fairies or elves, left in the places of human children who had been stolen from their families by the creatures.</u> (6) If an individual's family began to notice strange behaviors in the individual, they would assume he or she had been kidnapped and replaced with a changeling. (7) This provided, at least, some answers to families whose children suffered from unexplained ailments or disabilities.

(8) Many families believed there were specific actions that would encourage the changeling to leave and return the human child. (9) In Germany, Ireland, and Wales, for example, it was thought that brewing egg shells would surprise the changeling into admitting his or her true identity. (10) Unfortunately, however, the belief that changelings could be convinced to leave was not just <u>an innocuous superstition. (11) On some occasions,</u> harm came to the individual who was thought to be a changeling.

**7**

**Which of the following is the best way to introduce sentence 3 (reproduced below)?**

*More recently, as recently as the last two centuries, many cultures have turned to folklore and superstition to explain odd occurrences and behaviors.*

A.   More recently,

B.   These days,

C.   Therefore,

D.   On the other hand,

**8**

**Which is the best revision for the underlined portion of sentence 4 (reproduced below)?**

*one creature in particular takes the blame when individuals, especially children, begin acting strangely, the changeling.*

A.  as it is now

B.  one creature in particular takes the blame when individuals, especially children, begin acting strangely: the changeling.

C.  one creature in particular takes the blame when individuals—especially children, begin acting strangely—the changeling.

D.  one creature in particular takes the blame when individuals especially children begin acting strangely. The changeling.

**9**

**Which of the following would NOT be an acceptable revision of the underlined portion of sentence 5 (reproduced below)?**

*changelings were the children of fairies or elves, left in the places of human children who had been stolen from their families by the creatures.*

A.  changelings were the children of fairies or elves, who were left in the places of human children who had been stolen from their families by the creatures.

B.  changelings were the children of fairies or elves; they were left in the places of human children who had been stolen from their families by the creatures.

C.  changelings were the children of fairies or elves, they were left in the places of human children who had been stolen from their families by the creatures.

D.  changelings were the children of fairies or elves—left in the places of human children who had been stolen from their families by the creatures.

**10**

**Which revision to sentence 7 (reproduced below) is most needed?**

*This provided, at least, some answers to families whose children suffered from unexplained ailments or disabilities.*

A.  delete the sentence

B.  insert *explanation* after *this* and before *provided*

C.  change *families* to *family's*

D.  change *whose* to *who's*

**Go on**

**11**

**What is the best placement for sentence 8 (reproduced below)?**

*Many families believed there were specific actions that would encourage the changeling to leave and return the human child.*

A.    where it is now

B.    at the end of the second paragraph

C.    after sentence 9

D.    after sentence 10

**12**

**Which is the best way to revise and combine sentences 10 and 11 (reproduced below) at the underlined point?**

*Unfortunately, however, the belief that changelings could be convinced to leave was not just __an innocuous superstition. On some occasions,__ harm came to the individual who was thought to be a changeling.*

A.    an innocuous superstition, on some occasions,

B.    an innocuous superstition, so on some occasions,

C.    an innocuous superstition, but on some occasions,

D.    an innocuous superstition: on some occasions,

**13**

**Which of the following phrases would be most appropriate to use in the blank below?**

**Typically, water that has evaporated _____ before falling to Earth again as precipitation.**

A.    remain in the sky in cloud form for fewer than ten days

B.    remain in the sky in cloud form for fewer then ten days

C.    remains in the sky in cloud form for fewer than ten days

D.    will remain in the sky in cloud form for fewer then ten days

**14**

**Which of the following punctuation marks would be most appropriate to use in the blank in the excerpt below?**

**James had already been awake for nineteen hours___ after a twelve-hour work day, when he received the news.**

A.    period ( . )

B.    semicolon ( ; )

C.    comma ( , )

D.    dash ( — )

**15**

Which of the following nouns is written in the correct plural form?

A.  vertebraes

B.  gooses

C.  octopusses

D.  bronchi

**16**

Which of the following phrases would be most appropriate to use in the blank below?

Unlike a traditional comic book, which would likely be released as part of a periodical or series, a graphic novel is released as _____, either in the form of one long story or in the form of an anthology.

A.  only one single publication

B.  only a publication

C.  a single publication

D.  a single, unique publication

**17**

Which of the following sentences is correctly punctuated?

A.  In addition to the disastrous effects an active volcano can have on it's immediate surroundings, an eruption can also pose a threat to passing aircraft.

B.  In addition to the disastrous effects an active volcano can have on it's immediate surroundings: an eruption can also pose a threat to passing aircraft.

C.  In addition to the disastrous effects an active volcano can have on its immediate surroundings: an eruption can also pose a threat to passing aircraft!

D.  In addition to the disastrous effects an active volcano can have on its immediate surroundings, an eruption can also pose a threat to passing aircraft.

**18**

Which of the following words is misspelled?

A.  astrophysicists

B.  astronemers

C.  techniques

D.  technology

**19**

**Which of the following phrases would be most appropriate to use in the blank below?**

**Though organized firefighting groups existed as early as Ancient Egypt, the first fully state-run brigade was created by Emperor Augustus of Rome _____ as the nation's official police force.**

A.   which also functioned

B.   and also functioned

C.   also functioning

D.   that also functioned

**20**

**Which of the following sentences correctly combines the two clauses?**

A.   While these incidents sometimes end in funny or heartwarming stories, at other times they end in fear and destruction.

B.   While these incidents sometimes end in funny or heartwarming stories; at other times they end in fear and destruction.

C.   While these incidents sometimes end in funny or heartwarming stories: at other times they end in fear and destruction.

D.   While these incidents sometimes end in funny or heartwarming stories—at other times they end in fear and destruction.

**21**

**Which of the following phrases would be most appropriate to use in the blank below?**

**In 1903, Pennsylvania _____ in response, however, artists like Walt McDougall began depicting politicians in an even less flattering light—as inanimate objects such as trees and mugs.**

A.   depicting politicians as animals, passed a law prohibiting cartoonists in order to curb criticism by the press;

B.   prohibiting cartoonists from depicting politicians as animals, passed a law in order to curb criticism by the press;

C.   passed a law prohibiting cartoonists from depicting politicians in order to curb criticism as animals by the press;

D.   passed a law prohibiting cartoonists from depicting politicians as animals in order to curb criticism by the press;

**22**

Which of the following words or phrases would be most appropriate to use in the blank below?

In today's professional baseball leagues, strict regulations have standardized the design of bats; in the early days of baseball, _____, players often shaped their own bats, leading to a wide range of shapes, sizes, and weights.

A. although

B. on the other hand

C. nevertheless

D. in consequence

**23**

Which phrase from the excerpt contains an error in capitalization?

The *Chicago Tribune* is famous for many reasons: in 1948, the paper published an erroneous headline about the winner of the Presidential election, and in 1974, it called for President Nixon's resignation.

A. *Chicago Tribune*

B. the paper

C. about the winner

D. Presidential election

**24**

Which of the following phrases would be most appropriate to use in the blank below?

Vivariums are controlled, enclosed spaces designed to replicate a particular _____ aquariums and terrariums are fairly common, insectariums (for keeping insects) and penguinariums (for keeping penguins) are less so.

A. habitat, and while

B. habitat; and while

C. habitat, while

D. habitat: and while

**25**

Which of the following phrases follows the rules of capitalization?

A. President Carter and his advisers

B. Robert Jones, the senior Senator from California

C. my Aunt and Uncle who live out west

D. the party on New Year's eve

**26**

**Which of the following phrases would be most appropriate to use in the blank below?**

L.L. Zamenhof, an ophthalmologist in the late 1800s, invented a language called Esperanto with the goal of creating a universal second language that could be taught around the world in order _____ international communications and relations.

A.   to instill

B.   to improve

C.   to initiate

D.   to invite

**27**

**Which of the following phrases would be most appropriate to use in the blank below?**

_____ research into automating vehicle processes began as early as the 1920s.

A.   Before self-driving vehicles are just now being introduced on the automotive market,

B.   Though self-driving vehicles are just now being introduced on the automotive market,

C.   Because self-driving vehicles are just now being introduced on the automotive market,

D.   Self-driving vehicles are just now being introduced on the automotive market,

**28**

**Which of the following sentences contains a comma usage error?**

A.   On her way home she stopped to pick up groceries, pay her electric bill, and buy some flowers.

B.   I used to drink coffee every morning but my office took away the coffee machine.

C.   Elizabeth will order the cake for the party after she orders the hats.

D.   My cousin, who lives in Indiana, is coming to visit this weekend.

**29**

**Which of the following phrases would be most appropriate to use in the blank below?**

When determining the conservation status of a species, biologists consider many _____ size, changes in population size over time, geographical range of existing population, rate of reproduction, and known threats to the population.

A.    factors including; population

B.    factors including, population

C.    factors. Including population

D.    factors, including population

**30**

**Which of the following is a complex sentence?**

A.    Engineers designed seat belts to stop the inertia of traveling bodies by applying an opposing force to the driver and passengers during a collision.

B.    Hurricanes cost the United States roughly $5 billion per year in damages and have been the cause of almost two million deaths in the last two hundred years.

C.    Woodstock appeared in the *Peanuts* comic strips as early as April 1967, but he was not named until June 1970, ten months after the famous music festival of the same name, Woodstock.

D.    Although organized firefighting groups existed as early as ancient Egyptian times, the first fully state-run brigade was created by Emperor Augustus of Rome.

**31**

**Which of the following phrases would be most appropriate to use in the blank below?**

Despite an extremely competitive acceptance rate at Chinese universities—_____almost one-third of college graduates have trouble finding and establishing permanent careers.

A.    with less then 20 percent of students being allowed to continue there educations after high school—

B.    with less than 20 percent of students being allowed to continue there educations after high school—

C.    with less than 20 percent of students being allowed to continue their educations after high school—

D.    with less than 20 percent of students being allowed to continue their educations after high school,

**32**

**Which of the following words contains an error in spelling?**

A.   potatos

B.   onions

C.   saliva

D.   conservators

**33**

**Which of the following phrases would be most appropriate to use in the blank below?**

**Though professional dental care is _____ in the developed world, the prevalence of cavities is much higher there than in the developing world due to higher rates of sugar consumption.**

A.   relatively wide available

B.   relative widely available

C.   relatively wide availability

D.   relatively widely available

**34**

**Which of the following parts of speech is *travels* as used in the sentence?**

**Abby's travels in Asia provided her the opportunity to try many foods that she would not have been able to try at home in the United States.**

A.   verb

B.   noun

C.   adjective

D.   adverb

**35**

**Which of the following phrases would be most appropriate to use in the blank below?**

**The Cult Awareness Network, created to provide the public _____ about groups whose activities were considered cult-like, was disbanded in 1996 after a series of lawsuits brought on by members of the Church of Scientology forced the organization to declare bankruptcy.**

A.   with facts and information

B.   with facts, figures, and information

C.   with facts and detailed information

D.   with information

**36**

**Which of the following phrases would be most appropriate to use in the blank below?**

The exotic pet _____ is a significant concern for environmentalists and animal rights advocates around the world.

A.   trade, which involves both the capturing of wild animals and the captive breeding of wild species,

B.   trade, which involves both the capturing of wild animals and they breed wild species in captivity,

C.   trade involves both the capturing of wild animals and the captive breeding of wild species, it

D.   trade, it involves both the capturing of wild animals and the captive breeding of wild species,

**37**

**Which of the following phrases would be most appropriate to use in the blank below?**

Though the term *nomad* is often associated with early primitive _____ even today, especially in Europe and Asia.

A.   populations; nomadic cultures continue to exist

B.   populations: nomadic cultures continue to exist

C.   populations, nomadic cultures continue to exist

D.   populations nomadic cultures continue to exist

**38**

**Which of the following phrases would be most appropriate to use in the blank below?**

Freediving, which is done without breathing supports like SCUBA gear, is sometimes _____ other underwater activities such as underwater photography, underwater football, underwater hockey, and even underwater target shooting.

A.   combined of

B.   combined in

C.   combined with

D.   combined over

**39**

**Which of the following punctuation marks is used incorrectly?**

In many European countries such as, France, Spain, and Italy, hot chocolate is made with real melted chocolate; this creates a beverage that is thick and rich.

A. the comma after *as*

B. the comma after *France*

C. the comma after *Italy*

D. the semicolon after *chocolate*

**40**

**Which of the following is an appropriate synonym for *traditional* as it is used in the sentence?**

Unlike a traditional comic book, a graphic novel is released as one single publication, either in the form of one long story or in the form of an anthology.

A. old-fashioned

B. conventional

C. expensive

D. popular

SENTENCE CORRECTION

Rewrite the following sentence, addressing the two errors in grammar and mechanics it contains while retaining its original meaning.

You can't have either the cake nor the cookie.

Rewrite the following sentence, addressing the two errors in grammar and mechanics it contains while retaining its original meaning.

Make a study plan learn the parts of the respiratory system the muscles and the heart.

## CONSTRUCTED RESPONSE

**Prompt**

In recent years, catastrophic hurricanes and typhoons around the world have resulted in large-scale destruction and loss of life. However, rapid population growth and the urban development necessary to accommodate the growth have continued in areas vulnerable to storms and flooding, putting millions at risk. Is it possible to allow for economic growth even while keeping people safe?

# Mathematics

Work the problem, and choose the most correct answer.

---

**1**

Simplify:  $(1.2 \times 10^{-3})(1.13 \times 10^{-4})$

A.   $1.356 \times 10^{-7}$

B.   $1.356 \times 10^{-1}$

C.   $1.356 \times 10$

D.   $1.356 \times 10^{12}$

---

**2**

Which inequality is represented by the following graph?

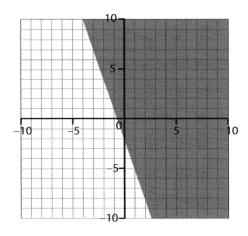

A.   $y \geq -3x - 2$

B.   $y \geq 3x - 2$

C.   $y > -3x - 2$

D.   $y \leq -3x - 2$

---

**3**

If $\triangle ABD \sim \triangle DEF$ and the similarity ratio is 3:4, what is the measure of *DE* if *AB* = 12?

A.   9

B.   16

C.   96

D.   12

---

**4**

If $j = 4$, what is the value of $2(j-4)^4 - j + \frac{1}{2}j$?

A.   0

B.   −2

C.   2

D.   4

---

**5**

The average speed of cars on a highway (*s*) is inversely proportional to the number of cars on the road (*n*). If a car drives at 65 mph when there are 250 cars on the road, how fast will a car drive when there are 325 cars on the road?

A.   50 mph

B.   55 mph

C.   60 mph

D.   85 mph

---

**6**

The height of students at Glenwood High School is normally distributed. If the average height of a student is 5.5 feet with a standard deviation of 0.25 feet, a student picked at random has the highest probability of being in which group?

A.   Students with heights from 5 to 5.25 feet.

B.   Students with heights from 5.25 to 5.5 feet.

C.   Students with heights from 5.75 to 6 feet.

D.   Students with heights from 6 to 6.25 feet.

**7**

The coordinates of point *A* are (7, 12) and the coordinates of point *C* are (−3, 10). If *C* is the midpoint of $\overline{AB}$, what are the coordinates of point *B*?

A.   (2, 11)

B.   (−13, 8)

C.   (17, 14)

D.   (−13, 11)

**8**

The pie graph below shows how a state's government plans to spend its annual budget of $3 billion. How much more money does the state plan to spend on infrastructure than education?

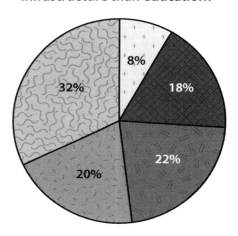

8%

32%

18%

20%

22%

⊕ Employees        ● Education

● Healthcare        ◯ Pension

◯ Infrastructure

A.   $60,000,000

B.   $120,000,000

C.   $300,000,000

D.   $600,000,000

**9**

Simplify: $(3^2 \div 1^3) - (4 - 8^2) + 2^4$

A.   −35

B.   −4

C.   28

D.   85

**10**

If the length of a rectangle is increased by 40% and its width is decreased by 40%, what is the effect on the rectangle's area?

A.   The area is the same.

B.   It increases by 16%.

C.   It increases by 20%.

D.   It decreases by 16%.

**11**

A high school cross country team sent 25 percent of its runners to a regional competition. Of these, 10 percent won medals. If 2 runners earned medals, how many members does the cross country team have?

A.   8

B.   80

C.   125

D.   1250

**12**

What is the *x*-intercept of the given equation?

$10x + 10y = 10$

A.   (1, 0)

B.   (0, 1)

C.   (0, 0)

D.   (1, 1)

**13**

W, X, Y, and Z lie on a circle with center A. If the diameter of the circle is 75, what is the sum of $\overline{AW}$, $\overline{AX}$, $\overline{AY}$, and $\overline{AZ}$?

A.   75

B.   300

C.   150

D.   106.5

**14**

Convert 55 meters to feet (round to the nearest tenth of a foot).

A.   16.8 feet

B.   21.7 feet

C.   139.7 feet

D.   180.4 feet

**15**

Which of the following is equivalent to $z^3(z + 2)^2 - 4z^3 + 2$?

A.   2

B.   $z^5 + 4z^4 + 4z^3 + 2$

C.   $z^6 + 4z^3 + 2$

D.   $z^5 + 4z^4 + 2$

**16**

Fifteen DVDs are to be arranged on a shelf. 4 of the DVDs are horror films, 6 are comedies, and 5 are science fiction. In how many ways can the DVDs be arranged if DVDs of the same genre must be placed together?

A.   2,073,600

B.   6,220,800

C.   12,441,600

D.   131,216,200

**17**

What is the value of z in the following system?

$z - 2x = 14$

$2z - 6x = 18$

A.   −7

B.   3

C.   5

D.   24

**18**

If $\dfrac{4x - 5}{3} = \dfrac{\frac{1}{2}(2x - 6)}{5}$, what is the value of x?

A.   $-\dfrac{2}{7}$

B.   $-\dfrac{4}{17}$

C.   $\dfrac{16}{17}$

D.   $\dfrac{8}{7}$

**19**

If a person reads 40 pages in 45 minutes, approximately how many minutes will it take her to read 265 pages?

A.   202

B.   236

C.   265

D.   298

**20**

A pair of 6-sided dice is rolled 10 times. What is the probability that in exactly 3 of those rolls, the sum of the dice will be 5?

A.   0.14%

B.   7.2%

C.   11.1%

D.   60%

**21**

In the figure below, there are six line segments that terminate at point $O$. If segment $\overline{DO}$ bisects $\angle AOF$ and segment $\overline{BO}$ bisects $\angle AOD$, what is the value of $\angle AOF$?

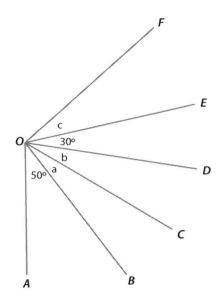

A.    140°

B.    160°

C.    170°

D.    200°

**22**

The line of best fit is calculated for a data set that tracks the number of miles that passenger cars traveled annually in the US from 1960 to 2010. In the model, $x = 0$ represents the year 1960, and $y$ is the number of miles traveled in billions. If the line of best fit is $y = 0.0293x + 0.563$, approximately how many additional miles were traveled for every 5 years that passed?

A.    0.0293 billion

B.    0.1465 billion

C.    0.563 billion

D.    0.710 billion

**23**

A worker was paid $15,036 for 7 months of work. If he received the same amount each month, how much was he paid for the first 2 months?

A.    $2,148

B.    $4,296

C.    $6,444

D.    $8,592

**24**

If the volume of a cube is 343 cubic meters, what is the cube's surface area?

A.    49 m²

B.    84 m²

C.    196 m²

D.    294 m²

**25**

What is the total number of 6-digit numbers in which each individual digit is less than 3 or greater than 6?

A.    38,880

B.    46,656

C.    80,452

D.    101,370

**26**

Which of the following is the solution set to the given inequality?

$$2x + 4 \geq 5(x - 4) - 3(x - 4)$$

A.    $(-\infty, \infty)$

B.    $(-\infty, 6.5]$

C.    $[6.5, -\infty)$

D.    $(-\infty, 6.5) \boxtimes (6.5, \infty)$

**27**

If an employee who makes $37,500 per year receives a 5.5% raise, what is the employee's new salary?

A. $35,437.50

B. $35,625

C. $39,375

D. $39,562.50

**28**

In the xy-coordinate plane, how many points have a distance of four from the origin?

A. 0

B. 2

C. 4

D. ∞

**29**

Simplify: $\dfrac{(3x^2y^2)^2}{3^3x^{-2}y^3}$

A. $3x^6y$

B. $\dfrac{x^6y}{3}$

C. $\dfrac{x^4}{3y}$

D. $\dfrac{3x^4}{y}$

**30**

The population of a city in 2008 was 1.25 million people. If the population is decreasing by 5% annually, in what year will the population reach 1 million?

A. 2011

B. 2012

C. 2013

D. 2014

**31**

The mean of 13 numbers is 30. The mean of 8 of these numbers is 42. What is the mean of the other 5 numbers?

A. 5.5

B. 10.8

C. 16.4

D. 21.2

**32**

What are the real zero(s) of the following polynomial?

$2n^2 + 2n - 12 = 0$

A. {2}

B. {−3, 2}

C. {2, 4}

D. There are no real zeros of n.

**33**

The vertices of quadrilateral PQRS are located at the points P (−6, −3), Q (−3, 2), R (0, 3), S (−1, 0). Quadrilateral PQRS is a

A. kite

B. parallelogram

C. trapezoid

D. rhombus

**34**

Which data set has a median larger than the mean and a standard deviation less than 2?

A. {5, 5, 5, 5, 5, 5}

B. {0, 0, 2, 8, 8, 8}

C. {1, 1, 5, 5, 10, 20}

D. {1, 2, 5, 5, 5, 6}

**35**

600 people between the ages of 15 and 45 were polled regarding their use of social media. 200 people from each age group were part of the study. The results are listed in the relative frequency table below.

| Hours Per Day Spent on Social Media | | | | |
|---|---|---|---|---|
| Age (years) | Less than 2 hours | 2 to 4 hours | More than 4 Hours | Total |
| 15 – 25 | 0.15 | 0.40 | 0.45 | 1.0 |
| 25 – 35 | 0.52 | 0.28 | 0.20 | 1.0 |
| 35 – 45 | 0.85 | 0.10 | 0.05 | 1.0 |
| Total | 0.51 | 0.26 | 0.23 | 1.0 |

**Which of the statements are true?**

I.   Of people 25 to 35 years old, 20% spend more than 4 hours per day on social media.

II.  Of the population of 15 to 45-year-olds, 26% spend 2 – 4 hours a day on social media.

III. Of people between the ages of 15 and 35, 67% spend 0 – 2 hours per day on social media.

IV.  5 people who reported using social media more than 4 hours per week were 35 to 45 years old.

A.   I and II

B.   I, II, and IV

C.   I, II, and III

D.   II, III, and IV

**36**

If the surface area of a cylinder with radius of 4 feet is $48\pi$ square feet, what is its volume?

A.   $1\pi$ ft.$^3$

B.   $16\pi$ ft.$^3$

C.   $32\pi$ ft.$^3$

D.   $64\pi$ ft.$^3$

# Answer Key

## Reading

### 1)

A.   Incorrect. The second paragraph states that "[t]he scarlet kingsnake, for example, has very similar markings to the venomous coral snake with whom it frequently shares a habitat. However, the kingsnake is actually nonvenomous[.]"

B.   Incorrect. The second paragraph states that "[t]he scarlet kingsnake, for example, has very similar markings to the venomous coral snake with whom it frequently shares a habitat. However, the kingsnake is actually nonvenomous[.]"

**C.   Correct.** The second paragraph states that "[t]he scarlet kingsnake, for example, has very similar markings to the venomous coral snake with whom it frequently shares a habitat. However, the kingsnake is actually nonvenomous[.]"

D.   Incorrect. The second paragraph states that "[t]he scarlet kingsnake, for example, has very similar markings to the venomous coral snake with whom it frequently shares a habitat. However, the kingsnake is actually nonvenomous[.]"

### 2)

**A.   Correct.** The passage indicates that a snakes'"intricate diamonds, stripes, and swirls help the animals hide from predators, but perhaps most importantly (for us humans, anyway), the markings can also indicate whether the snake is venomous."

B.   Incorrect. Though the author does mention one difference between the kingsnake and the coral snake, this is not the primary purpose of the passage.

C.   Incorrect. The author does not indicate why snakes are dangerous, only that some of them are.

D.   Incorrect. Though the author does provide some examples of this, this answer choice is more general, while the passage focused on snakes in particular.

**3)**

A. Incorrect. The author mentions that "the kingsnake is actually nonvenomous" but provides no more information about whether the kingsnake poses a danger to humans.

**B. Correct.** The final paragraph of the passage states that the two species "frequently [share] a habitat" and that "[a] predatory hawk or eagle, usually hunting from high in the sky, can't tell the difference between the two species, and so the kingsnake gets passed over and lives another day."

C. Incorrect. The author does not imply that it is easy to tell the difference between venomous and nonvenomous snakes, only that it is possible.

D. Incorrect. The final paragraph states that the kingsnake "has very similar marking to the venomous coral snake" and does not indicate that these markings change with circumstances.

**4)**

A. Incorrect. This is one detail from the passage but is not adequate as a summary.

B. Incorrect. This is one detail from the passage but is not adequate as a summary.

C. Incorrect. This is one detail from the passage but is not adequate as a summary.

**D. Correct.** This summary captures the main ideas of each paragraph.

**5)**

A. Incorrect. The second paragraph states that "[a] predatory hawk or eagle, usually hunting from high in the sky, can't tell the difference between the two species, and so the kingsnake gets passed over and lives another day."

B. Incorrect. The second paragraph states that "[t]he scarlet kingsnake, for example, has very similar markings to the venomous coral snake with whom it frequently shares a habitat."

**C. Correct.** The first paragraph states that "[w]hile it might seem counterintuitive for a venomous snake to stand out in bright red or blue, that fancy costume tells any nearby predator that approaching him would be a bad idea." The coral snake's markings do not allow it to hide from predators but rather to "ward [them] off[.]"

D. Incorrect. The second paragraph states that "the kingsnake is actually nonvenomous; it's merely pretending to be dangerous to eat."

**6)**

**A. Correct.** The passage states that "intricate diamonds, stripes, and swirls help the animals hide from predators[,]" implying that these markings are complex enough to allow the animals to blend in with their surroundings.

B. Incorrect. The passage indicates that colorful markings do not allow the animals to hide but rather to ward off predators, so the word *colorful* does not apply in the context of the sentence.

C. Incorrect. This answer choice does not fit in the context of the sentence, as the animals do not choose their markings.

D. Incorrect. The author does not suggest that animals' markings are changeable.

**7)**

A.   Incorrect. While the author points out that jazz is often associated with New Orleans, he does not indicate that this is a problem or that people should change how they think about jazz.

**B.   Correct.** The author writes that "[j]azz music was played by and for a more expressive and freed populace than the United States had previously seen." In addition to "the emergence of the flapper[,]" the 1920s saw "the explosion of African American art and culture now known as the Harlem Renaissance."

C.   Incorrect. Though this is mentioned in the passage, it is not the main idea.

D.   Incorrect. Though this is stated at the end of the passage, it is not the main idea.

**8)**

**A.   Correct.** The author writes that "[j]azz music was played by and for a more expressive and freed populace than the United States had previously seen." In addition to "the emergence of the flapper[,]" the 1920s saw "the explosion of African American art and culture now known as the Harlem Renaissance."

B.   Incorrect. Though these artists are mentioned in the passage, the author does not indicate that they were the most important jazz musicians of the Harlem Renaissance, only that they were important.

C.   Incorrect. Though women's suffrage is mentioned in the passage, the author gives no indication that jazz music was the cause of this change.

D.   Incorrect. Though these artists are mentioned in the passage, the author does not indicate that they supported the movement for women's suffrage.

**9)**

A.   Incorrect. The author writes, "Jazz music also provided the soundtrack for the explosion of African American art and culture now known as the Harlem Renaissance." However, this is not the primary purpose of the passage.

B.   Incorrect. Though the author names many of the important jazz musicians who were playing during the 1920s, this is not the primary purpose of the passage.

**C.   Correct.** The author opens the passage saying, "In recent decades, jazz has been associated with New Orleans and festivals like Mardi Gras, but in the 1920s, jazz was a booming trend whose influence reached into many aspects of American culture." He then goes on to elaborate on what these movements were.

D.   Incorrect. The author discusses the effects of jazz music on arts and culture in the 1920s but does not go into the history of the art.

**10)**

A.   Incorrect. In the first paragraph, the author writes, "In fact, the years between World War I and the Great Depression were known as the Jazz Age, a term coined by A. Scott Fitzgerald in his famous novel *The Great Gatsby*."

**B.   Correct.** At the end of the first paragraph, the author writes, "Ella Fitzgerald, for example, moved from Virginia to New York City to begin her much-lauded singing career, and jazz pioneer Louis Armstrong got his big break in Chicago."

C.   Incorrect. At the beginning of the second paragraph, the author writes, "Women gained the right to vote and were openly seen drinking and dancing to jazz music. This period marked the emergence of the flapper, a woman determined to make a statement about her new role in society."

D.   Incorrect. Toward the end of the second paragraph, the author writes, "Jazz music also provided the soundtrack for the explosion of African American art and culture now known as the Harlem Renaissance."

## 11)

A.   Incorrect. The author states that the term *Jazz Age* was "coined by A. Scott Fitzgerald in his famous novel *The Great Gatsby*" but does not elaborate on Fitzgerald's relationship to the artists of the age.

B.   Incorrect. The author does not discuss the current popularity of jazz, only that it is often associated with New Orleans.

**C.   Correct.** The author writes that "[j]azz music was played by and for a more expressive and freed populace than the United States had previously seen." In addition to "the emergence of the flapper[,]" the 1920s saw "the explosion of African American art and culture now known as the Harlem Renaissance."

D.   Incorrect. The passage does not indicate that flappers and African American musicians worked together, only that they both used jazz music as a way to express themselves.

## 12)

A.   Incorrect. The author states, "nothing struck me more forcibly than the general equality of conditions."

**B.   Correct.** The text states that equality of conditions "has no less empire over civil society than over the Government; it creates opinions, engenders sentiments, suggests the ordinary practices of life, and modifies whatever it does not produce."

C.   Incorrect. The passage states clearly that equal conditions exist, so at this time in American history, the government did not have to insist that people be treated equally.

D.   Incorrect. This is a detail or evidence of the main idea that equal conditions exist.

## 13)

A.   Incorrect. The text is not persuasive; the author is sharing what he observed.

B.   Incorrect. Although the author presents his viewpoint forcefully, he is not using rhetorical devices to engage readers. In addition, he is speaking about only one principle: equality.

C.   Incorrect. The author does not mention France, although America may have had more equality than France did at this time in history.

**D.   Correct.** The author is enthusiastic about the tremendous influence that belief in equality has in American life, thought, and government.

## 14)

A.   Incorrect. The author was impressed by the equality of conditions, suggesting that some people did not have more status than others.

B.   Incorrect. The author did not include any mention of social classes; he said, "[equality of conditions] has no less empire over civil society than over the Government."

C.   Incorrect. The author does not comment on this, but the desire to do well is not related to having equal rights or worth.

**D.**    **Correct.** Equality of conditions suggests that the conditions for people, in terms of economics and status, were equal. In the New World, people were not born as "nobles" or "commoners" as they were in the Old World.

**15)**

**A.**    **Correct.** The author writes that "[t]here's another class of symbiosis that is controversial among scientists" and goes on to say that "many scientists claim the relationships currently described as commensal are just mutualistic or parasitic in ways that haven't been discovered yet." This implies that scientists debate about the topic of commensalism.

B.    Incorrect. The author does not imply that scientists disapprove of or protest commensalism, only that they disagree about whether it truly exists.

C.    Incorrect. The author does not imply that scientists are confused about commensalism, only that they disagree about whether it truly exists.

D.    Incorrect. The author does not imply that scientists are upset about commensalism, only that they disagree about whether it truly exists.

**16)**

A.    Incorrect. Though the author explores this idea in the final paragraph, it is not the main focus of the passage as a whole.

**B.**    **Correct.** The author writes that "[a]s these communities have evolved, the species in them have developed complex, long-term interspecies interactions known as symbiotic relationships." She then goes on to describe the different types of symbiotic relationships that exist.

C.    Incorrect. Though the author introduces the passage with this idea, it is not the main focus of the passage as a whole.

D.    Incorrect. Though the author does provide examples of interspecies interaction, this is not the primary purpose of the passage; rather, the examples provide further detail about the main topic—symbiotic relationships.

**17)**

A.    Incorrect. The author writes, "In mutualism, both individuals benefit, while in synnecrosis, both organisms are harmed."

B.    Incorrect. The author writes, "In mutualism, both individuals benefit, while in synnecrosis, both organisms are harmed."

C.    Incorrect. The author writes, "Pollination, for example, is mutualistic[:]pollinators get nutrients from the flower, and the plant is able to reproduce[.]"

**D.**    **Correct.** The author writes, "Often, relationships described as commensal include one species that feeds on another species' leftovers; remoras, for instance, will attach themselves to sharks and eat the food particles they leave behind. It might seem like the shark gets nothing from the relationship, but a closer look will show that sharks in fact benefit from remoras, which clean the sharks' skin and remove parasites."

**18)**

A.    Incorrect. The author writes, "In mutualism, both individuals benefit[.]"

B.     Incorrect. The author writes, "As it's long been defined, commensalism is a relationship where one species benefits and the other is unaffected."

**C.     Correct.** The author writes, "A relationship where one individual benefits and the other is harmed is known as parasitism."

D.     Incorrect. The author writes, "In mutualism, both individuals benefit, while in synnecrosis, both organisms are harmed."

### 19)

**A.     Correct.** The author writes, "But is it possible for two species to interact and for one to remain completely unaffected?..."In fact, many scientists claim that relationships currently described as commensal are just mutualistic or parasitic in ways that haven't been discovered yet."

B.     Incorrect. The author does not indicate that scientists disagree about the classification of relationships, only that they recognize that they do not fully understand all relationships yet and may, therefore, be classifying some of them based on incomplete information.

C.     Incorrect. The author does not indicate that the example of remoras and sharks is the reason for the controversy about commensalism, only that it illustrates this controversy well.

D.     Incorrect. The author does indicate that the controversy around commensalism is limited to discussions of animal species only.

### 20)

A.     Incorrect. The author does not indicate that scientists disagree about the classification of relationships, only that they recognize that they do not fully understand all relationships yet and may, therefore, be classifying some of them based on incomplete information.

B.     Incorrect. The author provides no support for this in the passage.

C.     Incorrect. The author provides no support for this in the passage.

**D.     Correct.** The author writes, "The bacteria, fungi, insects, plants, and animals that live together in a habitat have evolved to share a pool of limited resources...As these communities have evolved, the species in them have developed complex, long-term interspecies interactions known as symbiotic relationships."

### 21)

A.     Incorrect. The author identifies the ideals associated with idealism but does not offer an opinion on or advocate for them.

**B.     Correct.** The purpose of the passage is to explain what an idealist believes in. The author does not offer any opinions or try to persuade readers about the importance of certain values.

C.     Incorrect. The author states that social and political discourse are "permeated with idealism" but does not suggest that this is destructive or wrong.

D.     Incorrect. The author provides the reader with information but does not seek to change the reader's opinions or behaviors.

**22)**

A.  Incorrect. The passage is about babies' senses in general; therefore this answer choice is too specific.

B.  Incorrect. The passage is about babies' senses in general; therefore this answer choice is too specific.

**C.  Correct.** The passage states that babies' senses are much like those of their adult counterparts with the exception of their vision, which develops later.

D.  Incorrect. The passage indicates that a baby's vision "changes significantly in its first year of life[,]" but suggests that other senses are relatively well-developed at birth.

**23)**

A.  Incorrect. The passage states that "vision does not become the dominant sense until around the age of 12 months."

**B.  Correct.** The passage states that "infants rely primarily on hearing."

C.  Incorrect. The sense of touch in not mentioned in the passage.

D.  Incorrect. The sense of smell is not mentioned in the passage.

**24)**

**A.  Correct.** The passage explains how a baby's senses develop and allow it to interact with the world.

B.  Incorrect. The passage does not tell a story.

C.  Incorrect. The passage is not intended to change the reader's opinions or behaviors.

D.  Incorrect. The passage provides facts, not descriptions.

**25)**

A.  Incorrect. The author states that the Aztec people popped popcorn both for special occasions ("in ceremonies") and for regular consumption ("as a food staple").

**B.  Correct.** The author states, "For the Aztec Indians who called the caves home, popcorn (or *momochitl*) played an important role in society, both as a food staple and in ceremonies." This implies that the Aztec people popped popcorn both for special occasions ("in ceremonies") and for regular consumption ("as a food staple").

C.  Incorrect. Though the author does describe the process the Aztec peoples used to cook popcorn, this definition does not fit in the context of the sentence, when the author contrasts the phrase "as a food staple" with the phrase "in ceremonies."

D.  Incorrect. This definition does not fit in the context of the sentence.

**26)**

**A.  Correct.** The author states that "popcorn continued to rule the snack food kingdom until the rise in popularity of home televisions during the 1950s" when the industry saw a "decline in sales" as a result of the changing pastimes of the American people.

B.  Incorrect. The author indicates that "the introduction of the mobile popcorn machine" occurred "at the World's Columbian Exposition" after the Great Depression.

C.  Incorrect. The author indicates that the primary reason people consumed popcorn during the Great Depression was the it was advertised as a "wholesome and economical food[,]...a luxury the downtrodden could afford." This implies that the cost, not the luxuriousness, of popcorn was its primary appeal.

D. Incorrect. The author indicates that "[t]he American love affair with popcorn began in 1912" and only after this did "popcorn move from the theatre into fairs and parks."

## 27)

A. Incorrect. Though the author does discuss the effect of the microwave on the popcorn industry ("it wasn't until microwave popcorn became commercially available in 1981 that at-home popcorn consumption began to grow exponentially"), this is not the primary purpose of the passage.

B. Incorrect. Though this may be true, it is not the primary purpose of the passage; the author traces the history of popcorn from ancient to modern times.

C. **Correct.** In the opening paragraph the author writes, "But popcorn isn't just for fun— it's also a multimillion-dollar-a-year industry with a long and fascinating history." The author then goes on to illustrate the history of popcorn from the ancient Aztecs, to early twentieth century America, to the present day.

D. Incorrect. Though the author discusses the ancient Aztecs, the rest of the passage is focused on popcorn's history in American culture.

## 28)

A. Incorrect. The author mentions that popcorn was consumed "both as a food staple and in ceremonies" in Aztec culture but does not tie this to the popcorn industry in the United States.

B. Incorrect. The author indicates that growth in popularity of home televisions actually hurt the popcorn industry: "Popcorn continued to rule the snack food kingdom until the rise in popularity of home televisions during the 1950s" when the industry saw "a decline in sales[.]"

C. **Correct.** The author writes, "The popcorn industry flourished during the Great Depression when it was advertised as a wholesome and economical food."

D. Incorrect. Though the nutritional value of popcorn is mentioned as a factor in its popularity during the Great Depression, the author does not indicate that this is the reason for its popularity in the United States.

## 29)

A. **Correct.** This statement summarizes the entire passage, including the brief history of popcorn in ancient cultures and the growth in the popularity of popcorn in America.

B. Incorrect. Though the author does mention the history of popcorn in ancient cultures, this is not an adequate summary of the passage as a whole.

C. Incorrect. Though the author discusses the history of popcorn in America, this is not an adequate summary of the passage as a whole.

D. Incorrect. Though the author does mention the versatility and popularity of popcorn as a snack food, this is not an adequate summary of the passage as a whole.

**30)**

A.   Incorrect. The author writes, "In 1948, Herbert Dick and Earle Smith discovered old popcorn dating back 4000 years in the New Mexico Bat Cave."

B.   Incorrect. The author writes, "The American love affair with popcorn began in 1912, when popcorn was first sold in theaters."

C.   **Correct.** The author writes, "However, it wasn't until microwave popcorn became commercially available in 1981 that at-home popcorn consumption began to grow exponentially. With the wide availability of microwaves in the United States, popcorn also began popping up in offices and hotel rooms."

D.   Incorrect. The author writes, "However, the home still remains the most popular popcorn eating spot: today, 70 percent of the 16 billion quarts of popcorn consumed annually in the United States are eaten at home."

**31)**

A.   **Correct.** A company that profits from private tutoring might introduce bias into a study on the effects of private tutoring in schools.

B.   Incorrect. A study showing the differences in standardized test scores between students in different neighborhoods would likely strengthen the author's argument by reinforcing the conclusion that private tutoring leads to educational inequality.

C.   Incorrect. Statements from local teachers would not weaken the author's argument about educational inequality because they are subjective and would not ensure equal opportunity.

D.   Incorrect. The study is not focused on college success.

**32)**

A.   Incorrect. The author does not employ emotional or figurative language to make her argument.

B.   Incorrect. The passage does not indicate that it is meant directed at people of authority.

C.   **Correct.** The author cites data from a study to support his or her argument.

D.   Incorrect. The author does not employee any rhetorical questions.

**33)**

A.   Incorrect. This is irrelevant because the plant produces offsets, which allow it to spread.

B.   Incorrect. Inactive roots suggest the plant would not multiply.

C.   Incorrect. Although the passage indicates that the plant needs moist soil, the soil may or may not stay moist throughout the year, depending on the weather.

D.   **Correct.** An offset is like a daughter plant that comes off the mother plant.

**34)**

A.   Incorrect. The author does not suggest that the narrative of the Civil War as "a battle for individual identity" is a complicated one, only that it is untrue.

B.   **Correct.** The author writes, "All other explanations for the war are either a direct consequence of the South's desire for wealth at the expense of her fellow man or a fanciful invention to cover up this sad portion of our nation's history."

C.    Incorrect. The author does not discuss the extent to which the attempt to "cover up this sad portion of our nation's history" was successful or unsuccessful.

D.    Incorrect. Though the author may agree that the invention of the identity narrative is unfortunate, this is not the best answer choice to highlight her main assertion that it is untrue.

## 35)

A.    **Correct.** The author writes, "But people who try to sell you this narrative are wrong. The Civil War was not a battle of cultural identities—it was a battle about slavery."

B.    Incorrect. Though the author describes the cultural differences between the North and South in the first half of the passage, her primary purpose is revealed when she states, "But people who try to sell you this narrative are wrong."

C.    Incorrect. The author makes no comment on the outcome of the Civil War.

D.    Incorrect. The author asserts that, despite the popular identity narrative, the cause of the Civil War was actually very clear: "The Civil War was not a battle of cultural identities—it was a battle about slavery."

## 36)

A.    Incorrect. The author asserts that, despite the popular narrative, cultural differences were not the cause of the Civil War.

B.    **Correct.** The author writes, "The Civil War was not a battle of cultural identities—it was a battle about slavery. All other explanations for the war are either a direct consequence of the South's desire for wealth at the expense of her fellow man or a fanciful invention to cover up this sad portion of our nation's history."

C.    Incorrect. The author does not discuss the strengths of the North or provide any reason for why it won the war.

D.    Incorrect. Though the author mentions these cultural beliefs, she does not suggest that these were the reasons the South was defeated.

# Writing

## MULTIPLE CHOICE

### 1)

A. **Correct.** This information is unnecessary and detracts from the point of the passage.

B. Incorrect. *Many* and *most* have similar meanings and are both grammatically correct in this case.

C. Incorrect. *Deceased* is a more formal word for *dead*, but neither is incorrect.

D. Incorrect. *Witnessed* is a more formal word for *saw*, but neither is incorrect.

### 2)

A. Incorrect. *Therefore* does not fit in the context of this sentence, as no cause-and-effect relationship exists.

B. **Correct.** *In fact* can be used correctly in this instance to draw attention to interesting information that builds on the previous sentence.

C. Incorrect. *However* does not fit in the context of this sentence, as no contradictory relationship exists.

D. Incorrect. *In addition* does not fit in the context of this sentence, as this sentence builds on the previous one and does not introduce a new idea.

### 3)

A. Incorrect. This choice is unnecessarily wordy, as *examined the facts* is implied in *debated*.

B. Incorrect. This choice is ambiguous, as *hemmed* and *hawed* are colloquial, which does not match the rest of the passage, whereas *debate* implies a more serious tone. Furthermore, this choice is wordy.

C. **Correct.** This is the clearest, most concise choice for communicating this idea.

D. Incorrect. *Hemmed and hawed* is a colloquial saying, which does not match the tone of the rest of the passage.

### 4)

A. Incorrect. The sentence provides important information about two scientists who point to science fiction as the inspiration for their work.

B. Incorrect. *Always* is unnecessary to the reader's understanding of the sentence.

C. **Correct.** *His* should become *their* because the work belongs to two people (Goddard and Szilard).

D. Incorrect. The phrase inside the dashes is not grammatically necessary, but it is helpful to the reader's understanding of the sentence.

### 5)

A. Incorrect. This choice is too specific, as only one sentence of the final paragraph relates to transportation.

B. Incorrect. This sentence adds very little to the meaning of the paragraph.

C.    Incorrect. The tone of this sentence is conversational, and it does not fit with the rest of the passage.

**D.    Correct.** This choice provides a brief but interesting overview of the information to come.

**6)**

**A.    Correct.** This sentence relates directly to the overall idea of the passage—that science fiction has a natural influence on real life.

B.    Incorrect. This sentence does not relate to the overall topic of the passage—the relationship between science fiction and reality.

C.    Incorrect. This sentence is inappropriately argumentative when compared with the rest of the passage, and it detracts from the main idea of the passage.

D.    Incorrect. This sentence is too general and provides no additional insight to the reader.

**7)**

**A.    Correct.** As it is written, *more recently* provides the reader with information about the time period being referred to as well as its relationship to the time period that was discussed in the previous sentence.

B.    Incorrect. *These days* in a colloquial expression used to refer to the present day; it does not agree with the meaning the author hopes to convey.

C.    Incorrect. *Therefore* incorrectly suggests a cause-and-effect relationship between this sentence and the preceding sentence.

D.    Incorrect. *On the other hand* incorrectly suggests a contradictory relationship between this sentence and the preceding sentence.

**8)**

A.    Incorrect. The final phrase *the changeling* is incorrectly set off from its descriptor with only a comma.

**B.    Correct.** The final phrase *the changeling* is appropriately set off from the rest of the sentence—its descriptor—with a colon.

C.    Incorrect. The dashes in this sentence incorrectly set off information that is essential to the meaning.

D.    Incorrect. This choice creates a fragment by placing *the changeling* in its own sentence.

**9)**

A.    Incorrect. This choice correctly turns the second clause into a subordinate clause by adding *who* and joins it to an independent clause with a comma.

B.    Incorrect. This choice correctly joins two related independent clauses with a comma.

**C.    Correct.** This choice incorrectly joins two independent clauses with a comma (*changelings were...* and *they were left...*).

D.    Incorrect. The dash correctly joins the subordinate clause (*left in the places...*) to the main sentence.

**10)**

A.  Incorrect. This choice provides a meaningful conclusion to the paragraph by explaining why people may have been invested in the changeling legend.

**B.**  **Correct.** *Explanation* adds an important detail about what the demonstrative pronoun *this* refers to.

C.  Incorrect. *Families* is used correctly in the sentence to signify multiple families and does not need to be changed.

D.  Incorrect. *Whose* is used correctly in the sentence to signify possession (the children of the families) and does not need to be changed.

**11)**

**A.**  **Correct.** As written, the sentence acts appropriately as an introductory sentence, providing a summary of the topic that will be discussed; additionally, it gives meaning to the phrase *for example* in sentence 9.

B.  Incorrect. The content of the sentence is better aligned with the content of the third paragraph, as encouraging the changelings to leave was not an idea that was discussed in paragraph 2.

C.  Incorrect. In this placement, the sentence above is notably vague compared to the sentences around it; as such, it works best as an introductory statement that summarizes the similarities between the various examples.

D.  Incorrect. In this placement, the sentence above is notably vague compared to the sentences around it; as such, it works best as an introductory statement that summarizes the similarities between the various examples.

**12)**

A.  Incorrect. This choice creates a comma splice by combining two independent clauses with a comma.

B.  Incorrect. This choice combines the independent clauses correctly with a comma and a conjunction; however, the meaning of the conjunction *so* suggests a cause-and-effect relationship, which does not exist here.

C.  Incorrect. This choice combines the independent clauses correctly with a comma and a conjunction; however, the meaning of the conjunction *but* suggests a contradictory relationship, which does not exist here.

**D.**  **Correct.** The choice correctly joins the independent clauses with a colon, signifying that the information in the second clause somehow builds or expands on the first.

**13)**

A.  Incorrect. *Remain* is a plural, present-tense verb that does not agree with its subject *water*.

B.  Incorrect. *Then*, meaning "at that time," is used incorrectly here to express inequality.

**C.**  **Correct.** *Remains* is a singular, present-tense verb that agrees with its subject *water*, which is noncountable and therefore singular; *than* is a conjunction used correctly here to express inequality between two things (amount of time the water is in the sky and ten days).

D.    Incorrect. *Will remain* is a future-tense verb, used incorrectly to communicate a general fact; *then* is also used incorrectly (see choice B).

**14)**

A.    Incorrect. Ending a sentence here turns the remaining words into a fragment that does not make good sense.

B.    Incorrect. Placing a semicolon here creates a too-long pause in the middle of the phrase *awake for nineteen hours, after a twelve-hour work day*.

**C.    Correct.** The writer uses a pair of commas to set apart the inessential phrase *after a twelve-hour work day*.

D.    Incorrect. When used like this, dashes should appear in pairs. Here, the writer incorrectly uses one dash and one comma to set apart the phrase *after a twelve-hour work day*.

**15)**

A.    Incorrect. The correct plural form of *vertebra* is *vertebrae*.

B.    Incorrect. The correct plural form of *goose* is *geese*.

C.    Incorrect. The correct plural form of *octopus* is *octopi*.

**D.    Correct.** The singular noun *bronchus* is made plural by changing the *–us* to *–i*.

**16)**

A.    Incorrect. Because *only one* and *single* have the same meaning, only one of the phrases is needed.

B.    Incorrect. This choice places emphasis incorrectly on *publication*.

**C.    Correct.** This choice is the clearest, most concise way to communicate the idea.

D.    Incorrect. Because *single* and *unique* have similar meanings in this context, only one of the phrases is needed.

**17)**

A.    Incorrect. There should be no apostrophe in *its*.

B.    Incorrect. There should be no apostrophe in *its*. The colon should be changed to a comma.

C.    Incorrect. The colon should be changed to a comma, and the exclamation point should be changed to a period.

**D.    Correct.** In this choice, a comma correctly sets off the introductory phrase, and a period correctly ends the sentence.

**18)**

A.    Incorrect. *Astrophysicists* is spelled correctly.

**B.    Correct.** *Astronemers* should be spelled *astronomers*.

C.    Incorrect. *Techniques* is spelled correctly.

D.    Incorrect. *Technology* is spelled correctly.

## 19)

A. Incorrect. *Which also functioned* does not clearly modify the brigade; instead, it incorrectly seems to modify *Emperor Augustus of Rome.*

**B. Correct.** *And also functioned* introduces the second part of a compound verb phrase (*was created and functioned*).

C. Incorrect. *Also functioning* does not clearly modify the brigade; instead, it incorrectly seems to modify *Emperor Augustus of Rome.*

D. Incorrect. *That also functioned* does not clearly modify the brigade; instead, it incorrectly seems to modify *Emperor Augustus of Rome.*

## 20)

**A. Correct.** The first clause is dependent and the second is independent, so they are correctly joined by a comma.

B. Incorrect. The semicolon should be changed to a comma.

C. Incorrect. The colon should be changed to a comma.

D. Incorrect. The em dash should be changed to a comma.

## 21)

A. Incorrect. Modifying relationships are unclear in this sentence. *Pennsylvania* is separated from its verb *passed.*

B. Incorrect. Modifying relationships are unclear in this sentence. *Pennsylvania* is separated from its verb *passed.*

C. Incorrect. Modifying relationships are unclear in this sentence. *As animals* incorrectly modifies *criticism.*

**D. Correct.** Modifying relationships are clear: *Pennsylvania* is followed by its verb *passed* and the description of the law (*prohibiting cartoonists from...*) immediately follows the word *law*; the reason for the law (*in order to...*) comes after the description of the law.

## 22)

A. Incorrect. *Although*, meaning "despite," is used incorrectly here.

**B. Correct.** *On the other hand* appropriately signifies the opposing ideas in the two pieces of information.

C. Incorrect. *Nevertheless*, meaning "in spite of," is used incorrectly here.

D. Incorrect. *In consequence*, used to show cause-and-effect relationships, is used incorrectly here.

## 23)

A. Incorrect. The newspaper's name is a proper noun, so it is correctly capitalized.

B. Incorrect. The phrase *the paper* contains an article and a common noun. Both words are correctly lowercased.

C. Incorrect. The phrase *about the winner* contains a preposition, an article, and a common noun. All three words are correctly lowercased.

**D. Correct.** *Presidential* is an adjective that modifies the common noun *election*; neither word should be capitalized.

**24)**

A.    **Correct.** This choice correctly joins two independent clauses.

B.    Incorrect. Though the semicolon can be used to join independent clauses, it should not be used with a conjunction (*and*).

C.    Incorrect. This choice incorrectly joins two independent clauses with a comma.

D.    Incorrect. As with a semicolon, colons should not be used with conjunctions (*and*).

**25)**

A.    **Correct.** *President* is a title and should be capitalized when it refers to a specific person.

B.    Incorrect. *Senator* functions here as a common noun, not as a title or proper noun; it should not be capitalized.

C.    Incorrect. *Aunt* and *uncle* should not be capitalized here. They function as common nouns, not as parts of proper nouns such as *Aunt Julie* or *Uncle Michael*.

D.    Incorrect. The word *eve* should be capitalized here because it is part of a proper noun, the name of a specific holiday: New Year's Eve.

**26)**

A.    Incorrect. *To instill* suggests *international communications and relations* is a new area of concern.

B.    **Correct.** *To improve* correctly communicates the goal of Zamenhof to make better something that already exists.

C.    Incorrect. *To initiate* suggests *international communications and relations* is a new area of concern.

D.    Incorrect. *To invite* suggests *international communications and relations* are encouraged, but not important.

**27)**

A.    Incorrect. Having *before* and *now* in the same clause creates confusion; it also does not highlight the contradiction between the two clauses.

B.    **Correct.** *Though* is used correctly in this sentence to show a slight contradiction between the assumption (that self-driving cars are new) and the truth (that vehicle automation has been a topic of study for many decades).

C.    Incorrect. *Because* is used incorrectly in this sentence to show a cause-and-effect relationship.

D.    Incorrect. This choice creates a comma splice by making the first clause independent.

**28)**

A.    Incorrect. *Groceries* and *bill* should each be followed by a comma since they are items in a series.

B.    **Correct.** This compound sentence requires a comma before the conjunction *but*.

C.    Incorrect. This sentence requires no commas.

D.    Incorrect. Two commas correctly frame the phrase *who lives in Indiana*.

**29)**

- A.  Incorrect. The semicolon cannot be used to set off a list.
- B.  Incorrect. *Including* should not be separated from the list it introduces by a comma.
- C.  Incorrect. This choice creates two dependent clauses that cannot stand alone (fragments).
- **D.  Correct.** This choice creates a complete, uninterrupted sentence, since what follows *factors* is nonessential. The sentence make sense without listing the factors.

**30)**

- A.  Incorrect. This sentence has one independent clause; it has no dependent clauses.
- B.  Incorrect. This sentence has one subject and two predicates; it has no dependent clauses.
- C.  Incorrect. This sentence has two independent clauses connected by a comma and a conjunction.
- **D.  Correct.** The sentence has an independent clause (*the fully...of Rome*) and a dependent clause (*Although organized...Egyptian times*). The two are connected with a comma following the word *times*.

**31)**

- A.  Incorrect. *Then* is used incorrectly in this sentence to show comparison; *there* is used incorrectly to show possession.
- B.  Incorrect. *There* is used incorrectly in this sentence to show possession.
- **C.  Correct.** *Than* is used correctly to show comparison, while *their* is used correctly to show possession; the dash correctly closes off the appositive phrase.
- D.  Incorrect. A comma is used incorrectly in this sentence to close off an appositive phrase that was set off with a dash.

**32)**

- **A.  Correct.** *Potatos* should be spelled *potatoes*.
- B.  Incorrect. *Onions* is spelled correctly.
- C.  Incorrect. *Saliva* is spelled correctly.
- D.  Incorrect. *Conservators* is spelled correctly.

**33)**

- A.  Incorrect. *Available* is an adjective, which cannot be modified by another adjective (*wide*).
- B.  Incorrect. *Widely* is an adverb, which must be modified by another adverb (*relatively*).
- C.  Incorrect. *Availability* is a noun; *professional dental care is* should be followed by an adjective.
- **D.  Correct.** *Relatively* is an adverb that modifies *widely*, an adverb that modifies the adjective *available*.

**34)**

- A.  Incorrect. *Travels* functions as a noun, not as a verb like *provided*.
- **B.  Correct.** *Travels* functions as a noun; it is the subject of the sentence.

C.    Incorrect. *Travels* functions as a noun, not as an adjective like *spicy.*

D.    Incorrect. *Travels* functions as a noun, not as an adverb like *adventurously.*

**35)**

A.    Incorrect. *Facts* and *information* have roughly the same meaning in this context, so only one of the words is needed.

B.    Incorrect. *Facts*, *figures*, and *information* have roughly the same meaning in this context, so only one of the words is needed.

C.    Incorrect. *Facts* and *information* have roughly the same meaning in this context, so only one of the words is needed; *detailed* provides an additional unnecessary fact.

**D.    Correct.** This is the clearest and most concise way to covey the meaning of this sentence.

**36)**

**A.    Correct.** The appositive phrase is correctly enclosed with commas; the items inside the commas are parallel (*the capturing of wild animals and the captive breeding of wild species*).

B.    Incorrect. The two items in this list do not have parallel structures; *the capturing of wild animals* should be followed by another gerund.

C.    Incorrect. This choice creates a comma splice, with two independent clauses being joined by a comma.

D.    Incorrect. This choice creates a comma splice, with two independent clauses being joined by a comma.

**37)**

A.    Incorrect. The first clause (*Though the term...*) is dependent and cannot be joined to the second with a semicolon.

B.    Incorrect. The first clause (*Though the term...*) is dependent and cannot be joined to the second with a colon.

**C.    Correct.** The first clause (*Though the term...*) is correctly joined to the second (independent) clause with a comma.

D.    Incorrect. This choice fails to set off the dependent clause (*Though the term...*) from the sentence's main clause (*nomadic cultures continue...*).

**38)**

A.    Incorrect. *Of* is the incorrect preposition and fails to communicate the meaning of this sentence.

B.    Incorrect. *In* is the incorrect preposition and fails to communicate the meaning of this sentence.

**C.    Correct.** *With* is the correct preposition for completing the prepositional idiom *combined with* and for communicating the intended meaning (that two things are combined *with* each other).

D.    Incorrect. *Over* is the incorrect preposition and fails to communicate the meaning of this sentence.

**39)**

A.  **Correct.** The comma is not needed to separate *such as* from the list it introduces.

B.  Incorrect. This comma and the one following *Spain* are needed to separate items in a series.

C.  Incorrect. This comma is needed to set apart an introductory phrase.

D.  Incorrect. This semicolon is needed to connect two related short sentences.

**40)**

A.  Incorrect. *Traditional* and *old-fashioned* are synonyms, but the second word does not make good sense here.

B.  **Correct.** *Conventional* best expresses the idea that the usual kind of comic book is told in many episodes about an established set of characters.

C.  Incorrect. *Traditional* and *expensive* are not synonyms.

D.  Incorrect. *Traditional* and *popular* are not synonyms.

## SENTENCE CORRECTION

1. You can have either the cake or the cookie.
2. Make a study plan to learn the parts of the respiratory system, the muscles and the heart.

## CONSTRUCTED RESPONSE

Violent storms are a huge risk to human life and property; they also have a strong impact on the economy, interfering with economic activity and sometimes damaging infrastructure. However, natural disasters are a fact of life on our planet, and it's impossible for economic development and growth to cease due to the possibility of a powerful storm. Still, rapid urban development is occurring in particularly storm-prone areas in Asia and even in North America, putting millions of people at risk. While the risks of a calamitous storm should never be underestimated, the solution is not to halt migration and slow economic growth, but to encourage investment in urban planning and public safety.

Centers of population in storm-prone areas in Indonesia, the Philippines, the United States East and Gulf Coasts, and elsewhere are indeed growing; natural resources and urban areas in these places are essential to local and national economies and even the global economy. During this time of change, especially in areas that are newly developing, opportunities for proper urban planning abound. Before growing urban areas get even larger, governments must take action to prevent the proliferation of slums, improve existing infrastructure to meet the needs of growing cities (or develop new infrastructure), and put policies into place for good urban management. Given the importance of these urban and industrial areas, especially for billion-dollar sectors like the oil and gas industry, there may even be opportunities for major companies to get involved in sponsoring urban development and safety in the economic zones and cities relevant to their interests around the world.

Furthermore, with economic growth also comes innovation and technology. Today, there are more opportunities than ever to develop products and procedures to ensure safety. From engineering to preparedness to emergency medical treatment, there are a plethora of approaches to storm readiness and flood control. Urban planning can take into account flooding and geographical impediments to emergency response time. There are more products on the market to help families survive for several days without help (for instance, water purifiers and other survival gear). Governments, civic organizations, and NGOs could be involved in emergency preparedness efforts and enlisted to distribute preparedness items during storm seasons, especially to those poor and working people who are the most likely to be affected and who would most likely be harmed. Using good technology and wise community coordination would ensure that vulnerable workers and their families are as safe as possible during storm season, so that they could benefit year-round from economic growth.

While storms and other natural disasters are and will remain a threat to human life, it's unrealistic to imagine that all economic activity will stop for the sake of safety. Thanks to economic growth and innovation, we can develop planning, technology, policy, and coordination to ensure the safety of communities as they drive the economic growth of those regions affected by major storms. That way, development can continue in as safe an environment as possible.

# Mathematics

## 1)

**A.** Multiply the digits and add the exponents.

$(1.2 \times 10^{-3})(1.13 \times 10^{-4})$

$1.2 \times 1.13 = 1.356$

$-3 + (-4) = -7$

**$1.356 \times 10^{-7}$**

## 2)

Eliminate answer choices that don't match the graph.

**A.** Correct.

**B.** The graph has a negative slope while this inequality has a positive slope.

**C.** The line on the graph is solid, so the inequality should include the "or equal to" symbol.

**D.** The shading is above the line, meaning the inequality should be "y is greater than."

## 3)

**B.** Set up a proportion and solve.

$\frac{AB}{DE} = \frac{3}{4}$

$\frac{12}{DE} = \frac{3}{4}$

$3(DE) = 48$

**$DE = 16$**

## 4)

**B.** Plug 4 in for $j$ and simplify.

$2(j - 4)^4 - j + \frac{1}{2}j$

$2(4 - 4)^4 - 4 + \frac{1}{2}(4) = \mathbf{-2}$

## 5)

**A.** Use the formula for inversely proportional relationships to find $k$ and then solve for $s$.

$sn = k$

$(65)(250) = k$

$k = 16,250$

$s(325) = 16,250$

$s = \mathbf{50}$

## 6)

**B.** On a normal distribution curve, the group of students with a height between 5.25 and 5.5 feet is one standard deviation from the mean. More students will be in this group than any of the others, which are all more than one standard deviation from the mean.

## 7)

**B.** Use the midpoint formula to find point $B$.

$M_x: \frac{(7 + x)}{2} = -3$

$x = -13$

$M_y: \frac{(12 + y)}{2} = 10$

$y = 8$

$B = \mathbf{(-13, 8)}$

## 8)

**A.** Find the amount the state will spend on infrastructure and education, and then find the difference.

$infrastructure = 0.2(3,000,000,000) = 600,000,000$

$education = 0.18(3,000,000,000) = 540,000,000$

$600,000,000 - 540,000,000 = $ **$60,000,000**

## 9)

**D.** Simplify using PEMDAS.

$(3^2 \div 1^3) - (4 - 8^2) + 2^4$

$= (9 \div 1) - (4 - 64) + 16$

$= 9 - (-60) + 16 = \mathbf{85}$

**10)**

**D.** Use the formula for the area of a rectangle to find the increase in its size.

$A = lw$

$A = (1.4l)(0.6w)$

$A = 0.84lw$

The new area will be 84% of the original area, a decrease of **16%**.

**11)**

**B.** Work backwards to find the number of runners in the competition ($c$) and then the number of runners on the team ($r$).

$\frac{2}{c} = \frac{10}{100}$

$c = 20$

$\frac{20}{r} = \frac{25}{100}$

$r = 80$

**12)**

**A.** Plug 0 in for $y$ and solve for $x$.

$10x + 10y = 10$

$10x + 10(0) = 10$

$x = 1$

The $x$-intercept is at **(1, 0)**.

**13)**

**C.** All the points lie on the circle, so each line segment is a radius. The sum of the 4 lines will be 4 times the radius.

$r = \frac{75}{2} = 37.5$

$4r = 150$

**14)**

**D.** Multiply by the converstion factor to get from meters to feet.

$55 \text{ m} \left(\frac{3.28 \text{ ft.}}{1 \text{ m}}\right) = 180.4 \text{ feet}$

**15)**

**D.** Simplify using PEMDAS.

$z^3(z + 2)^2 - 4z^3 + 2$

$z^3(z^2 + 4z + 4) - 4z^3 + 2$

$z^5 + 4z^4 + 4z^3 - 4z^3 + 2$

$z^5 + 4z^4 + 2$

**16)**

**C.** Use the fundamental counting principle to determine how many ways the DVDs can be arranged within each category and how many ways the 3 categories can be arranged.

*ways to arrange horror* $= 4! = 24$

*ways to arrange comedies* $= 6! = 720$

*ways to arrange science fiction* $= 5! = 120$

*ways to arrange categories* $= 3! = 6$

$(24)(720)(120)(6) = 12{,}441{,}600$

**17)**

**D.** Solve the system using substitution.

$z - 2x = 14 \rightarrow z = 2x + 14$

$2z - 6x = 18$

$2(2x + 14) - 6x = 18$

$4x + 28 - 6x = 18$

$-2x = -10$

$x = 5$

$z - 2(5) = 14$

$z = 24$

**18)**

**C.** Cross multiply and solve for x.

$\frac{4x - 5}{3} = \frac{\frac{1}{2}(2x - 6)}{5}$

$5(4x - 5) = \frac{3}{2}(2x - 6)$

$20x - 25 = 3x - 9$

$17x = 16$

$x = \frac{16}{17}$

**19)**

**D.** Write a proportion and then solve for $x$.

$\frac{40}{45} = \frac{265}{x}$

$40x = 11,925$

$x = 298.125 \approx \textbf{298}$

**20)**

**B.** Use the equation for Bernoulli trials (binomial distribution).

$P = {}_nC_r(p^r)(q^{n-r})$

$n = 10$

$r = 3$

$p = \dfrac{4}{36} = \dfrac{1}{9}$

$q = \dfrac{8}{9}$

$P = {}_{10}C_3\left(\dfrac{1}{9}\right)^3\left(\dfrac{8}{9}\right)^7 = 0.072 = \textbf{7.2\%}$

**21)**

**D.** Set up a system of equations.

$OD$ bisects $\angle AOF$: $50 + a + b = 30 + c$

$BO$ bisects $\angle AOD$: $50 = a + b$

Substitute and solve.

$50 + 50 = 30 + c$

$c = 70$

Add each angle to find m$\angle AOF$.

$\angle AOF = 50° + a° + b° + 30° + c°$

$\angle AOF = 50° + 50° + 30° + 70°$

$\angle AOF = \textbf{200°}$

**22)**

**B.** The slope 0.0293 gives the increase in passenger car miles (in billions) for each year that passes. Muliply this value by 5 to find the increase that occurs over 5 years: $5(0.0293) = $ **0.1465 billion miles**.

**23)**

**B.** Write a proportion and then solve for $x$.

$\dfrac{15,036}{7} = \dfrac{x}{2}$

$7x = 30,072$

$x = \textbf{4,296}$

**24)**

**D.** Use the volume to find the length of the cube's side.

$V = s^3$

$343 = s^3$

$s = 7\,\text{m}$

Find the area of each side and multiply by 6 to find the total surface area.

$7(7) = 49\,\text{m}$

$49(6) = \textbf{294 m}^2$

**25)**

**A.** There are six digits that can be used to make up the 6-digit number: 0, 1, 2, 7, 8, and 9. However, 0 cannot be used for the first digit. Use the fundamental counting principle: $(5)(6)(6)(6)(6)(6) = \textbf{38,880}$.

**26)**

**A.** Simplify the inequality.

$2x + 4 \geq 5x - 20 - 3x + 12$

$2x + 4 \geq 2x - 8$

$4 \geq -8$

Since the inequality is always true, the solution is all real numbers, $(-\infty, \infty)$.

**27)**

**D.** Find the amount of change and add to the original amount.

*amount of change = original amount × percent change*

$= 37,500 \times 0.055 = 2,062.50$

$37,500 + 2,062.50 = \textbf{\$39,562.50}$

**28)**

**D.** There are an infinite number of points with distance four from the origin, all of which lie on a circle centered at the origin with a radius of 4.

**29)**

**B.** Use the rules of exponents to simplify the expression.

$$\frac{(3x^2y^2)^2}{3^3x^{-2}y^3} = \frac{3^2x^4y^4}{3^3x^{-2}y^3} = \frac{x^6y}{3}$$

**30)**

**C.** Use the equation for exponential decay to find the year the population reached 1 million.

$$y = a(1 - r)^t$$

$$y = 1250000(1 - 0.05)^t$$

$$1,000,000 = 1250000(1 - 0.05)^t$$

$$0.8 = 0.95^t$$

$$\log_{0.8} 0.8 = \log_{0.8} 0.95^t$$

$$1 = t \times \frac{\log 0.95}{\log .8}$$

$$t = 4.35$$

**The population will reach 1 million in 2013.**

**31)**

**B.** Find the sum of the 13 numbers whose mean is 30.

$$13 \times 30 = 390$$

Find the sum of the 8 numbers whose mean is 42.

$$8 \times 42 = 336$$

Find the sum and mean of the remaining 5 numbers.

$$390 - 336 = 54$$

$$\frac{54}{5} = \mathbf{10.8}$$

**32)**

**B.** Factor the trinomial and set each factor equal to 0.

$$2n^2 + 2n - 12 = 0$$

$$2(n^2 + n - 6) = 0$$

$$2(n + 3)(n - 2) = 0$$

$$n = \mathbf{-3} \text{ and } n = \mathbf{2}$$

**33)**

**A.** Find the distance between consecutive points to determine the side length.

$$PQ = \sqrt{(-3 - (-6))^2 + (2 - (-3))^2} = \sqrt{9 + 25} = \sqrt{34}$$

$$QR = \sqrt{(0 - (-3))^2 + (3 - (2))^2} = \sqrt{9 + 1} = \sqrt{10}$$

$$RS = \sqrt{-1 - (0))^2 + (0 - (3))^2} = \sqrt{1 + 9} = \sqrt{10}$$

$$SP = \sqrt{-1 - (-6))^2 + (0 - (-3))^2} = \sqrt{25 + 9} = \sqrt{34}$$

The figure has two sets of congruent sides, so it is a **kite**.

**34)**

**D.** This problem can be solved by calculating the needed values, but it's faster to examine the general shape of each data set.

**A.** Incorrect: All the values are the same, so the mean and median will have the same value.

**B.** Incorrect: The majority of the data points are not close to the mean, so the standard deviation will be high.

**C.** Incorrect: The high outlier will make the mean larger than the median.

**D.** Correct: The mean is slightly lower than the median, and the spread is small.

**35)**

**A.** I. True: The row "25 – 35 year-olds" and the column "more than 4 hours" show a relative frequency of 0.20 or 20%.

II. True: The total relative frequency of participants who spend 2 to 4 hours on social media a day is 0.26 or 26%.

III. False: These percentages cannot be added because the "whole" is not the same. To calculate the percentage of people aged 15 – 35 who use social media less than 2 hours a day, find the total number of people in each category and divide by the total number of people in both categories.

*people 15 – 25 years old spending < 2 hrs.* = 0.15(200) = 30 *people 25 – 35 years old spending < 2 hrs.* = 0.52(200) = 104

*percentage of people 15 – 35 years old spending < 2 hrs.* = $\frac{30 + 104}{400}$ = 0.34 = 34%

IV. False: The number of people aged 35 – 45 who used social media more than 4 hours a day is 0.05(200) = 10.

**36)**

**C.** Find the height of the cylinder using the equation for surface area.

$SA = 2\pi rh + 2\pi r^2$

$48\pi = 2\pi(4)h + 2\pi(4)^2$

$h = 2$

Find the volume using the volume equation.

$V = \pi r^2 h$

$V = \pi(4)^2(2) = \mathbf{32\pi\ ft.^3}$

Follow the link below to take your PECT PAPA practice test and to access other online study resources:

**www.cirrustestprep.com/pect–papa–online–resources**

46447831R00149

Made in the USA
Lexington, KY
26 July 2019